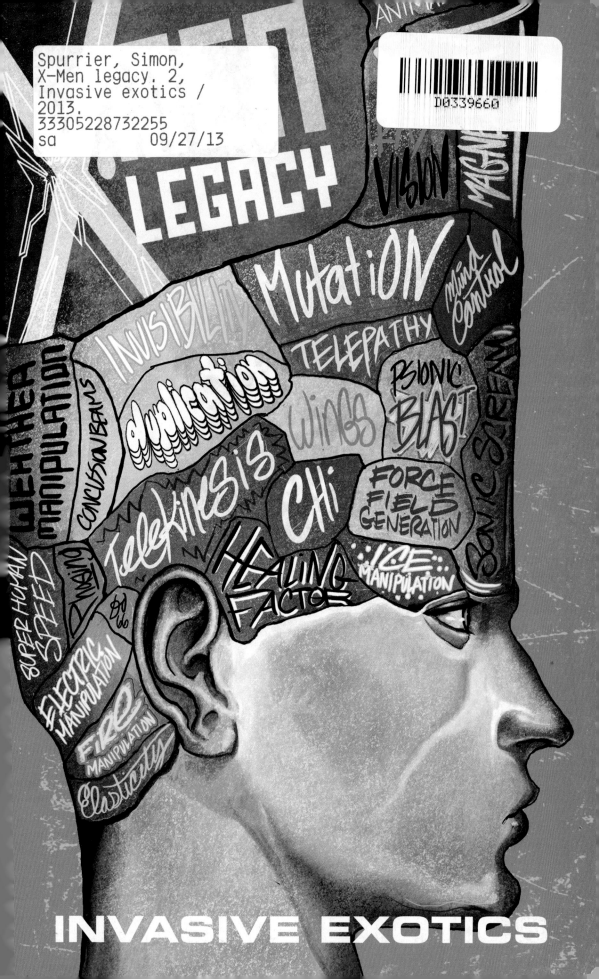

LEGACY

VISION

MAGNET

MUTATION

Mind Control

INVISIBILITY

TELEPATHY

duplication

BIONIC BLAST

WEATHER MANIPULATION

CONCUSSION BEAMS

WINGS

SONIC SCREAM

Telekinesis

CHI

FORCE FIELD GENERATION

SUPER HUMAN SPEED

PHASING

HEALING FACTOR

ICE MANIPULATION

ELECTRIC MANIPULATION

FIRE MANIPULATION

Elasticity

INVASIVE EXOTICS

INVASIVE EXOTICS

writer **SIMON SPURRIER**
pencilers **TAN ENG HUAT** (#7-9 & #11)
& **PAUL DAVIDSON** (#10-12)
inkers **CRAIG YEUNG** (#7-9 & #11), **PAUL DAVIDSON** (#10-11)
& **JAY LEISTEN** (finishes, #12)
colorists **JOSÉ VILLARRUBIA** (#7-9), **RACHELLE ROSENBERG** (#10-11)
& **CRIS PETER** (#12)
letterer **VC'S CORY PETIT**
cover artist **MIKE DEL MUNDO**
assistant editor **JENNIFER M. SMITH**
editor **DANIEL KETCHUM**
x-men group editor **NICK LOWE**

Collection Editor: Mark D. Beazley • Assistant Editors: Alex Starbuck & Nelson Ribeiro
Editor, Special Projects: Jennifer Grünwald • Senior Editor, Special Projects: Jeff Youngquist
SVP of Print & Digital Publishing Sales: David Gabriel

Editor in Chief: Axel Alonso • Chief Creative Officer: Joe Quesada
Publisher: Dan Buckley • Executive Producer: Alan Fine

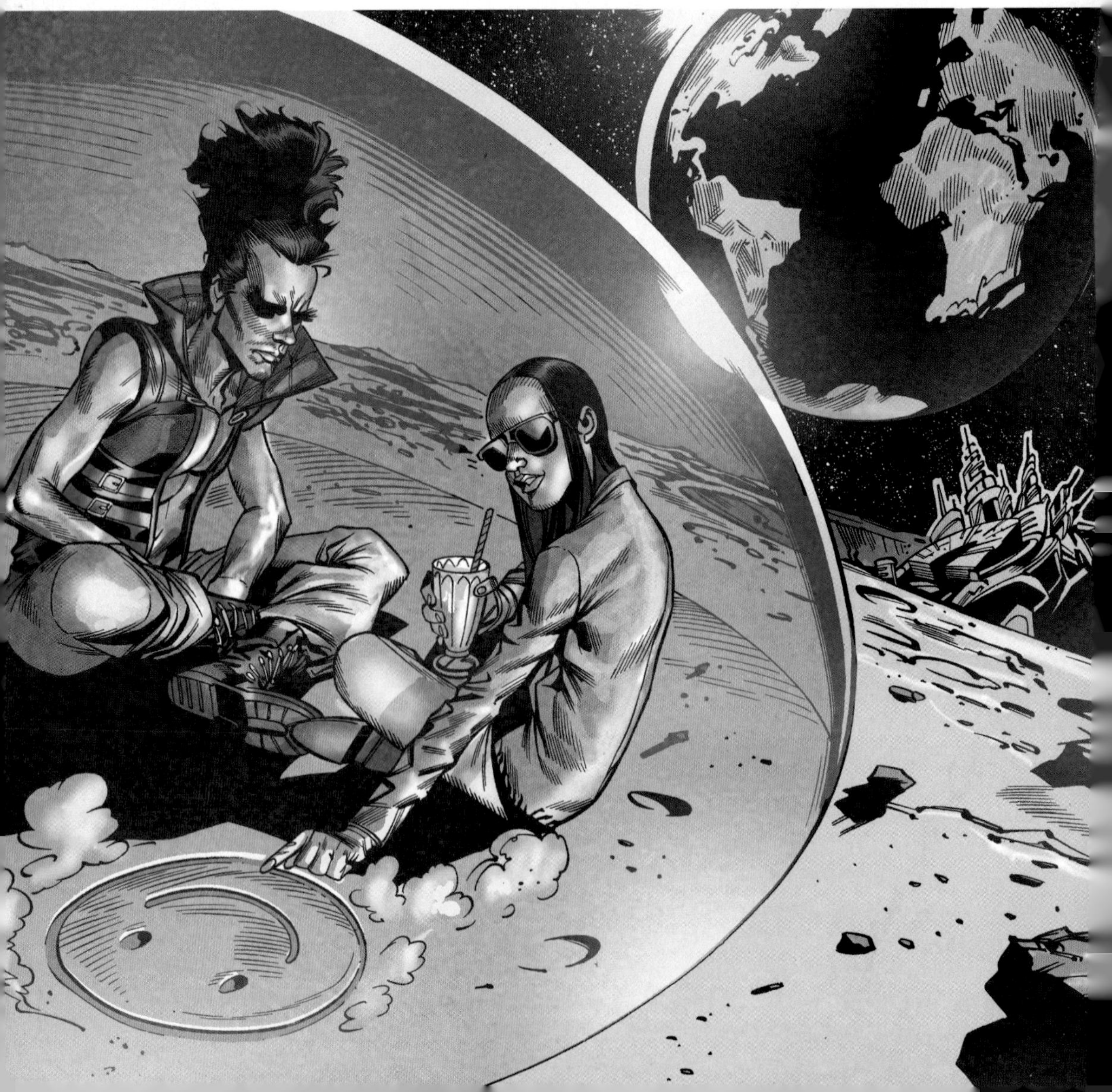

CHARLES XAVIER'S MUTANT SON DAVID HALLER WOULD BE NEARLY OMNIPOTENT IF HE COULD LOCK HIS MULTIPLE PERSONALITIES AWAY IN AN EFFECTIVE MENTAL PRISON. BUT THAT TASK SEEMS INSURMOUNTABLE IN THE WAKE OF HIS FATHER'S UNTIMELY DEATH. NOW, DAVID FIGHTS TO KEEP HIS MIND AND POWERS UNDER CONTROL AS HE WORKS TO UPHOLD HIS FATHER'S LEGACY.

Previously

BEFORE DAVID MET HIM AS A PAIR OF EYEBALLS, LUCA ALDINE HAD BEEN BORN-AGAIN TWICE. HIS FIRST CONVERSION — AT THE HANDS OF RELIGIOUS FANATICS — WAS FROM DRUG-ADDICT DIRTBAG TO MUTANT-HATING, MOTHER-MURDERING FUNDAMENTALIST. THEN, WHILE SHUFFLING OFF THE MORTAL COIL VIA LETHAL INJECTION, HE FILCHED SOME PSYCHIC POWER FROM HIS SISTER RUTH, A.K.A. BLINDFOLD, A STUDENT AT THE JEAN GREY SCHOOL AND DAVID'S TENTATIVE LOVE INTEREST. WITH THAT PSYCHIC THEFT, LUCA BECAME AN INCORPOREAL SPIRIT WITH VISIONS OF THE FUTURE — VISIONS THAT WOULD LEAD DAVID TO A CONFRONTATION WITH THE X-MEN AND WITH BLINDFOLD HERSELF.

AFTER A BATTLE WITH LUCA THAT SEEMED TO END IN DAVID'S VICTORY, WOLVERINE LET DAVID WALK AWAY FREELY. NOW, ALONE AGAIN, DAVID PURSUES HIS FATHER'S LEGACY WITH A SECRETIVE, PROACTIVE AGENDA...

X-MEN LEGACY VOL. 2: INVASIVE EXOTICS. Contains material originally published in magazine form as X-MEN LEGACY #7-12. First printing 2013. ISBN# 978-0-7851-6718-1. Published by MARVEL WORLDWIDE, INC., a subsidiary of MARVEL ENTERTAINMENT, LLC. OFFICE OF PUBLICATION: 135 West 50th Street, New York, NY 10020. Copyright © 2013 Marvel Characters, Inc. All rights reserved. All characters featured in this issue and the distinctive names and likenesses thereof, and all related indicia are trademarks of Marvel Characters, Inc. No similarity between any of the names, characters, persons, and/or institutions in this magazine with those of any living or dead person or institution is intended, and any such similarity which may exist is purely coincidental. **Printed in the U.S.A.** ALAN FINE, EVP - Office of the President, Marvel Worldwide, Inc. and EVP & CMO Marvel Characters B.V.: DAN BUCKLEY, Publisher & President - Print, Animation & Digital Divisions; JOE QUESADA, Chief Creative Officer; TOM BREVOORT, SVP of Publishing; DAVID BOGART, SVP of Operations & Procurement, Publishing; C.B. CEBULSKI, SVP of Creator & Content Development; DAVID GABRIEL, SVP of Print & Digital Publishing Sales; JIM O'KEEFE, VP of Operations & Logistics; DAN CARR, Executive Director of Publishing Technology; SUSAN CRESPI, Editorial Operations Manager; ALEX MORALES, Publishing Operations Manager; STAN LEE, Chairman Emeritus. For information regarding advertising in Marvel Comics or on Marvel.com, please contact Niza Disla, Director of Marvel Partnerships, at ndisla@marvel.com. For Marvel subscription inquiries, please call 800-217-9158. Manufactured between 7/5/2013 and 8/12/2013 by QUAD/GRAPHICS ST. CLOUD, ST. CLOUD, MN, USA.

10 9 8 7 6 5 4 3 2 1

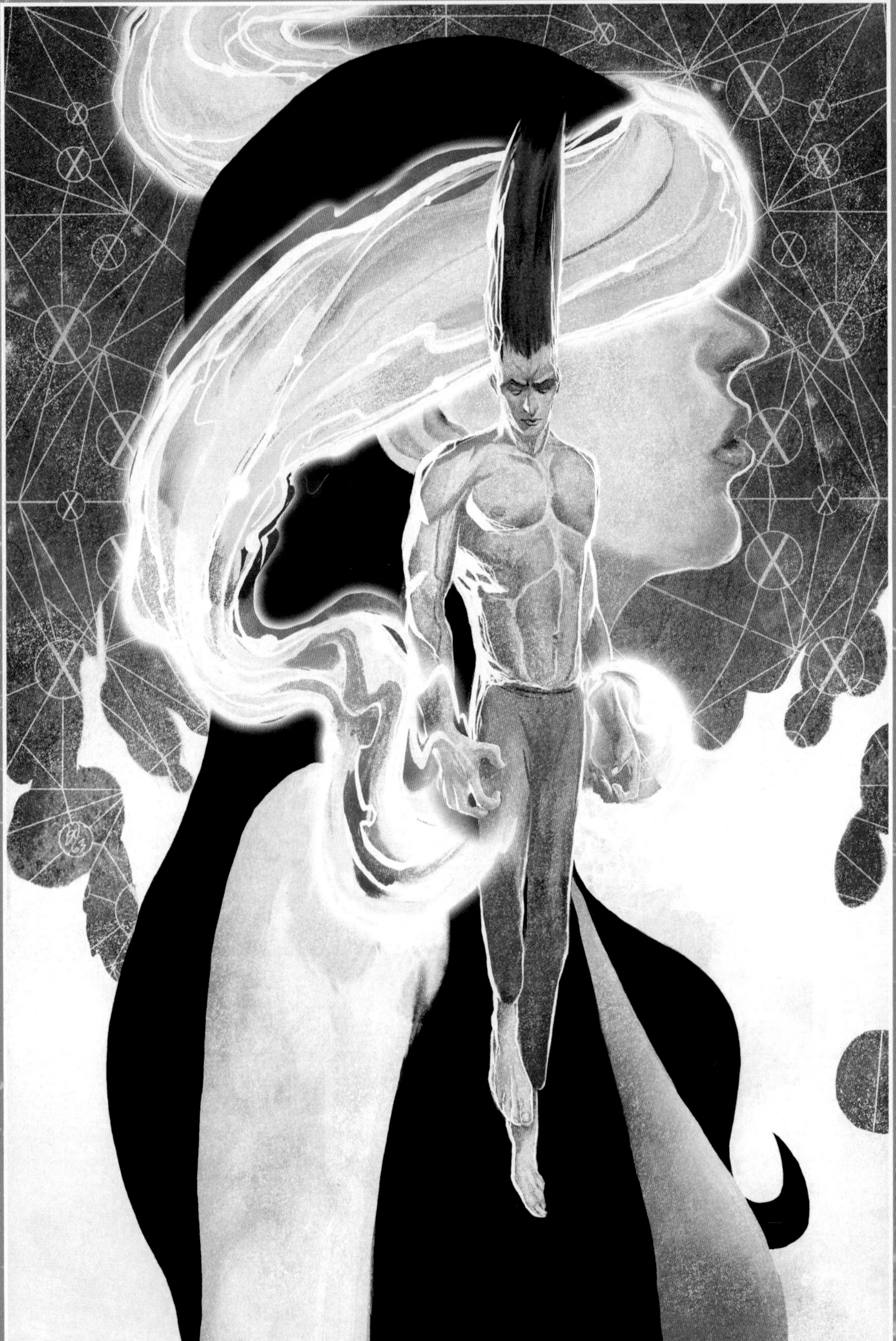

SEVEN

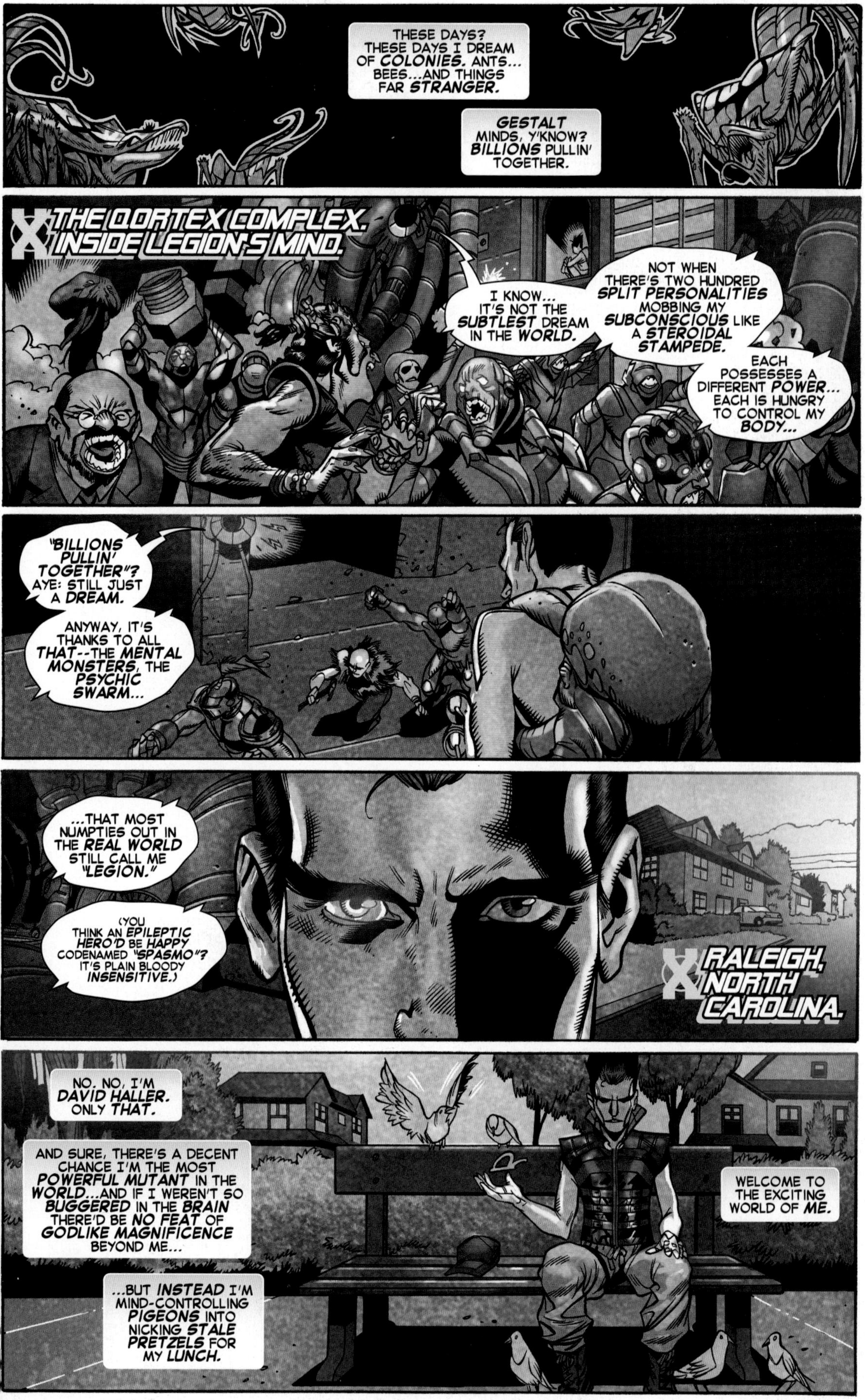
THESE DAYS? THESE DAYS I DREAM OF COLONIES. ANTS... BEES...AND THINGS FAR STRANGER.
GESTALT MINDS, Y'KNOW? BILLIONS PULLIN' TOGETHER.
THE QORTEX COMPLEX. INSIDE LEGION'S MIND.
I KNOW... IT'S NOT THE SUBTLEST DREAM IN THE WORLD.
NOT WHEN THERE'S TWO HUNDRED SPLIT PERSONALITIES MOBBING MY SUBCONSCIOUS LIKE A STEROIDAL STAMPEDE.
EACH POSSESSES A DIFFERENT POWER... EACH IS HUNGRY TO CONTROL MY BODY...
"BILLIONS PULLIN' TOGETHER"? AYE: STILL JUST A DREAM.
ANYWAY, IT'S THANKS TO ALL THAT--THE MENTAL MONSTERS, THE PSYCHIC SWARM...
...THAT MOST NUMPTIES OUT IN THE REAL WORLD STILL CALL ME "LEGION."
(YOU THINK AN EPILEPTIC HERO'D BE HAPPY CODENAMED "SPASMO"? IT'S PLAIN BLOODY INSENSITIVE.)
RALEIGH, NORTH CAROLINA.
NO. NO, I'M DAVID HALLER. ONLY THAT.
AND SURE, THERE'S A DECENT CHANCE I'M THE MOST POWERFUL MUTANT IN THE WORLD...AND IF I WEREN'T SO BUGGERED IN THE BRAIN THERE'D BE NO FEAT OF GODLIKE MAGNIFICENCE BEYOND ME...
...BUT INSTEAD I'M MIND-CONTROLLING PIGEONS INTO NICKING STALE PRETZELS FOR MY LUNCH.
WELCOME TO THE EXCITING WORLD OF ME.

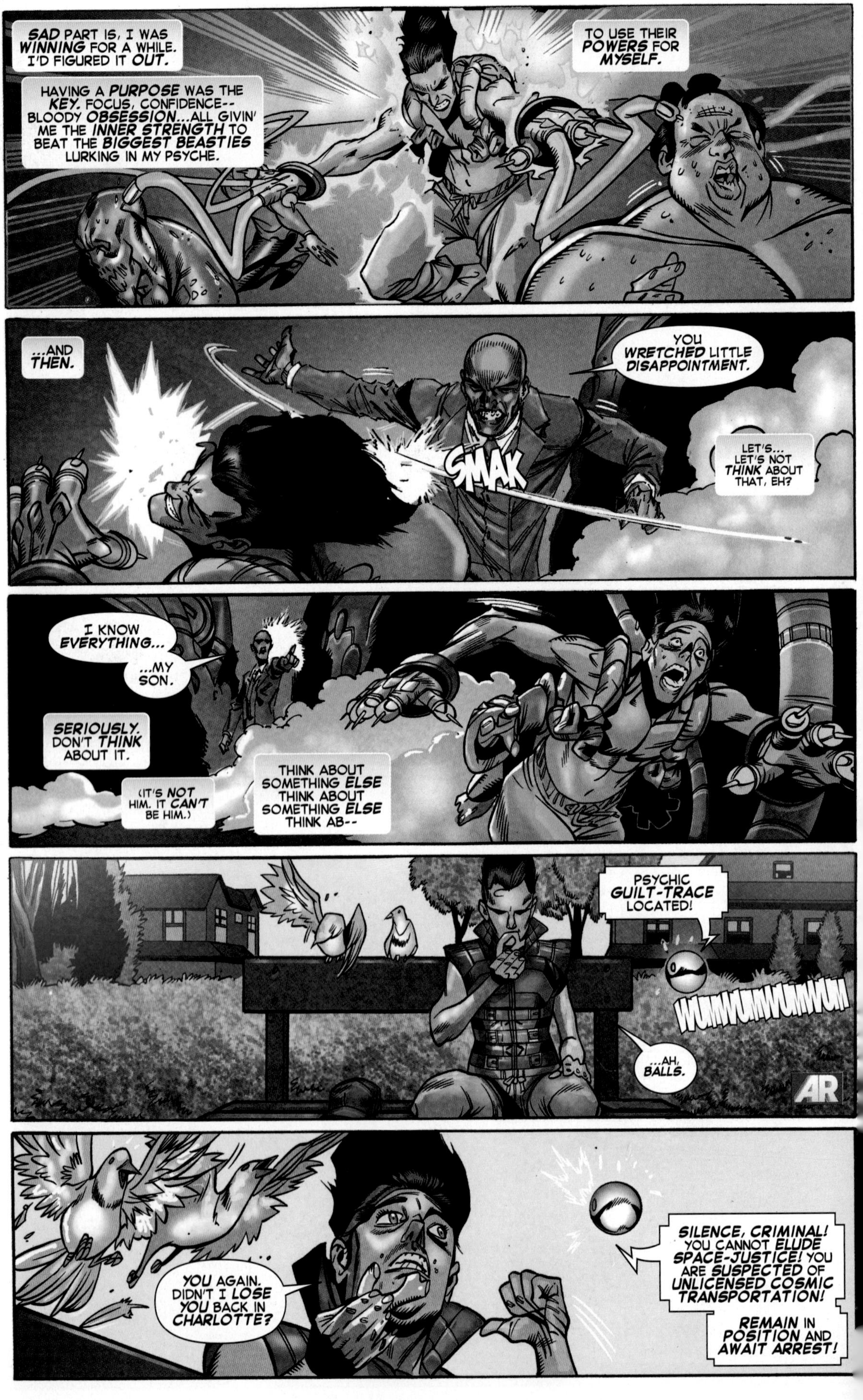
SAD PART IS, I WAS WINNING FOR A WHILE. I'D FIGURED IT OUT.
HAVING A PURPOSE WAS THE KEY. FOCUS, CONFIDENCE-- BLOODY OBSESSION...ALL GIVIN' ME THE INNER STRENGTH TO BEAT THE BIGGEST BEASTIES LURKING IN MY PSYCHE.
TO USE THEIR POWERS FOR MYSELF.
...AND THEN.
YOU WRETCHED LITTLE DISAPPOINTMENT.
SMAK
LET'S... LET'S NOT THINK ABOUT THAT, EH?
I KNOW EVERYTHING...
...MY SON.
SERIOUSLY. DON'T THINK ABOUT IT.
(IT'S NOT HIM. IT CAN'T BE HIM.)
THINK ABOUT SOMETHING ELSE THINK ABOUT SOMETHING ELSE THINK AB--
PSYCHIC GUILT-TRACE LOCATED!
WUMWUMWUMWUM
...AH, BALLS.
AR
YOU AGAIN. DIDN'T I LOSE YOU BACK IN CHARLOTTE?
SILENCE, CRIMINAL! YOU CANNOT ELUDE SPACE-JUSTICE! YOU ARE SUSPECTED OF UNLICENSED COSMIC TRANSPORTATION!
REMAIN IN POSITION AND AWAIT ARREST!

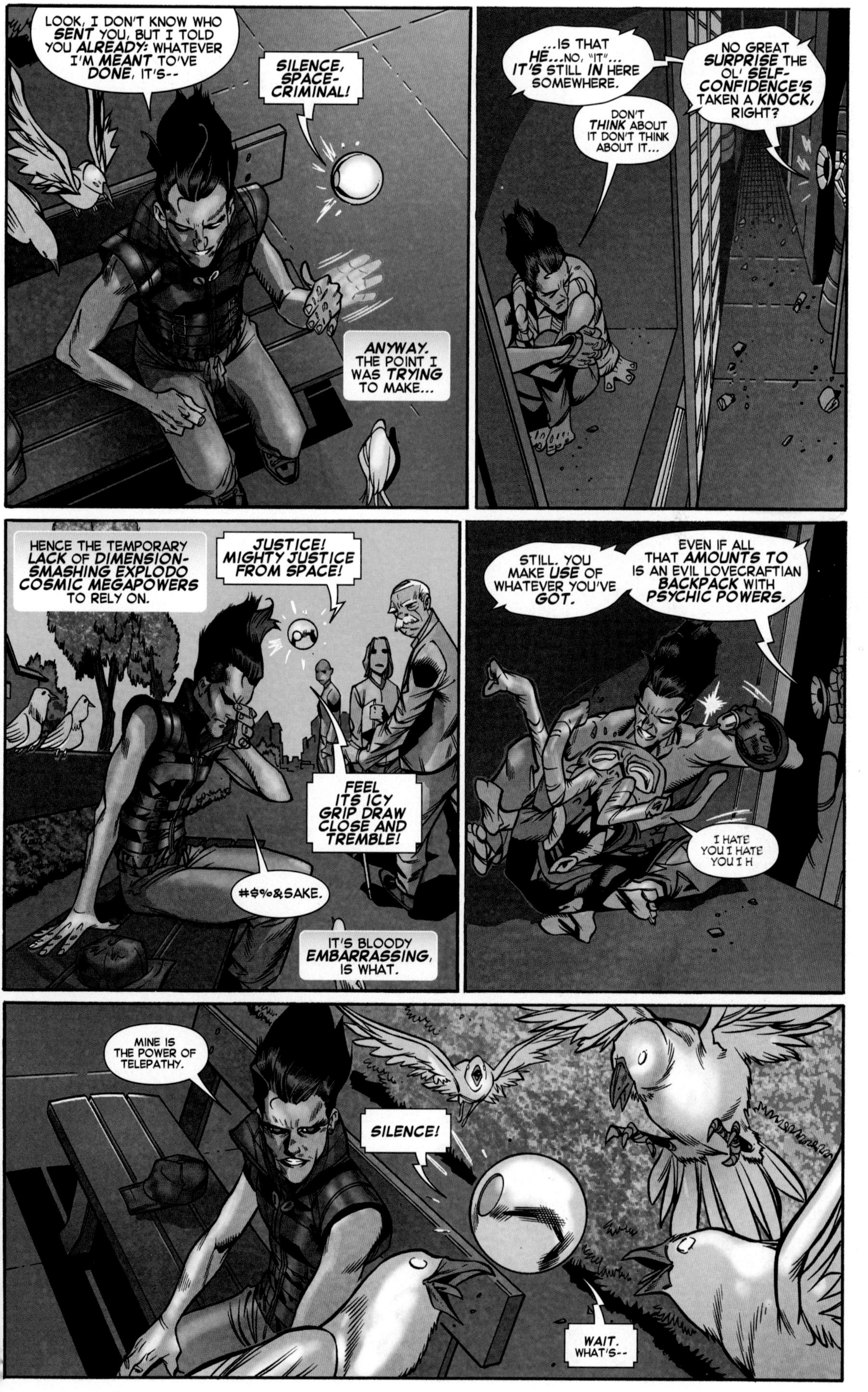
LOOK, I DON'T KNOW WHO SENT YOU, BUT I TOLD YOU ALREADY: WHATEVER I'M MEANT TO'VE DONE, IT'S--
SILENCE, SPACE-CRIMINAL!
ANYWAY. THE POINT I WAS TRYING TO MAKE...
...IS THAT HE...NO, "IT"... IT'S STILL IN HERE SOMEWHERE.
DON'T THINK ABOUT IT DON'T THINK ABOUT IT...
NO GREAT SURPRISE THE OL' SELF-CONFIDENCE'S TAKEN A KNOCK, RIGHT?
HENCE THE TEMPORARY LACK OF DIMENSION-SMASHING EXPLODO COSMIC MEGAPOWERS TO RELY ON.
JUSTICE! MIGHTY JUSTICE FROM SPACE!
FEEL ITS ICY GRIP DRAW CLOSE AND TREMBLE!
#$%&SAKE.
IT'S BLOODY EMBARRASSING, IS WHAT.
STILL. YOU MAKE USE OF WHATEVER YOU'VE GOT.
EVEN IF ALL THAT AMOUNTS TO IS AN EVIL LOVECRAFTIAN BACKPACK WITH PSYCHIC POWERS.
I HATE YOU I HATE YOU I H
MINE IS THE POWER OF TELEPATHY.
SILENCE!
WAIT. WHAT'S--

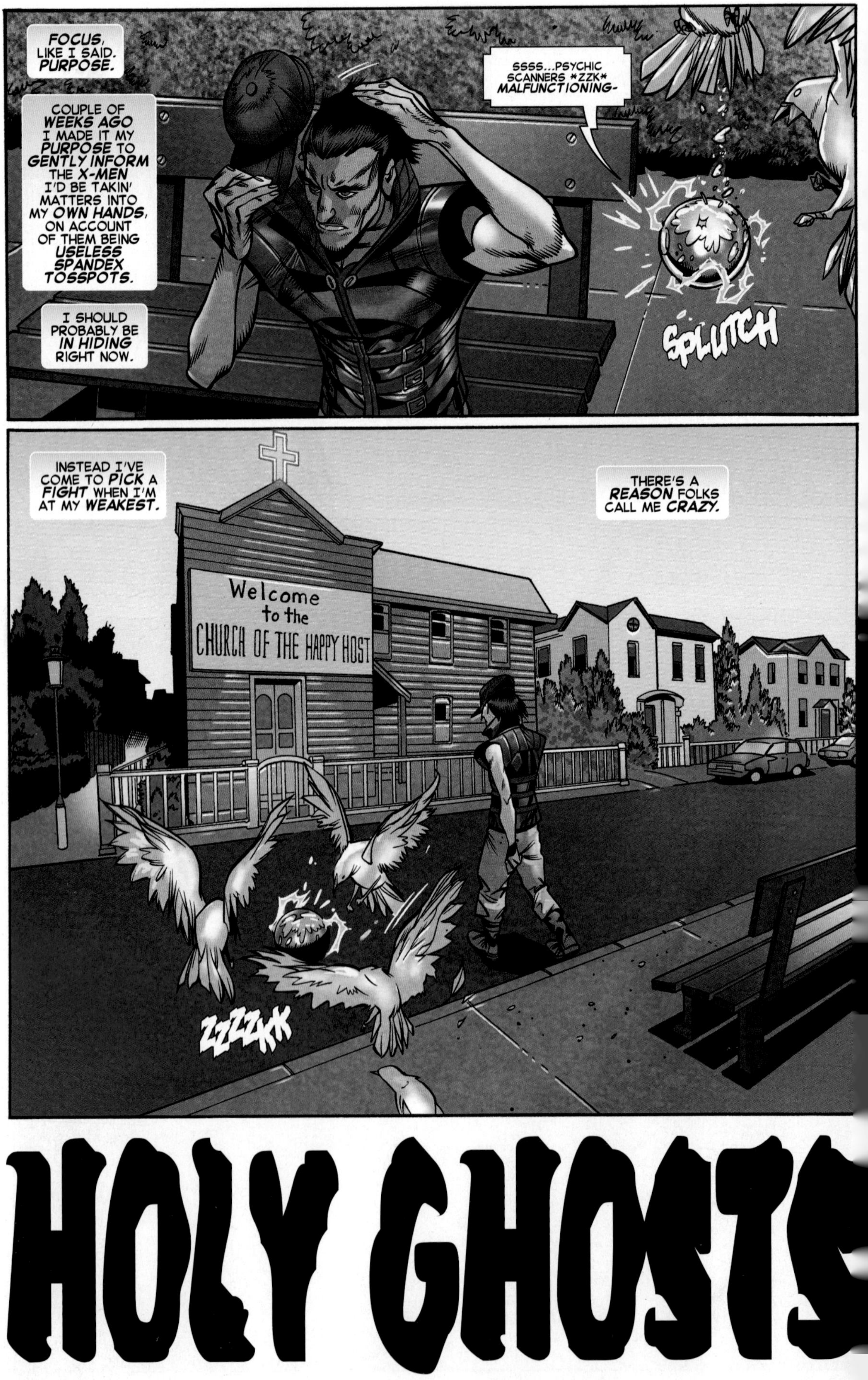
FOCUS, LIKE I SAID. PURPOSE.
COUPLE OF WEEKS AGO I MADE IT MY PURPOSE TO GENTLY INFORM THE X-MEN I'D BE TAKIN' MATTERS INTO MY OWN HANDS, ON ACCOUNT OF THEM BEING USELESS SPANDEX TOSSPOTS.
I SHOULD PROBABLY BE IN HIDING RIGHT NOW.
SSSS...PSYCHIC SCANNERS *ZZK* MALFUNCTIONING-
SPLUTCH
INSTEAD I'VE COME TO PICK A FIGHT WHEN I'M AT MY WEAKEST.
THERE'S A REASON FOLKS CALL ME CRAZY.
Welcome to the CHURCH OF THE HAPPY HOST
ZZZZKK

HOLY GHOSTS

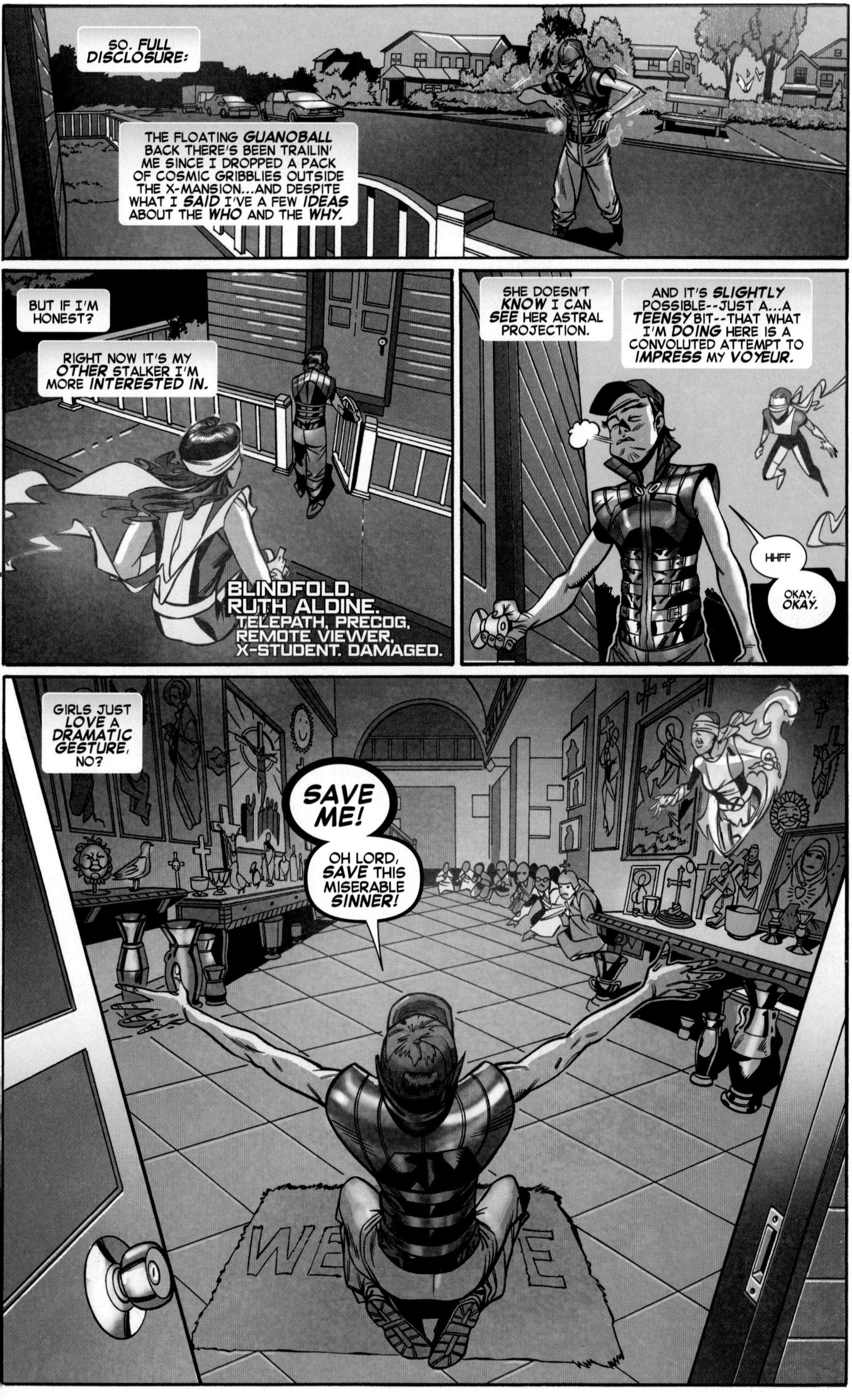
SO. FULL DISCLOSURE:
THE FLOATING GUANOBALL BACK THERE'S BEEN TRAILIN' ME SINCE I DROPPED A PACK OF COSMIC GRIBBLIES OUTSIDE THE X-MANSION...AND DESPITE WHAT I SAID I'VE A FEW IDEAS ABOUT THE WHO AND THE WHY.
BUT IF I'M HONEST?
RIGHT NOW IT'S MY OTHER STALKER I'M MORE INTERESTED IN.
BLINDFOLD. RUTH ALDINE.
TELEPATH, PRECOG, REMOTE VIEWER, X-STUDENT. DAMAGED.
SHE DOESN'T KNOW I CAN SEE HER ASTRAL PROJECTION.
AND IT'S SLIGHTLY POSSIBLE--JUST A...A TEENSY BIT--THAT WHAT I'M DOING HERE IS A CONVOLUTED ATTEMPT TO IMPRESS MY VOYEUR.
HHFF
OKAY. OKAY.
GIRLS JUST LOVE A DRAMATIC GESTURE, NO?
SAVE ME!
OH LORD, SAVE THIS MISERABLE SINNER!

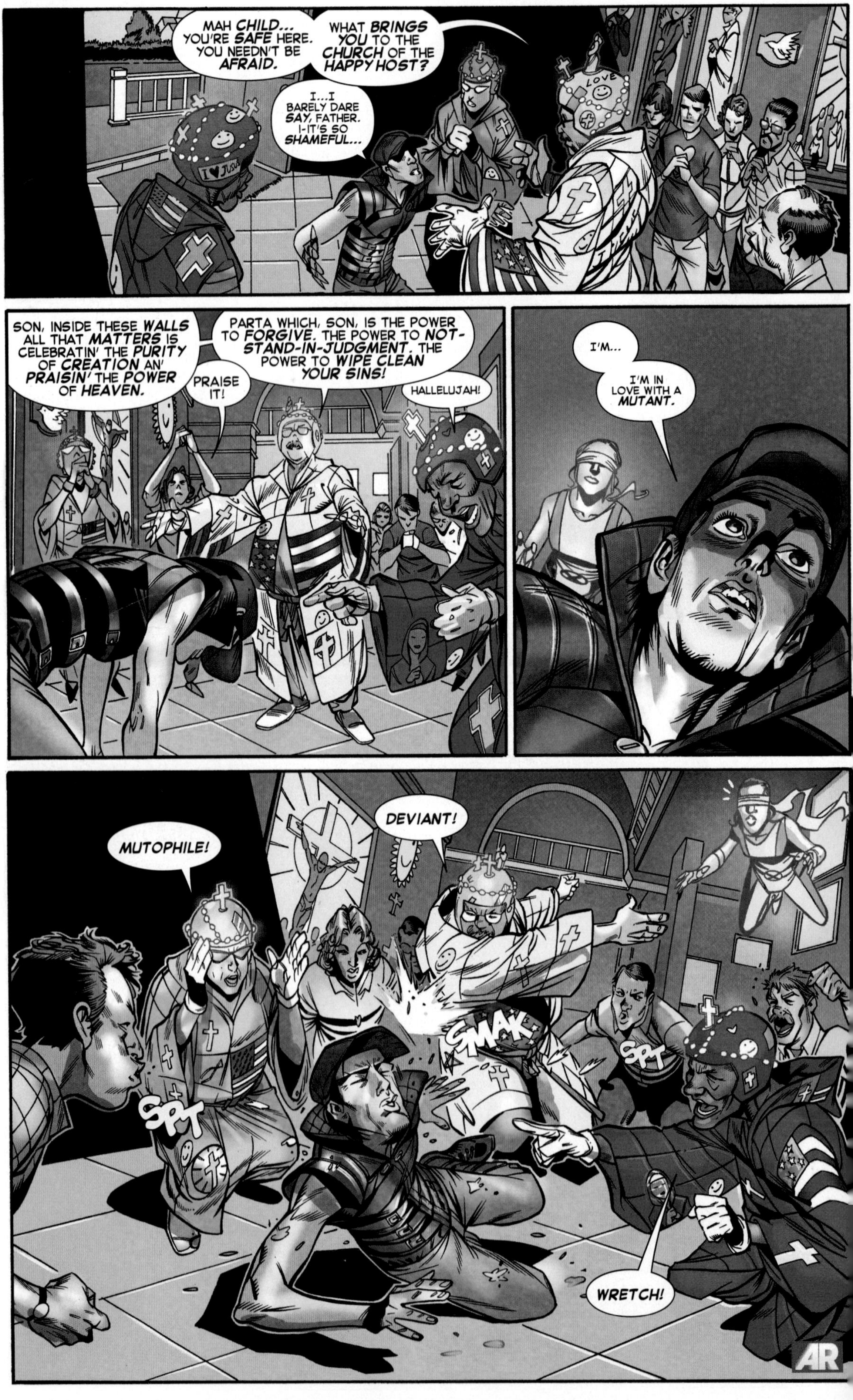
MAH CHILD... YOU'RE SAFE HERE. YOU NEEDN'T BE AFRAID.
WHAT BRINGS YOU TO THE CHURCH OF THE HAPPY HOST?
I...I BARELY DARE SAY, FATHER. I-IT'S SO SHAMEFUL...
SON, INSIDE THESE WALLS ALL THAT MATTERS IS CELEBRATIN' THE PURITY OF CREATION AN' PRAISIN' THE POWER OF HEAVEN.
PARTA WHICH, SON, IS THE POWER TO FORGIVE. THE POWER TO NOT-STAND-IN-JUDGMENT. THE POWER TO WIPE CLEAN YOUR SINS!
PRAISE IT!
HALLELUJAH!
I'M...
I'M IN LOVE WITH A MUTANT.
MUTOPHILE!
DEVIANT!
SMAK
SPT
SPT
WRETCH!

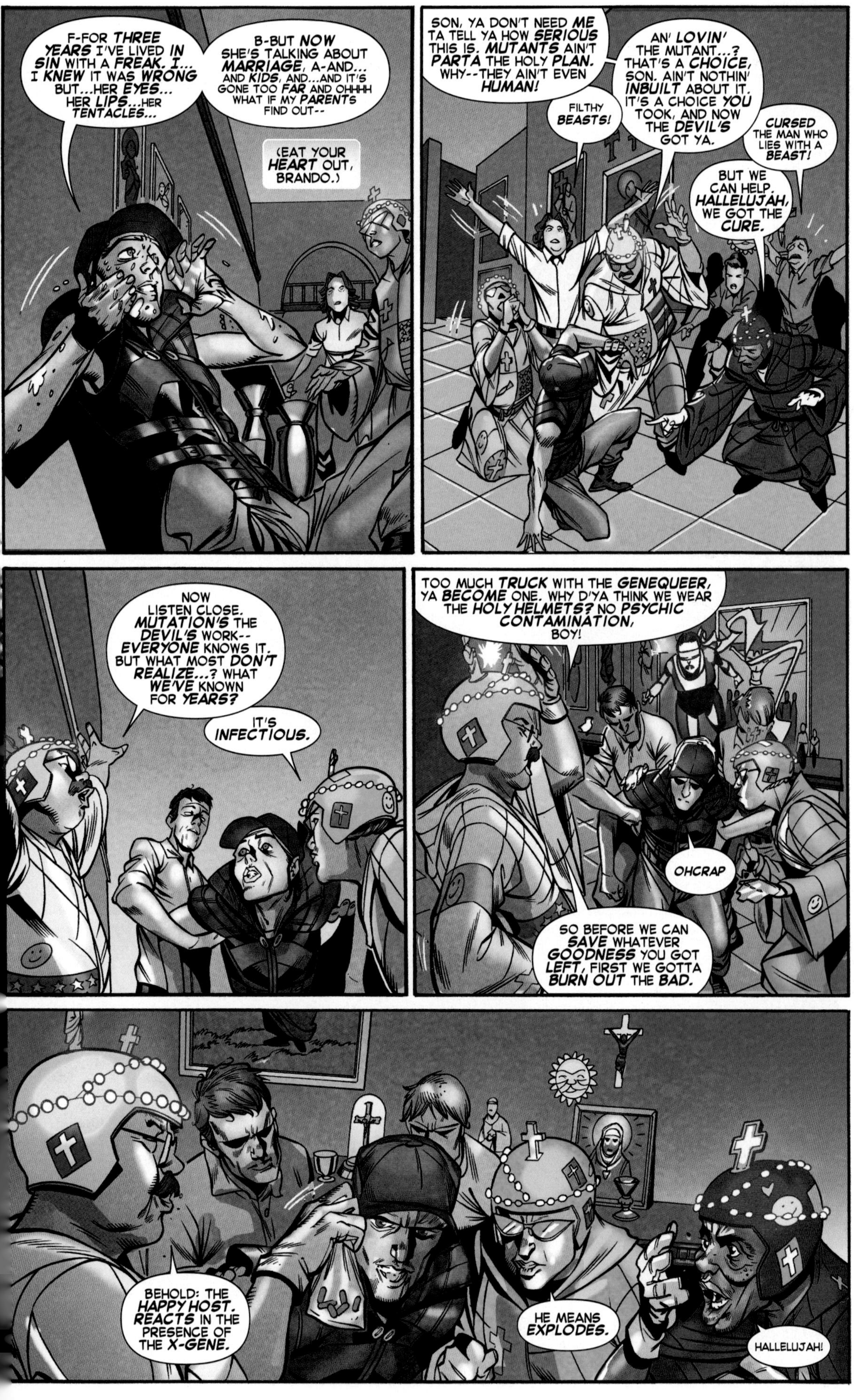
F-FOR THREE YEARS I'VE LIVED IN SIN WITH A FREAK. I... I KNEW IT WAS WRONG BUT...HER EYES... HER LIPS...HER TENTACLES...
B-BUT NOW SHE'S TALKING ABOUT MARRIAGE, A-AND... AND KIDS, AND...AND IT'S GONE TOO FAR AND OHHHH WHAT IF MY PARENTS FIND OUT--
(EAT YOUR HEART OUT, BRANDO.)
SON, YA DON'T NEED ME TA TELL YA HOW SERIOUS THIS IS. MUTANTS AIN'T PARTA THE HOLY PLAN. WHY--THEY AIN'T EVEN HUMAN!
FILTHY BEASTS!
AN' LOVIN' THE MUTANT...? THAT'S A CHOICE, SON. AIN'T NOTHIN' INBUILT ABOUT IT. IT'S A CHOICE YOU TOOK, AND NOW THE DEVIL'S GOT YA.
CURSED THE MAN WHO LIES WITH A BEAST!
BUT WE CAN HELP. HALLELUJAH, WE GOT THE CURE.
NOW LISTEN CLOSE. MUTATION'S THE DEVIL'S WORK-- EVERYONE KNOWS IT. BUT WHAT MOST DON'T REALIZE...? WHAT WE'VE KNOWN FOR YEARS?
IT'S INFECTIOUS.
TOO MUCH TRUCK WITH THE GENEQUEER, YA BECOME ONE. WHY D'YA THINK WE WEAR THE HOLY HELMETS? NO PSYCHIC CONTAMINATION, BOY!
OHCRAP
SO BEFORE WE CAN SAVE WHATEVER GOODNESS YOU GOT LEFT, FIRST WE GOTTA BURN OUT THE BAD.
BEHOLD: THE HAPPY HOST. REACTS IN THE PRESENCE OF THE X-GENE.
HE MEANS EXPLODES.
HALLELUJAH!

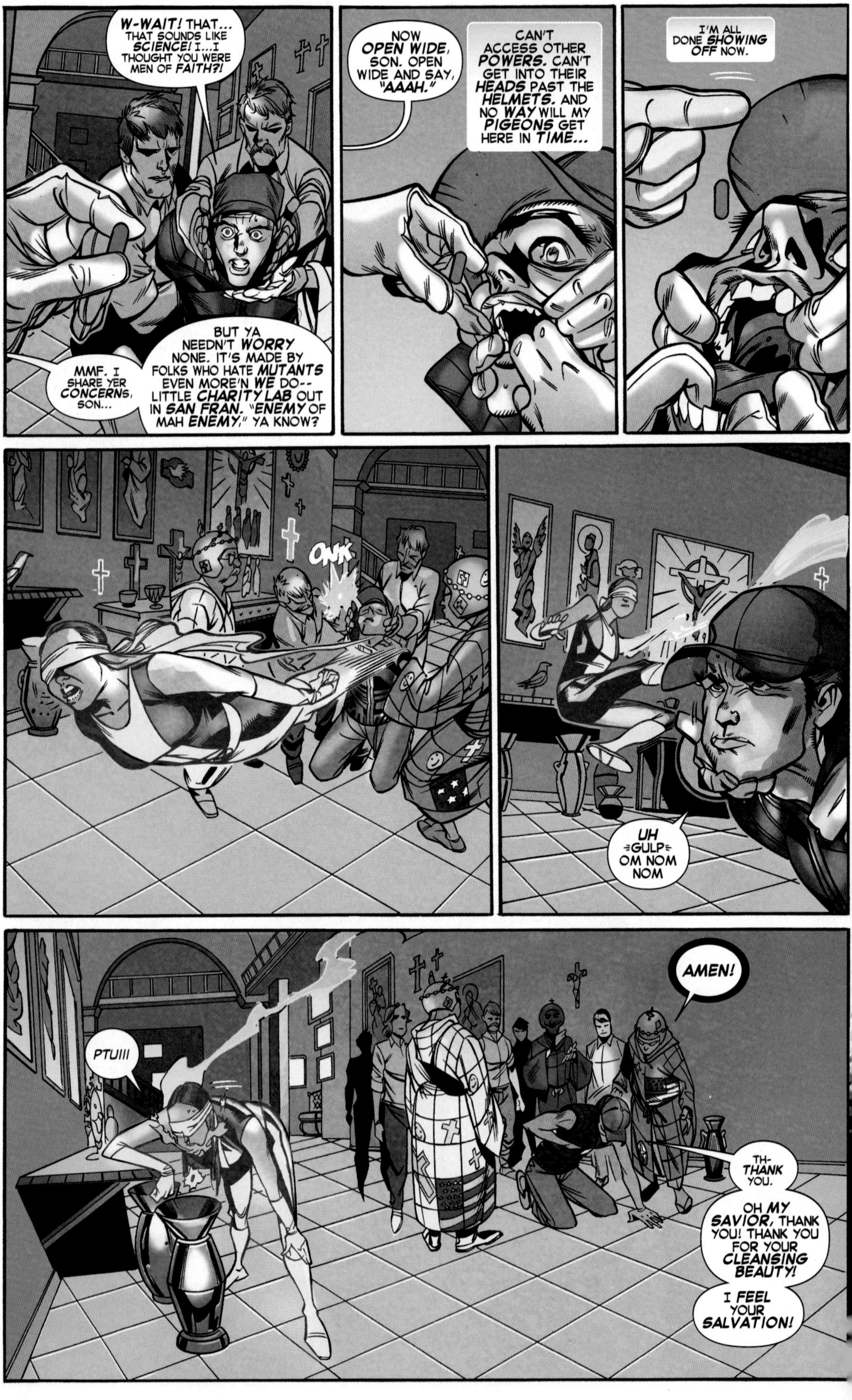
W-WAIT! THAT... THAT SOUNDS LIKE SCIENCE! I...I THOUGHT YOU WERE MEN OF FAITH?!
MMF. I SHARE YER CONCERNS, SON...
BUT YA NEEDN'T WORRY NONE. IT'S MADE BY FOLKS WHO HATE MUTANTS EVEN MORE'N WE DO-- LITTLE CHARITY LAB OUT IN SAN FRAN. "ENEMY OF MAH ENEMY," YA KNOW?
NOW OPEN WIDE, SON. OPEN WIDE AND SAY, "AAAH."
CAN'T ACCESS OTHER POWERS. CAN'T GET INTO THEIR HEADS PAST THE HELMETS. AND NO WAY WILL MY PIGEONS GET HERE IN TIME...
I'M ALL DONE SHOWING OFF NOW.
ONK
UH GULP OM NOM NOM
PTUIII
AMEN!
TH-THANK YOU.
OH MY SAVIOR, THANK YOU! THANK YOU FOR YOUR CLEANSING BEAUTY!
I FEEL YOUR SALVATION!

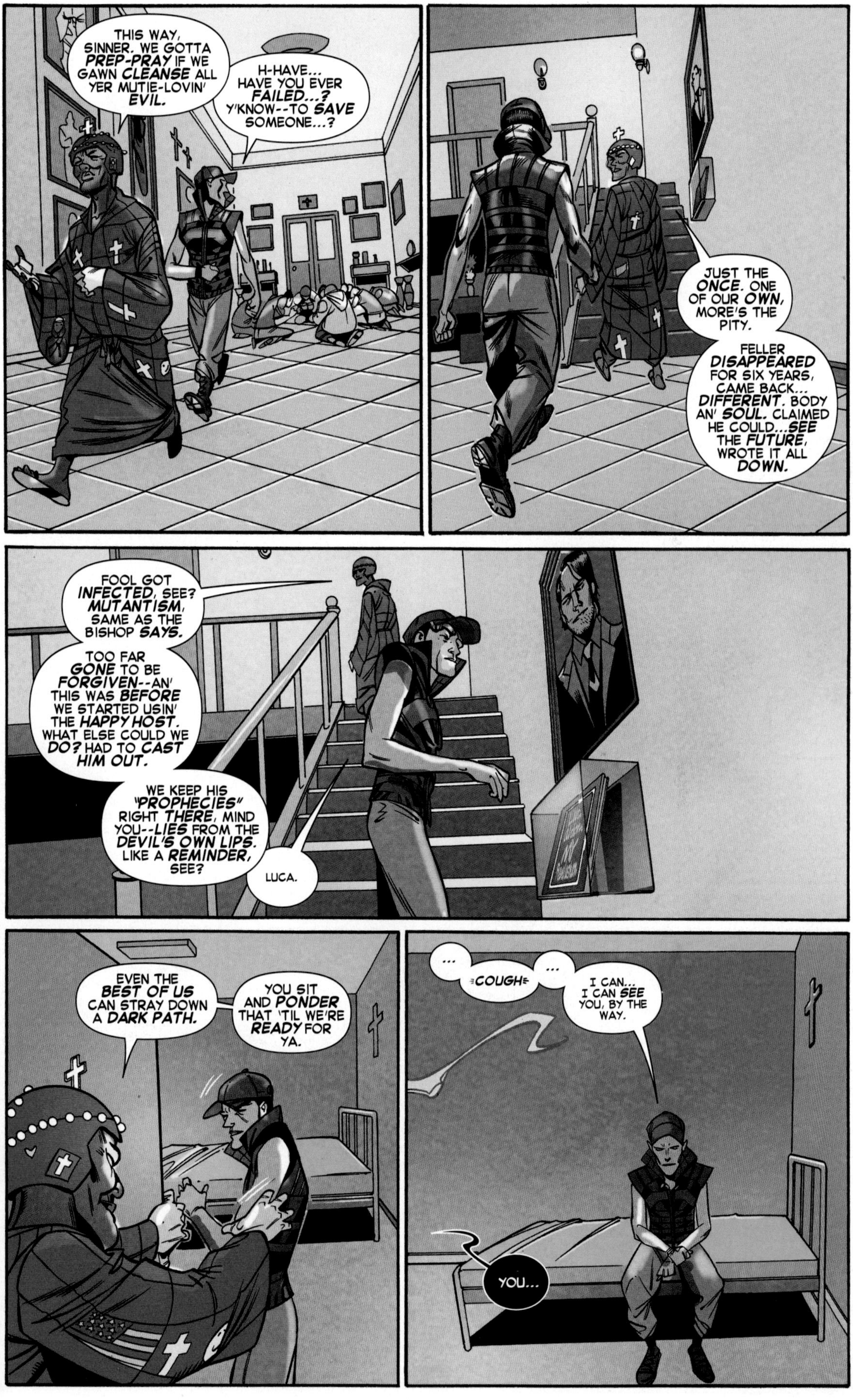
THIS WAY, SINNER. WE GOTTA PREP-PRAY IF WE GAWN CLEANSE ALL YER MUTIE-LOVIN' EVIL.
H-HAVE... HAVE YOU EVER FAILED...? Y'KNOW--TO SAVE SOMEONE...?
JUST THE ONCE. ONE OF OUR OWN, MORE'S THE PITY.
FELLER DISAPPEARED FOR SIX YEARS, CAME BACK... DIFFERENT. BODY AN' SOUL. CLAIMED HE COULD...SEE THE FUTURE, WROTE IT ALL DOWN.
FOOL GOT INFECTED, SEE? MUTANTISM, SAME AS THE BISHOP SAYS.
TOO FAR GONE TO BE FORGIVEN--AN' THIS WAS BEFORE WE STARTED USIN' THE HAPPY HOST. WHAT ELSE COULD WE DO? HAD TO CAST HIM OUT.
WE KEEP HIS "PROPHECIES" RIGHT THERE, MIND YOU--LIES FROM THE DEVIL'S OWN LIPS. LIKE A REMINDER, SEE?
LUCA.
EVEN THE BEST OF US CAN STRAY DOWN A DARK PATH.
YOU SIT AND PONDER THAT 'TIL WE'RE READY FOR YA.
...
COUGH
...
I CAN... I CAN SEE YOU, BY THE WAY.
YOU...

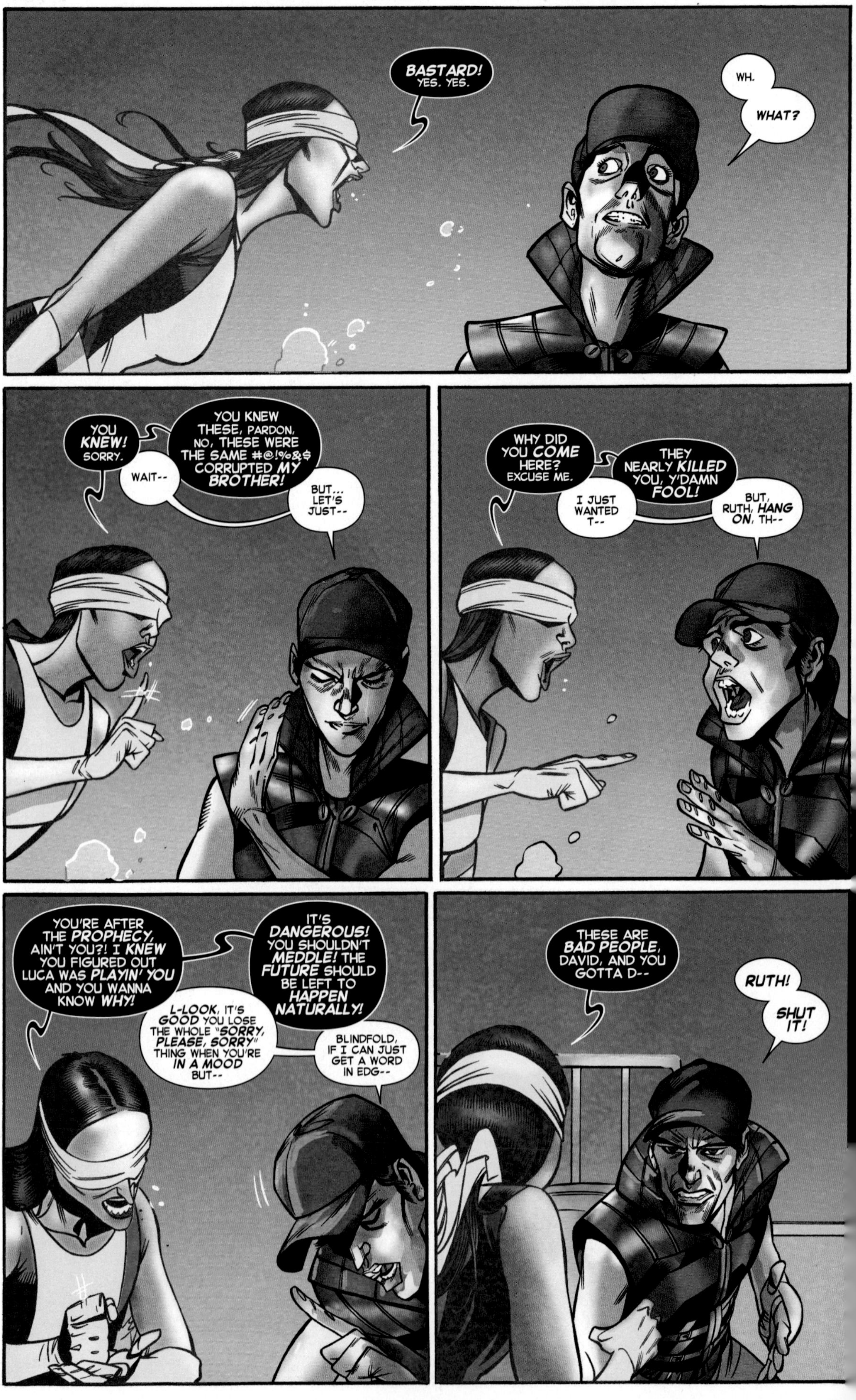
BASTARD! YES. YES.
WH.
WHAT?
YOU KNEW! SORRY.
WAIT--
YOU KNEW THESE, PARDON, NO, THESE WERE THE SAME #@!%&$ CORRUPTED MY BROTHER!
BUT... LET'S JUST--
WHY DID YOU COME HERE? EXCUSE ME.
I JUST WANTED T--
THEY NEARLY KILLED YOU, Y'DAMN FOOL!
BUT, RUTH, HANG ON, TH--
YOU'RE AFTER THE PROPHECY, AIN'T YOU?! I KNEW YOU FIGURED OUT LUCA WAS PLAYIN' YOU AND YOU WANNA KNOW WHY!
L-LOOK, IT'S GOOD YOU LOSE THE WHOLE "SORRY, PLEASE, SORRY" THING WHEN YOU'RE IN A MOOD BUT--
IT'S DANGEROUS! YOU SHOULDN'T MEDDLE! THE FUTURE SHOULD BE LEFT TO HAPPEN NATURALLY!
BLINDFOLD, IF I CAN JUST GET A WORD IN EDG--
THESE ARE BAD PEOPLE, DAVID, AND YOU GOTTA D--
RUTH!
SHUT IT!

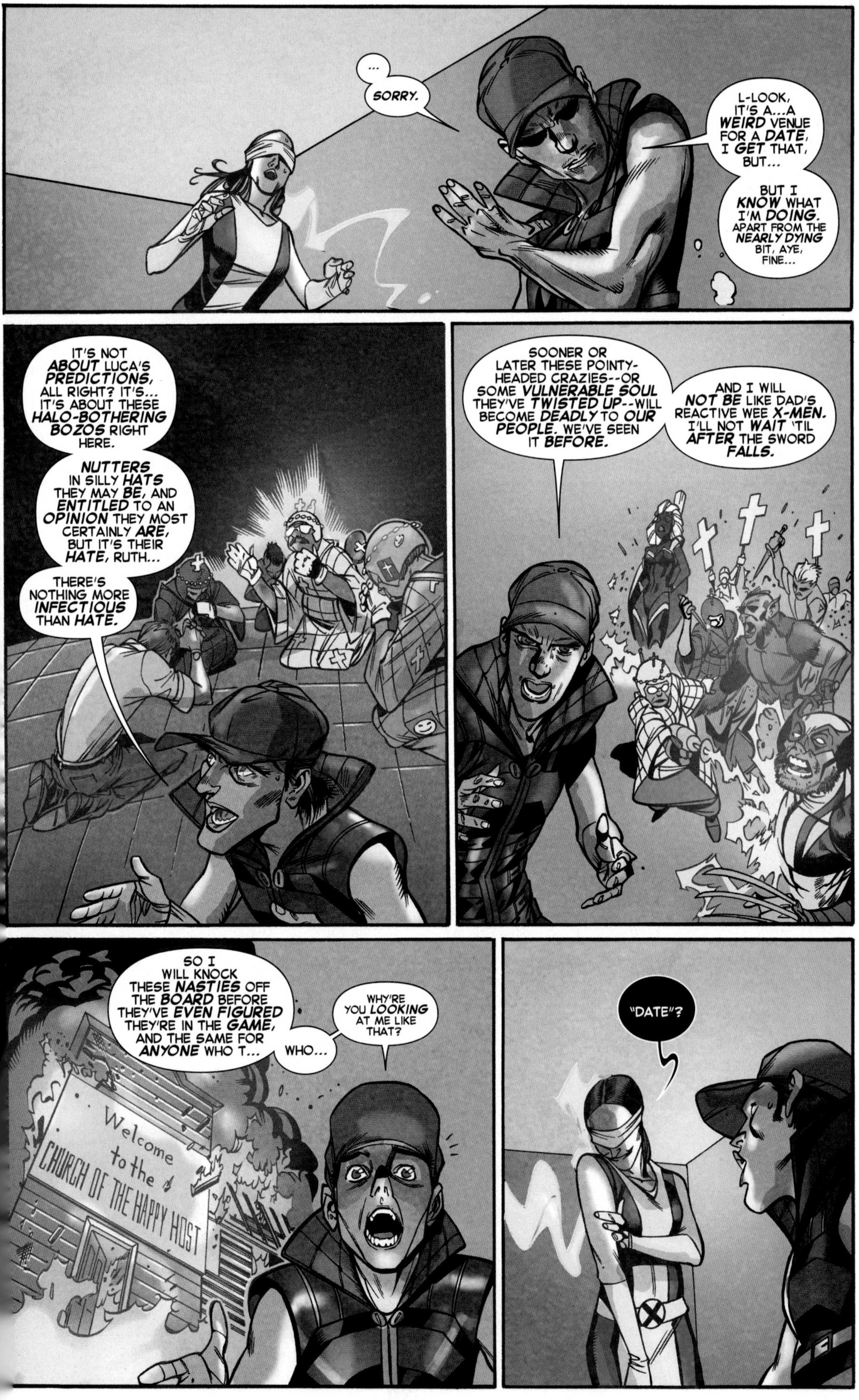
...
SORRY.
L-LOOK, IT'S A...A WEIRD VENUE FOR A DATE, I GET THAT, BUT...
BUT I KNOW WHAT I'M DOING. APART FROM THE NEARLY DYING BIT, AYE, FINE...
IT'S NOT ABOUT LUCA'S PREDICTIONS, ALL RIGHT? IT'S... IT'S ABOUT THESE HALO-BOTHERING BOZOS RIGHT HERE.
NUTTERS IN SILLY HATS THEY MAY BE, AND ENTITLED TO AN OPINION THEY MOST CERTAINLY ARE, BUT IT'S THEIR HATE, RUTH...
THERE'S NOTHING MORE INFECTIOUS THAN HATE.
SOONER OR LATER THESE POINTY-HEADED CRAZIES--OR SOME VULNERABLE SOUL THEY'VE TWISTED UP--WILL BECOME DEADLY TO OUR PEOPLE. WE'VE SEEN IT BEFORE.
AND I WILL NOT BE LIKE DAD'S REACTIVE WEE X-MEN. I'LL NOT WAIT 'TIL AFTER THE SWORD FALLS.
SO I WILL KNOCK THESE NASTIES OFF THE BOARD BEFORE THEY'VE EVEN FIGURED THEY'RE IN THE GAME, AND THE SAME FOR ANYONE WHO T...
WHO...
WHY'RE YOU LOOKING AT ME LIKE THAT?
Welcome to the CHURCH OF THE HAPPY HOST
"DATE"?

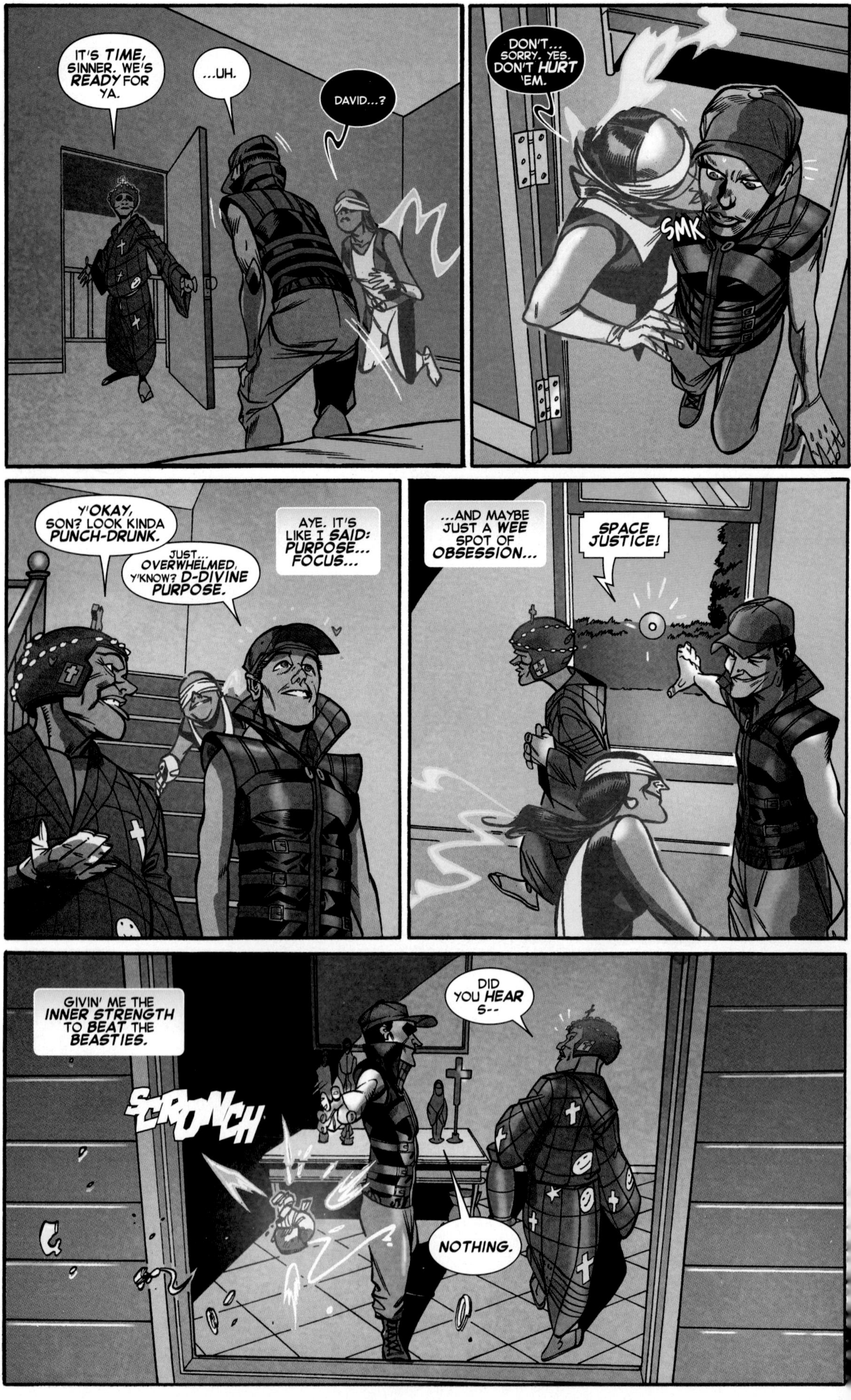
IT'S TIME, SINNER. WE'S READY FOR YA.
...UH.
DAVID...?
DON'T... SORRY. YES. DON'T HURT 'EM.
SMK
Y'OKAY, SON? LOOK KINDA PUNCH-DRUNK.
JUST... OVERWHELMED, Y'KNOW? D-DIVINE PURPOSE.
AYE. IT'S LIKE I SAID: PURPOSE... FOCUS...
...AND MAYBE JUST A WEE SPOT OF OBSESSION...
SPACE JUSTICE!
GIVIN' ME THE INNER STRENGTH TO BEAT THE BEASTIES.
DID YOU HEAR S--
SCRONCH
NOTHING.

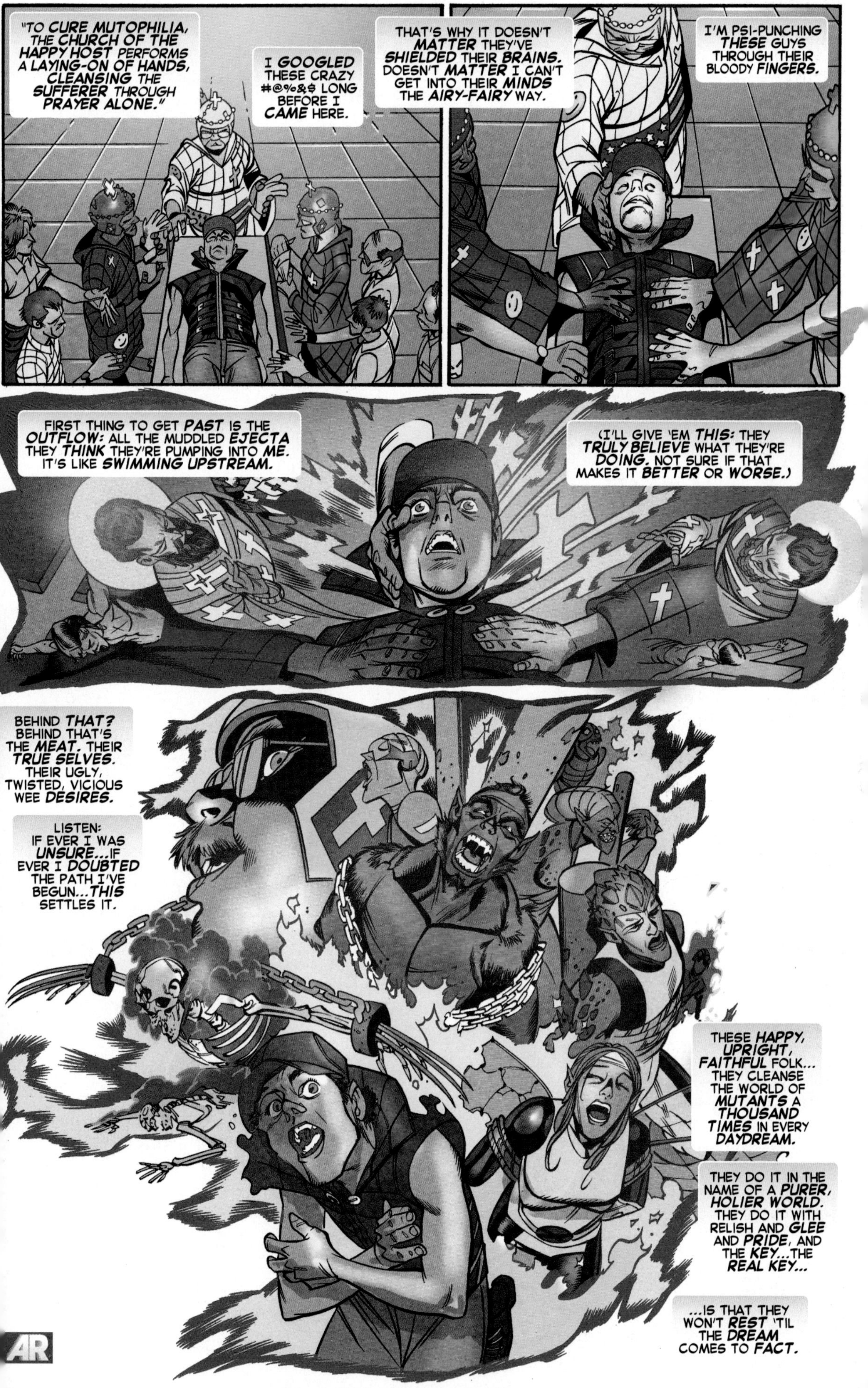
"TO CURE MUTOPHILIA, THE CHURCH OF THE HAPPY HOST PERFORMS A LAYING-ON OF HANDS, CLEANSING THE SUFFERER THROUGH PRAYER ALONE."
I GOOGLED THESE CRAZY #@%&$ LONG BEFORE I CAME HERE.
THAT'S WHY IT DOESN'T MATTER THEY'VE SHIELDED THEIR BRAINS. DOESN'T MATTER I CAN'T GET INTO THEIR MINDS THE AIRY-FAIRY WAY.
I'M PSI-PUNCHING THESE GUYS THROUGH THEIR BLOODY FINGERS.
FIRST THING TO GET PAST IS THE OUTFLOW: ALL THE MUDDLED EJECTA THEY THINK THEY'RE PUMPING INTO ME. IT'S LIKE SWIMMING UPSTREAM.
(I'LL GIVE 'EM THIS: THEY TRULY BELIEVE WHAT THEY'RE DOING. NOT SURE IF THAT MAKES IT BETTER OR WORSE.)
BEHIND THAT? BEHIND THAT'S THE MEAT. THEIR TRUE SELVES. THEIR UGLY, TWISTED, VICIOUS WEE DESIRES.
LISTEN: IF EVER I WAS UNSURE...IF EVER I DOUBTED THE PATH I'VE BEGUN...THIS SETTLES IT.
THESE HAPPY, UPRIGHT, FAITHFUL FOLK... THEY CLEANSE THE WORLD OF MUTANTS A THOUSAND TIMES IN EVERY DAYDREAM.
THEY DO IT IN THE NAME OF A PURER, HOLIER WORLD. THEY DO IT WITH RELISH AND GLEE AND PRIDE, AND THE KEY...THE REAL KEY...
...IS THAT THEY WON'T REST 'TIL THE DREAM COMES TO FACT.

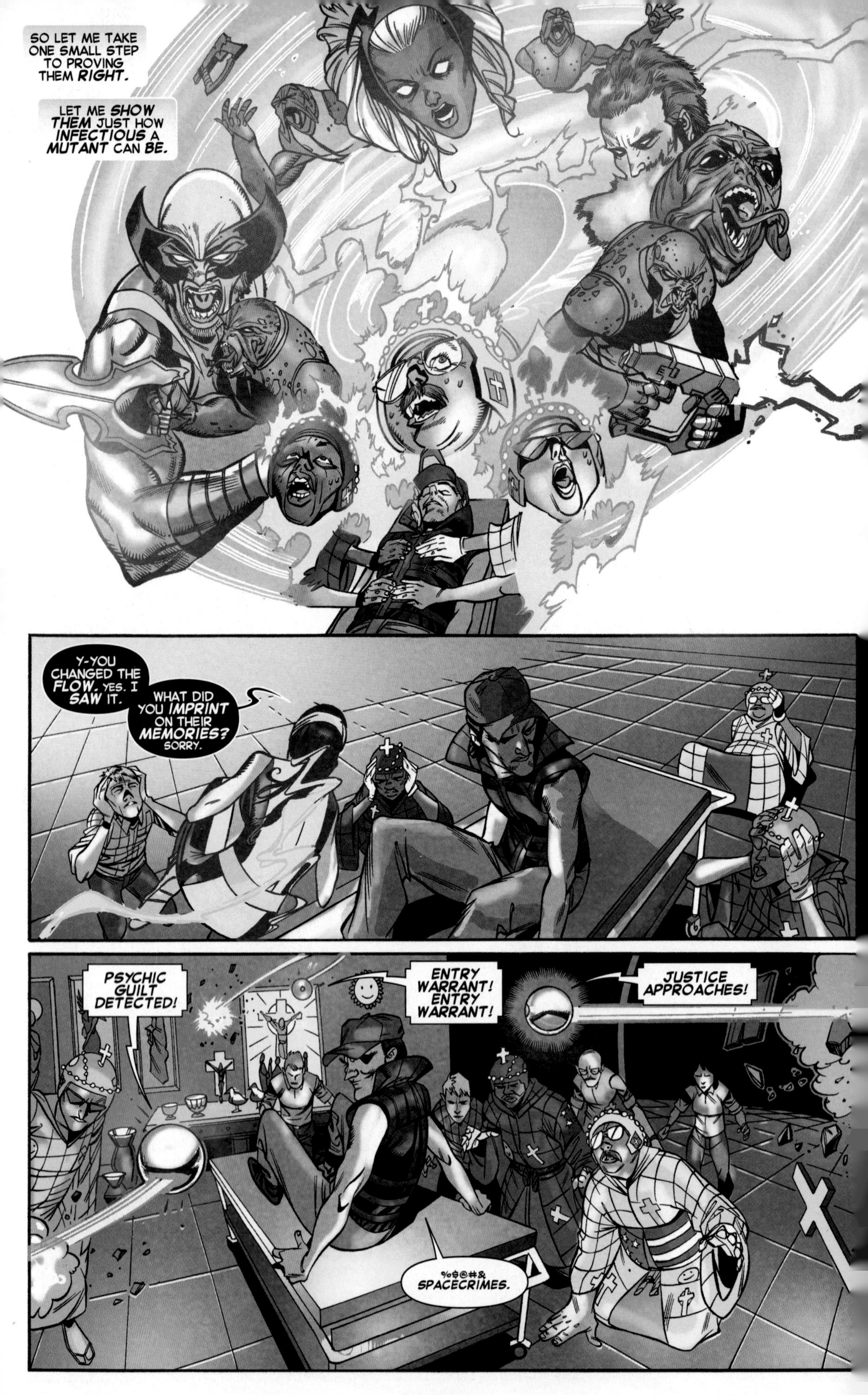
SO LET ME TAKE ONE SMALL STEP TO PROVING THEM *RIGHT.*
LET ME *SHOW THEM* JUST HOW *INFECTIOUS* A *MUTANT* CAN *BE.*
Y-YOU CHANGED THE *FLOW.* YES. I *SAW* IT.
WHAT DID YOU *IMPRINT* ON THEIR *MEMORIES?* SORRY.
PSYCHIC GUILT DETECTED!
ENTRY WARRANT! ENTRY WARRANT!
JUSTICE APPROACHES!
%$@#& *SPACECRIMES.*

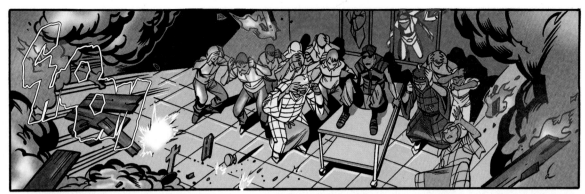

ONE: I HAVE IN MY HAND A *PORTABLE QUARK-ANNIHILATION DEVICE.*

SALIENT FACT TWO: MY *SERVICE RECORD* IS TRAGICALLY *TAINTED* BY A RECURRING *WEAKNESS* IN MY ABILITY TO *SUFFER FOOLS.*

LAST DIRTBAG TO LOSE THE *HILARIOUS HEADGEAR* GETS TO FIND OUT WHAT *LINKS* THE TWO FACTS.

WHAT'S... WHAT'S THE *MEANING* OF THIS?

ABIGAIL BRAND.
AGENT-COMMANDER OF S.W.O.R.D.
(SENTIENT WORLD OBSERVATION AND
RESPONSE DEPARTMENT). STARCOP.

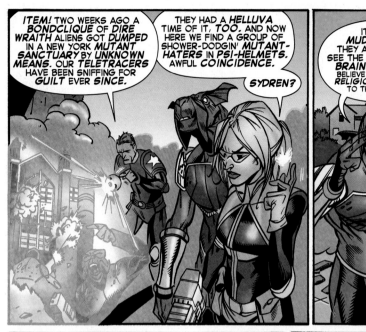

ITEM! TWO WEEKS AGO A *BONDCLIQUE* OF *DIRE WRAITH* ALIENS GOT *DUMPED* IN A NEW YORK *MUTANT SANCTUARY* BY UNKNOWN MEANS. OUR *TELETRACERS* HAVE BEEN SNIFFING FOR *GUILT* EVER *SINCE*.

THEY HAD A *HELLUVA* TIME OF IT, *TOO*. AND NOW HERE WE FIND A GROUP OF SHOWER-DODGIN' MUTANT-HATERS IN *PSI-HELMETS*. AWFUL *COINCIDENCE*.

SYDREN?

IT'SSSS... *MUDDLED*...BUT THEY ARE *GUILTY*. I SEE THE *CRIME* IN THEIR *BRAINSSS*. ALSSSO I BELIEVE THERE MAY BE A *RELIGIOUSSS ASSSPECT* TO THIS *CASSSE*.

SPOOKILY *PERCEPTIVE* AS EVER, *SYD.*

HOW *ABOUT* IT, *GODBOY?* YOU FEELIN' *CONFESSY?*

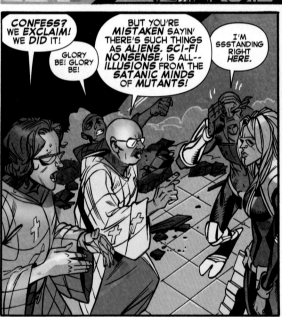

CONFESS? WE *EXCLAIM!* WE *DID* IT!

GLORY BE! GLORY BE!

BUT YOU'RE *MISTAKEN* SAYIN' THERE'S SUCH THINGS AS *ALIENS. SCI-FI NONSENSE,* IS ALL-- ILLUSIONS FROM THE *SATANIC MINDS* OF *MUTANTS!*

I'M *SSSTANDING RIGHT HERE.*

ALL WE DID WAS *INVOKE HEAVEN'S WRATH.* ASKED THE *ANGELS* TA...TA SEND *DEMONS* FROM HELL--COME *DRAG* THEM *MUTANTS BACK* TO WHERE THEY *BELONG!*

I *SSSENSE* THE HUMAN WISHES TO *ADMIT* THE *CRIME*.

YOU'RE *QUITE* SURE ABOUT THAT? YOU DON'T WANT A *SECOND OPINION* IN *GIANT NEON LETTERS?*

AND I AM NOW *COMPLETELY CCCERTAIN* THEY'RE *PRIESSSSSTS.*

SHUT UP. EVERYONE SHUT UP.

SOMETHING REEKS OF *RAT.*

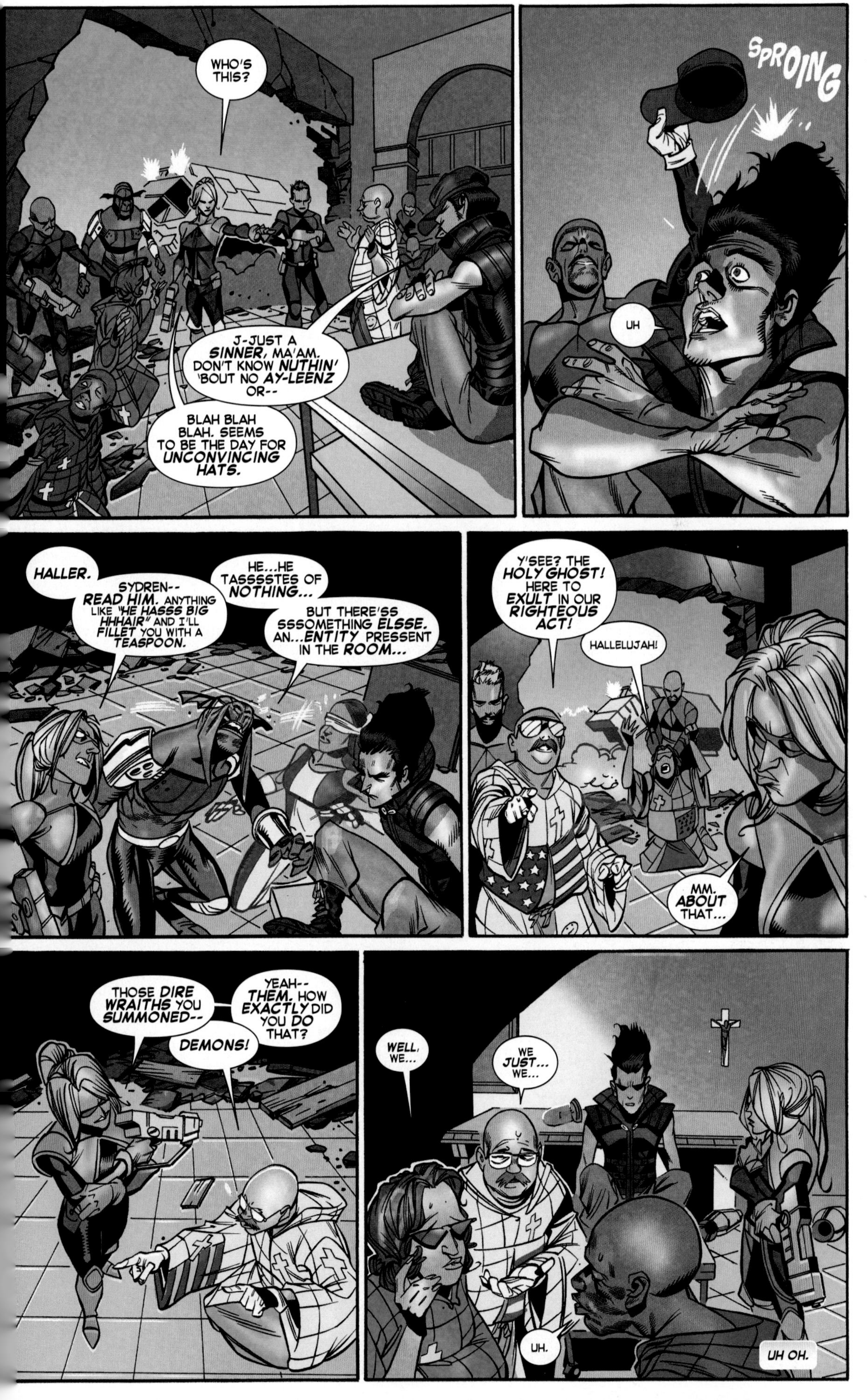

WHO'S THIS?
J-JUST A SINNER, MA'AM. DON'T KNOW NUTHIN' 'BOUT NO AY-LEENZ OR--
BLAH BLAH BLAH. SEEMS TO BE THE DAY FOR UNCONVINCING HATS.
SPROING
UH
HALLER.
SYDREN-- READ HIM. ANYTHING LIKE "HE HASSS BIG HHHAIR" AND I'LL FILLET YOU WITH A TEASPOON.
HE...HE TASSSSTES OF NOTHING...
BUT THERE'SS SSSOMETHING ELSSE. AN...ENTITY PRESSENT IN THE ROOM...
Y'SEE? THE HOLY GHOST! HERE TO EXULT IN OUR RIGHTEOUS ACT!
HALLELUJAH!
MM. ABOUT THAT...
THOSE DIRE WRAITHS YOU SUMMONED--
YEAH-- THEM. HOW EXACTLY DID YOU DO THAT?
DEMONS!
WELL, WE...
WE JUST... WE...
UH.
UH OH.

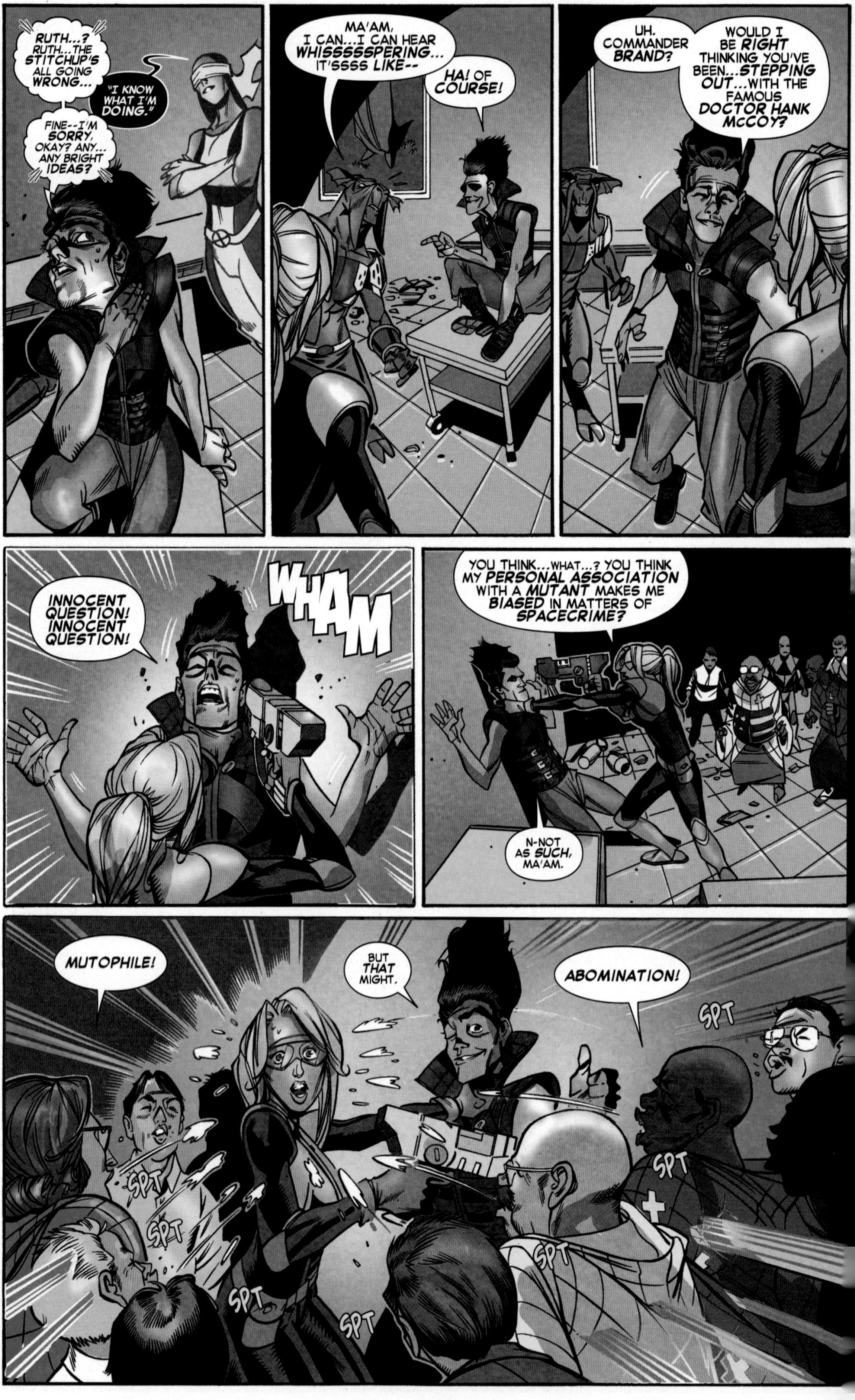

RUTH...? RUTH...THE STITCHUP'S ALL GOING WRONG...
"I KNOW WHAT I'M DOING."
FINE--I'M SORRY, OKAY? ANY... ANY BRIGHT IDEAS?
MA'AM, I CAN...I CAN HEAR WHISSSSSPERING... IT'SSSS LIKE--
HA! OF COURSE!
UH. COMMANDER BRAND?
WOULD I BE RIGHT THINKING YOU'VE BEEN...STEPPING OUT...WITH THE FAMOUS DOCTOR HANK McCOY?
INNOCENT QUESTION! INNOCENT QUESTION!
WHAM
YOU THINK...WHAT...? YOU THINK MY PERSONAL ASSOCIATION WITH A MUTANT MAKES ME BIASED IN MATTERS OF SPACECRIME?
N-NOT AS SUCH, MA'AM.
MUTOPHILE!
BUT THAT MIGHT.
ABOMINATION!
SPT
SPT
SPT
SPT
SPT
SPT
SPT
SPT

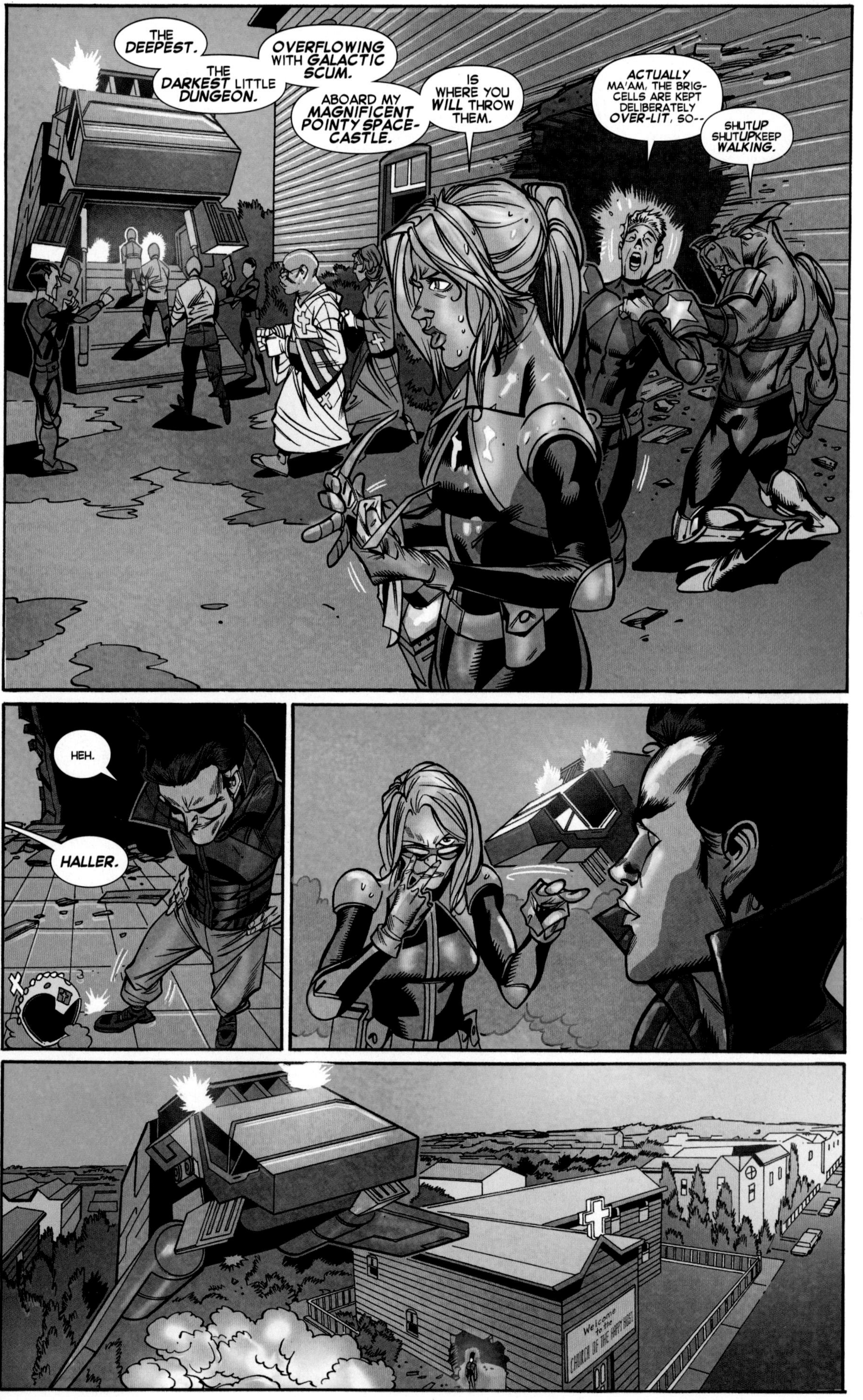
THE DEEPEST.
THE DARKEST LITTLE DUNGEON.
OVERFLOWING WITH GALACTIC SCUM.
ABOARD MY MAGNIFICENT POINTY SPACE-CASTLE.
IS WHERE YOU WILL THROW THEM.
ACTUALLY MA'AM, THE BRIG-CELLS ARE KEPT DELIBERATELY OVER-LIT, SO--
SHUTUP SHUTUPKEEP WALKING.
HEH.
HALLER.
Welcome to the CHURCH OF THE HAPPY HOST

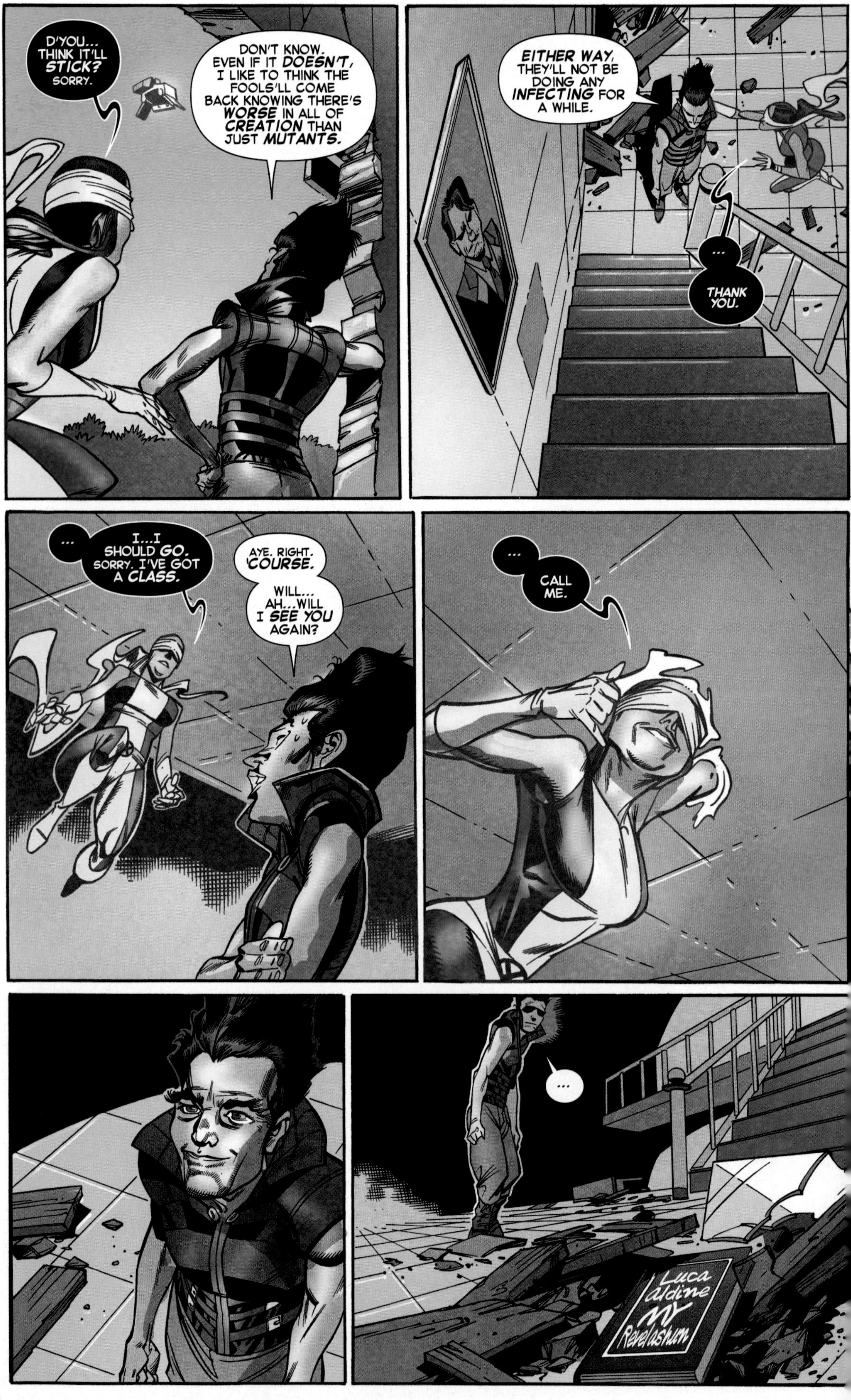
D'YOU... THINK IT'LL STICK? SORRY.
DON'T KNOW. EVEN IF IT DOESN'T, I LIKE TO THINK THE FOOLS'LL COME BACK KNOWING THERE'S WORSE IN ALL OF CREATION THAN JUST MUTANTS.
EITHER WAY, THEY'LL NOT BE DOING ANY INFECTING FOR A WHILE.
...
THANK YOU.
...
I...I SHOULD GO. SORRY. I'VE GOT A CLASS.
AYE. RIGHT. 'COURSE.
WILL... AH...WILL I SEE YOU AGAIN?
...
CALL ME.
...
Luca Aldine
MY Revelashun

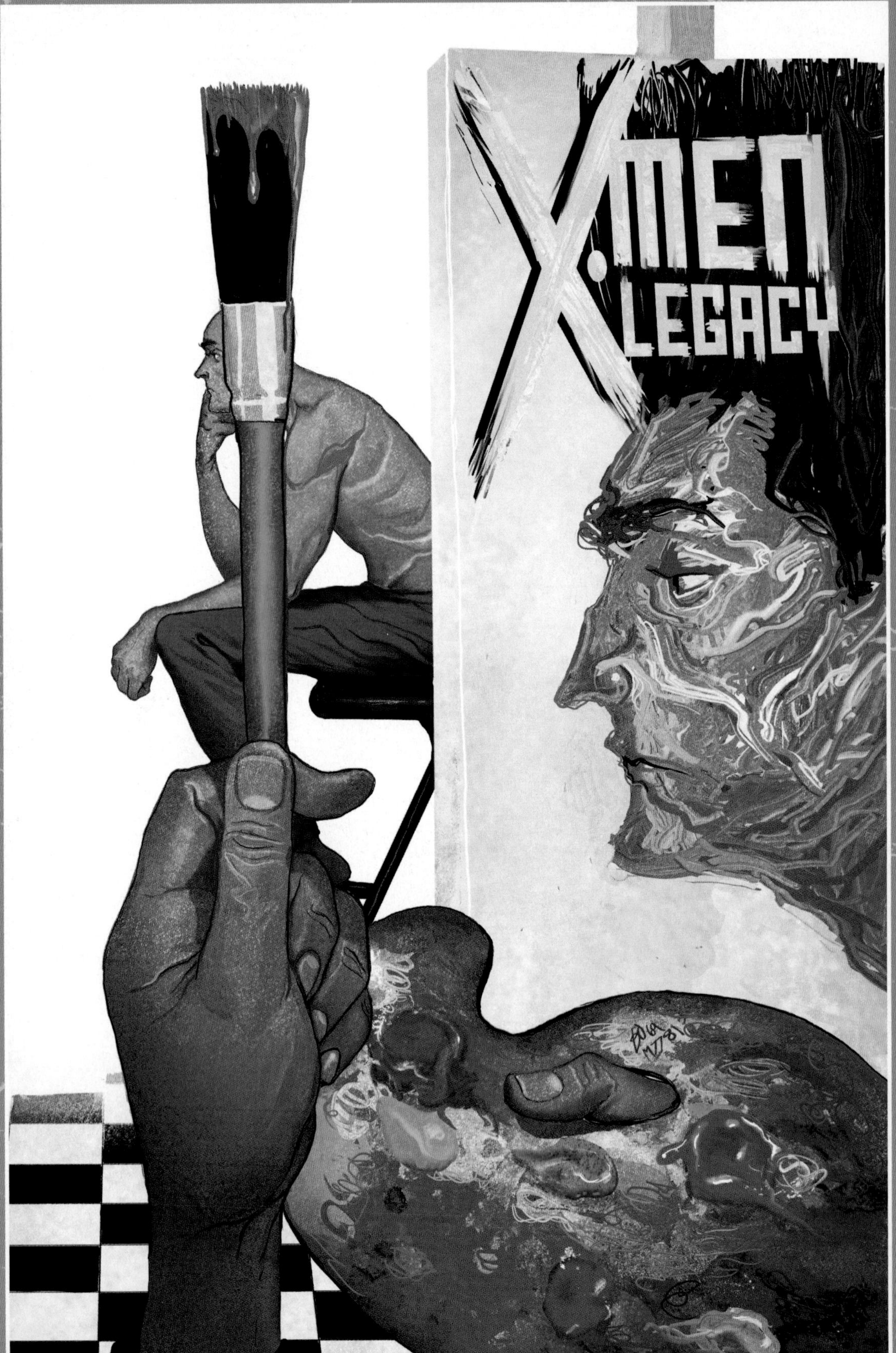
X-MEN
LEGACY

EIGHT

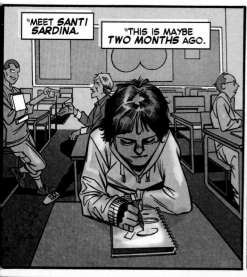

"MEET *SANTI SARDINA.*"

"THIS IS MAYBE *TWO MONTHS* AGO."

"SANTI'S WHAT YOU MIGHT CHARITABLY CALL A *LOSER.* AWKWARD, Y'KNOW? UNCOMFORTABLE IN HIS OWN *SKIN.*"

"AN *EASY-BLOODY-TARGET*--BUT A *DECENT LAD,* DESPITE IT ALL."

"OHHH, MAYBE HE'S *NOT* THE BRIGHTEST *BULB* IN THE *BOX*-- BUT HE'S NOT *DUMB.* SMART ENOUGH TO *HANG BACK* HEADIN' HOME. *SHIRK* THE *SHARKS.*"

"THAT'S HOW COME HE WASN'T *CAUGHT UP* IN IT ALL, WHEN IT HAPPENED."

A *CHOPPER!* YOU GET ME A %¢$&@# *CHOPPER* 'N' A %¢$&@# *PILOT!*

JUST... JUST STAY *CALM,* GORILLA-MAN! DON'T HURT THE K--

YOU THINK I WON'T *DO IT?!* YOU GET A *CHOPPER* HERE *NOW* OR THERE'S *KIDMEAT* INNA *STREETS* AND *HEADS* LIKE *BOTTLETOPS!*

"POOR OLD SANTI. *CLEAR RUN* AT THE BUGGER'S *BACK,* CONVENIENTLY DISCARDED *WEAPON,* DRAMATICALLY SWELLING *METAL MUSIC* IN HIS *EARS...*"

"...ALL THE *INGREDIENTS* OF A *HEROIC MOMENT...*"

"...AND THE *WEE SOD FROZE STIFF.*"

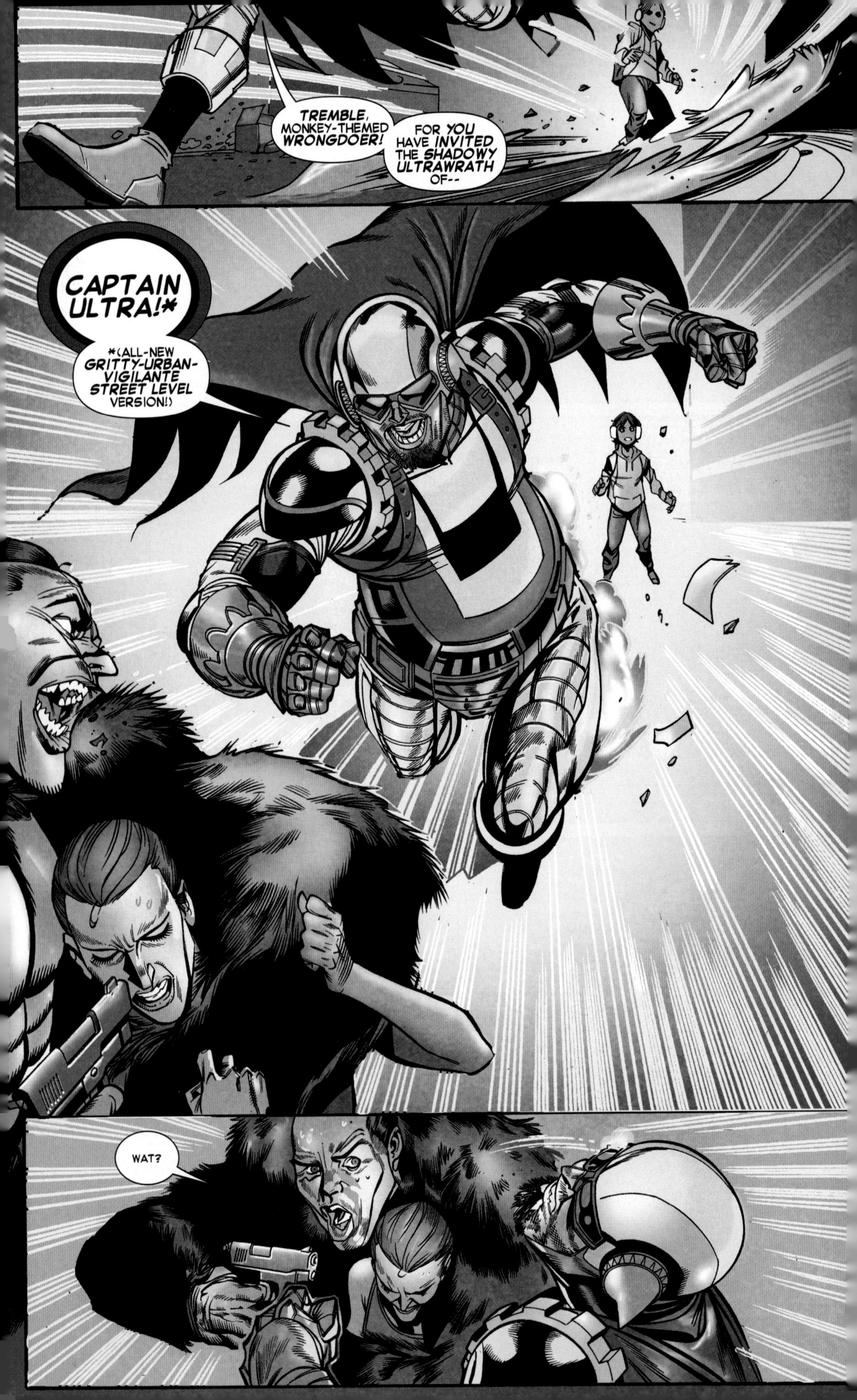
TREMBLE, MONKEY-THEMED WRONGDOER!
FOR YOU HAVE INVITED THE SHADOWY ULTRAWRATH OF--
CAPTAIN ULTRA!*
*(ALL-NEW GRITTY-URBAN-VIGILANTE STREET LEVEL VERSION!)
WAT?

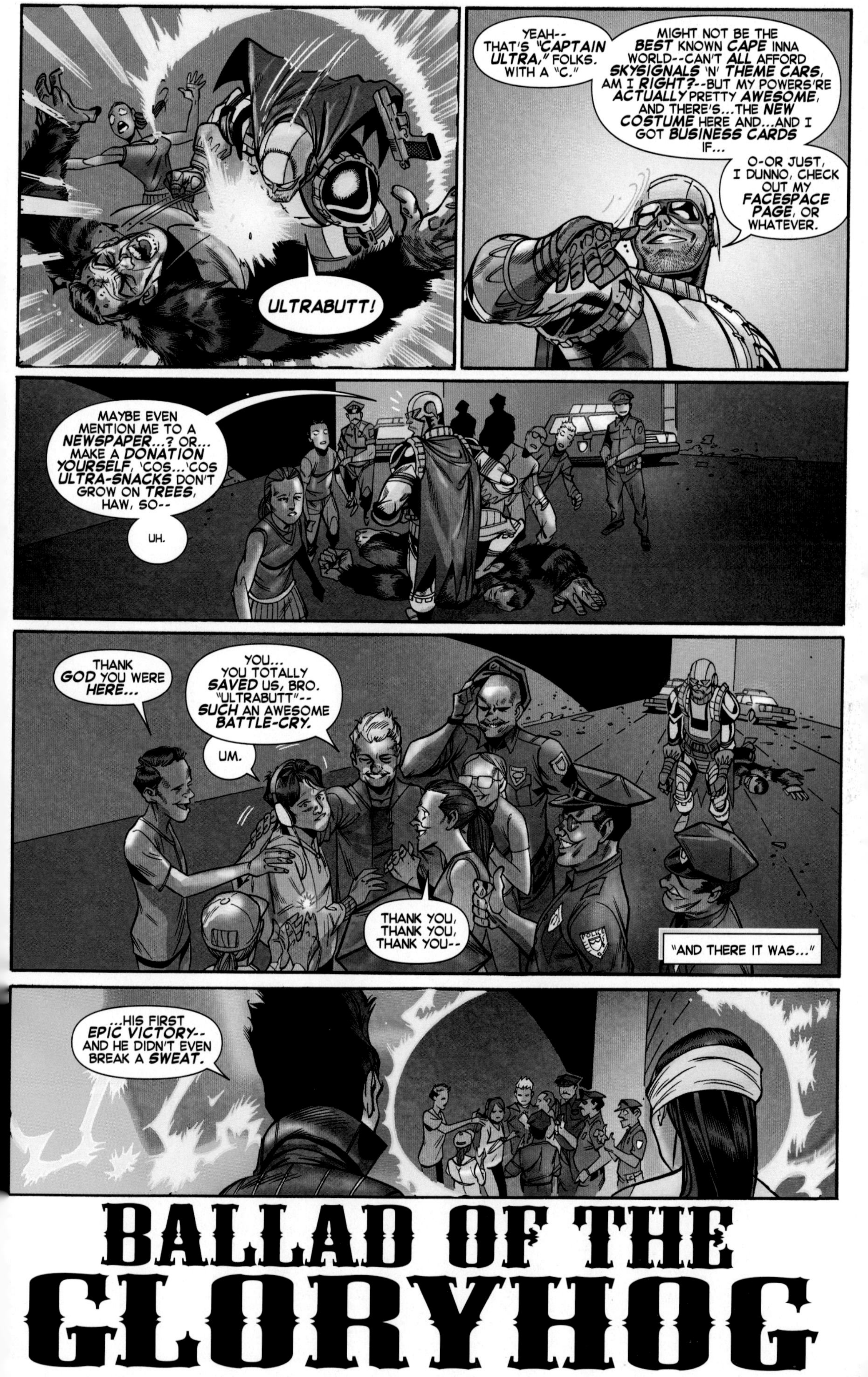
ULTRABUTT!
YEAH--THAT'S "CAPTAIN ULTRA," FOLKS. WITH A "C."
MIGHT NOT BE THE BEST KNOWN CAPE INNA WORLD--CAN'T ALL AFFORD SKYSIGNALS 'N' THEME CARS, AM I RIGHT?--BUT MY POWERS'RE ACTUALLY PRETTY AWESOME, AND THERE'S...THE NEW COSTUME HERE AND...AND I GOT BUSINESS CARDS IF...
O-OR JUST, I DUNNO, CHECK OUT MY FACESPACE PAGE, OR WHATEVER.
MAYBE EVEN MENTION ME TO A NEWSPAPER...? OR...MAKE A DONATION YOURSELF, 'COS...'COS ULTRA-SNACKS DON'T GROW ON TREES, HAW, SO--
UH.
THANK GOD YOU WERE HERE...
YOU... YOU TOTALLY SAVED US, BRO. "ULTRABUTT"--SUCH AN AWESOME BATTLE-CRY.
UM.
THANK YOU, THANK YOU, THANK YOU--
"AND THERE IT WAS..."
...HIS FIRST EPIC VICTORY--AND HE DIDN'T EVEN BREAK A SWEAT.

BALLAD OF THE GLORYHOG

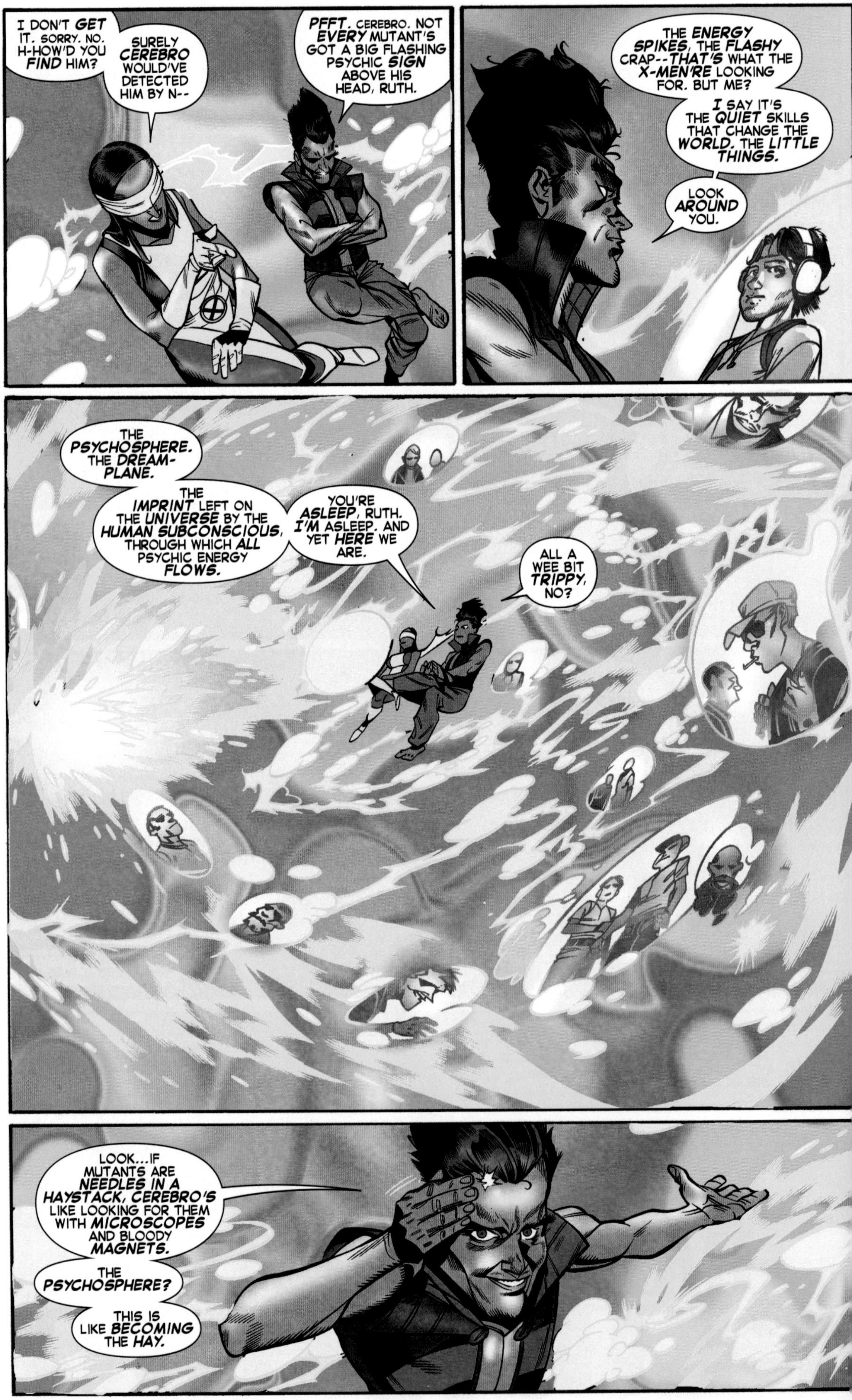
I DON'T GET IT. SORRY. NO. H-HOW'D YOU FIND HIM?
SURELY CEREBRO WOULD'VE DETECTED HIM BY N--
PFFT. CEREBRO. NOT EVERY MUTANT'S GOT A BIG FLASHING PSYCHIC SIGN ABOVE HIS HEAD, RUTH.
THE ENERGY SPIKES, THE FLASHY CRAP--THAT'S WHAT THE X-MEN'RE LOOKING FOR. BUT ME?
I SAY IT'S THE QUIET SKILLS THAT CHANGE THE WORLD. THE LITTLE THINGS.
LOOK AROUND YOU.
THE PSYCHOSPHERE. THE DREAM-PLANE.
THE IMPRINT LEFT ON THE UNIVERSE BY THE HUMAN SUBCONSCIOUS, THROUGH WHICH ALL PSYCHIC ENERGY FLOWS.
YOU'RE ASLEEP, RUTH. I'M ASLEEP. AND YET HERE WE ARE.
ALL A WEE BIT TRIPPY, NO?
LOOK...IF MUTANTS ARE NEEDLES IN A HAYSTACK, CEREBRO'S LIKE LOOKING FOR THEM WITH MICROSCOPES AND BLOODY MAGNETS.
THE PSYCHOSPHERE?
THIS IS LIKE BECOMING THE HAY.

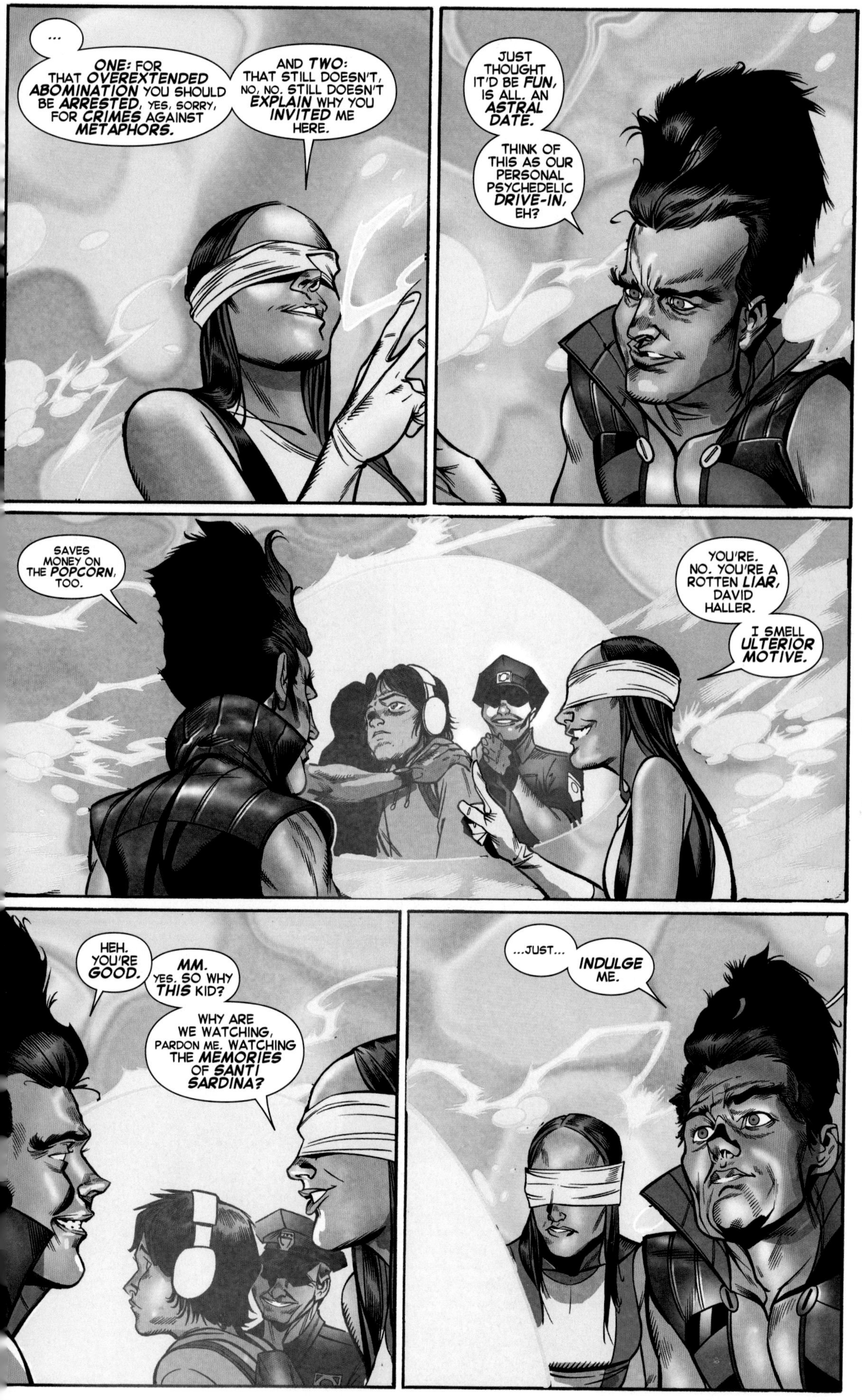
...
ONE: FOR THAT OVEREXTENDED ABOMINATION YOU SHOULD BE ARRESTED, YES, SORRY, FOR CRIMES AGAINST METAPHORS.
AND TWO: THAT STILL DOESN'T, NO, NO. STILL DOESN'T EXPLAIN WHY YOU INVITED ME HERE.
JUST THOUGHT IT'D BE FUN, IS ALL. AN ASTRAL DATE.
THINK OF THIS AS OUR PERSONAL PSYCHEDELIC DRIVE-IN, EH?
SAVES MONEY ON THE POPCORN, TOO.
YOU'RE. NO. YOU'RE A ROTTEN LIAR, DAVID HALLER.
I SMELL ULTERIOR MOTIVE.
HEH. YOU'RE GOOD.
MM. YES. SO WHY THIS KID?
WHY ARE WE WATCHING, PARDON ME. WATCHING THE MEMORIES OF SANTI SARDINA?
...JUST...
INDULGE ME.

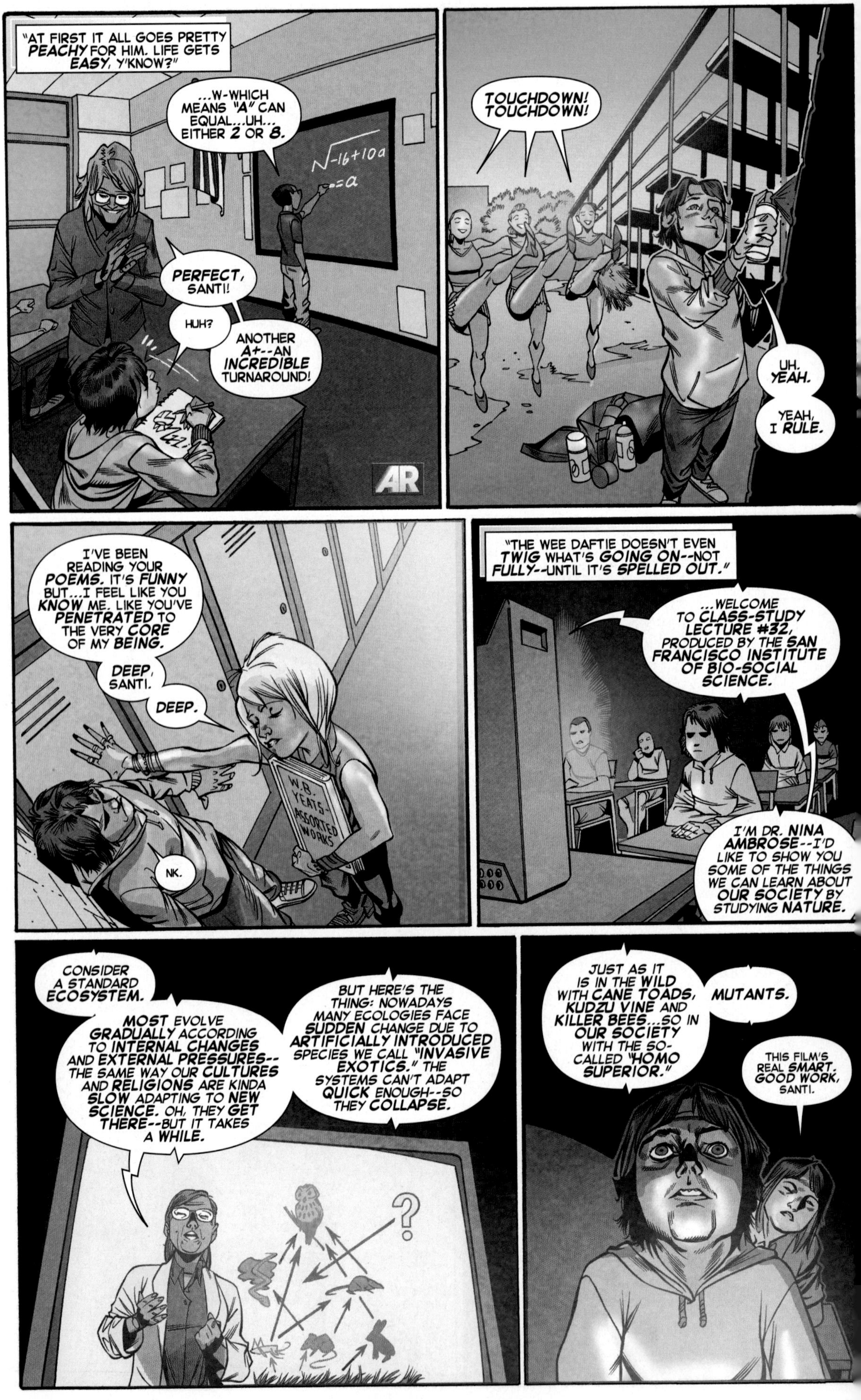
"AT FIRST IT ALL GOES PRETTY PEACHY FOR HIM. LIFE GETS EASY, Y'KNOW?"
...W-WHICH MEANS "A" CAN EQUAL...UH... EITHER 2 OR 8.
PERFECT, SANTI!
HUH?
ANOTHER A+--AN INCREDIBLE TURNAROUND!
AR
TOUCHDOWN! TOUCHDOWN!
UH. YEAH.
YEAH, I RULE.
I'VE BEEN READING YOUR POEMS. IT'S FUNNY BUT...I FEEL LIKE YOU KNOW ME. LIKE YOU'VE PENETRATED TO THE VERY CORE OF MY BEING.
DEEP, SANTI.
DEEP.
W.B. YEATS- ASSORTED WORKS
NK.
"THE WEE DAFTIE DOESN'T EVEN TWIG WHAT'S GOING ON--NOT FULLY--UNTIL IT'S SPELLED OUT."
...WELCOME TO CLASS-STUDY LECTURE #32, PRODUCED BY THE SAN FRANCISCO INSTITUTE OF BIO-SOCIAL SCIENCE.
I'M DR. NINA AMBROSE--I'D LIKE TO SHOW YOU SOME OF THE THINGS WE CAN LEARN ABOUT OUR SOCIETY BY STUDYING NATURE.
CONSIDER A STANDARD ECOSYSTEM.
MOST EVOLVE GRADUALLY ACCORDING TO INTERNAL CHANGES AND EXTERNAL PRESSURES--THE SAME WAY OUR CULTURES AND RELIGIONS ARE KINDA SLOW ADAPTING TO NEW SCIENCE. OH, THEY GET THERE--BUT IT TAKES A WHILE.
BUT HERE'S THE THING: NOWADAYS MANY ECOLOGIES FACE SUDDEN CHANGE DUE TO ARTIFICIALLY INTRODUCED SPECIES WE CALL "INVASIVE EXOTICS." THE SYSTEMS CAN'T ADAPT QUICK ENOUGH--SO THEY COLLAPSE.
?
JUST AS IT IS IN THE WILD WITH CANE TOADS, KUDZU VINE AND KILLER BEES...SO IN OUR SOCIETY WITH THE SO-CALLED "HOMO SUPERIOR."
MUTANTS.
THIS FILM'S REAL SMART. GOOD WORK, SANTI.

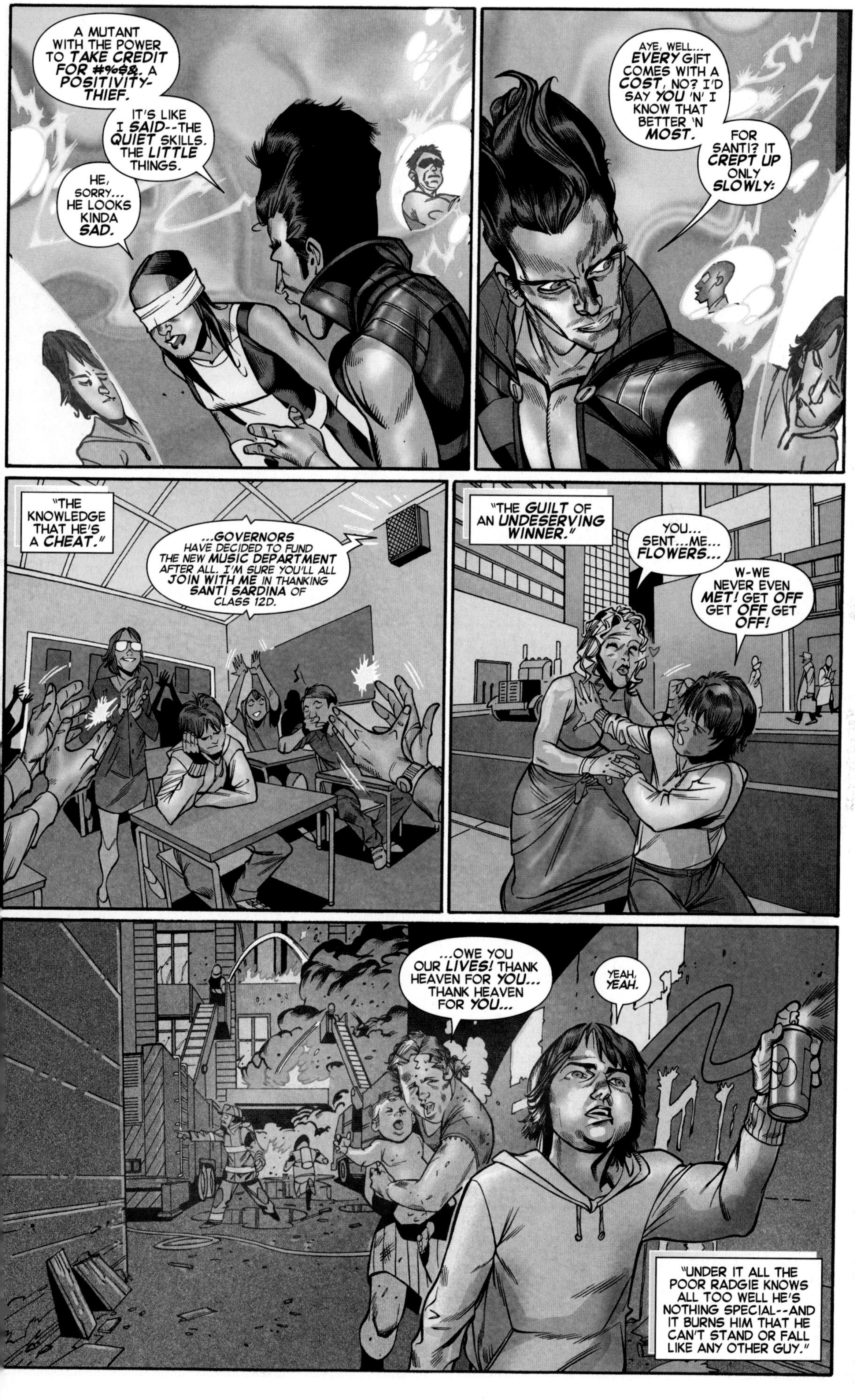
A MUTANT WITH THE POWER TO TAKE CREDIT FOR #%$&. A POSITIVITY-THIEF.
IT'S LIKE I SAID--THE QUIET SKILLS. THE LITTLE THINGS.
HE, SORRY... HE LOOKS KINDA SAD.
AYE, WELL... EVERY GIFT COMES WITH A COST, NO? I'D SAY YOU 'N' I KNOW THAT BETTER 'N MOST.
FOR SANTI? IT CREPT UP ONLY SLOWLY:
"THE KNOWLEDGE THAT HE'S A CHEAT."
...GOVERNORS HAVE DECIDED TO FUND THE NEW MUSIC DEPARTMENT AFTER ALL. I'M SURE YOU'LL ALL JOIN WITH ME IN THANKING SANTI SARDINA OF CLASS 12D.
"THE GUILT OF AN UNDESERVING WINNER."
YOU... SENT...ME... FLOWERS...
W-WE NEVER EVEN MET! GET OFF GET OFF GET OFF!
...OWE YOU OUR LIVES! THANK HEAVEN FOR YOU... THANK HEAVEN FOR YOU...
YEAH, YEAH.
"UNDER IT ALL THE POOR RADGIE KNOWS ALL TOO WELL HE'S NOTHING SPECIAL--AND IT BURNS HIM THAT HE CAN'T STAND OR FALL LIKE ANY OTHER GUY."

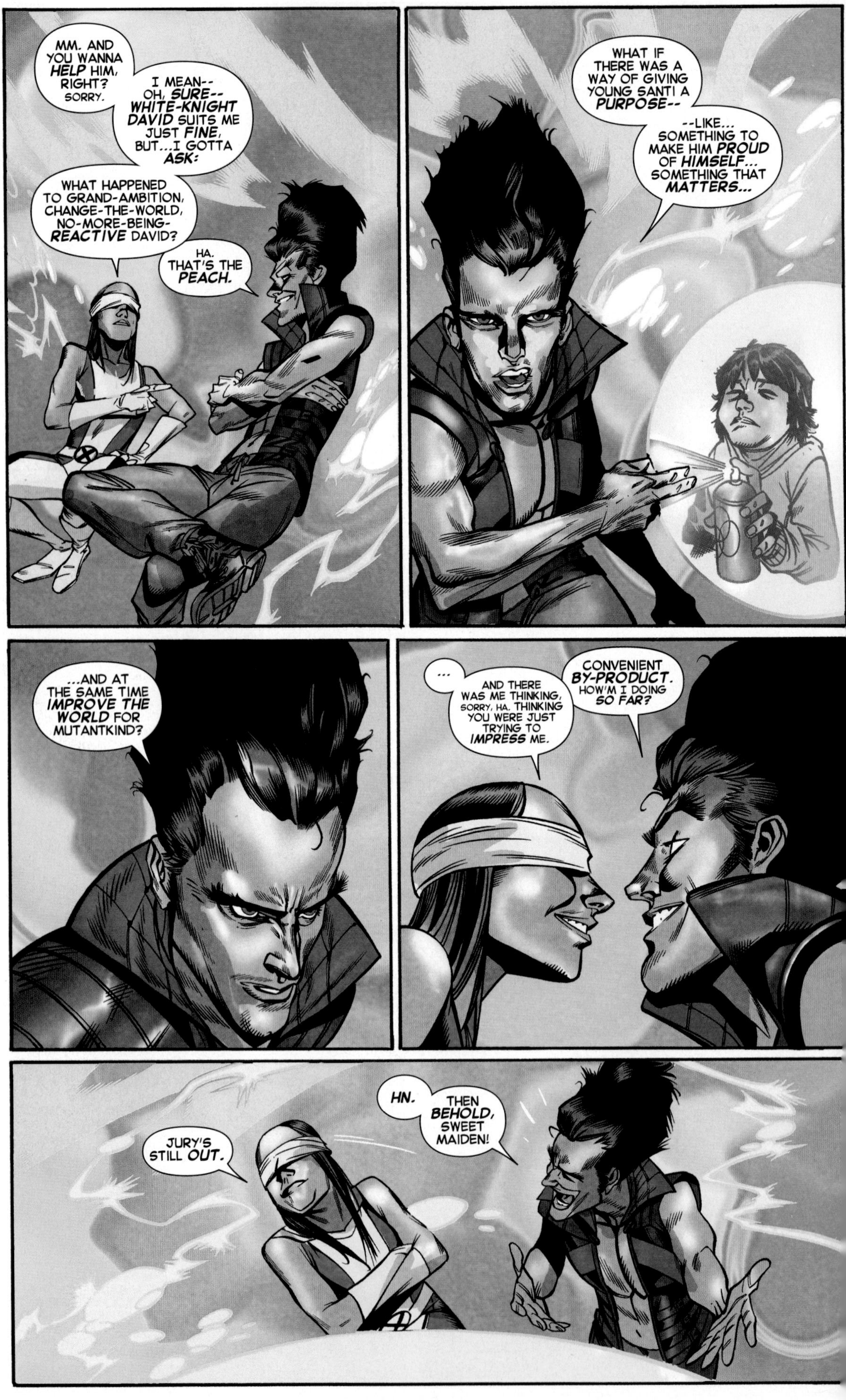
MM. AND YOU WANNA HELP HIM, RIGHT? SORRY.
I MEAN-- OH, SURE-- WHITE-KNIGHT DAVID SUITS ME JUST FINE, BUT...I GOTTA ASK:
WHAT HAPPENED TO GRAND-AMBITION, CHANGE-THE-WORLD, NO-MORE-BEING-REACTIVE DAVID?
HA. THAT'S THE PEACH.
WHAT IF THERE WAS A WAY OF GIVING YOUNG SANTI A PURPOSE--
--LIKE... SOMETHING TO MAKE HIM PROUD OF HIMSELF... SOMETHING THAT MATTERS...
...AND AT THE SAME TIME IMPROVE THE WORLD FOR MUTANTKIND?
...
AND THERE WAS ME THINKING, SORRY, HA. THINKING YOU WERE JUST TRYING TO IMPRESS ME.
CONVENIENT BY-PRODUCT. HOW'M I DOING SO FAR?
JURY'S STILL OUT.
HN.
THEN BEHOLD, SWEET MAIDEN!

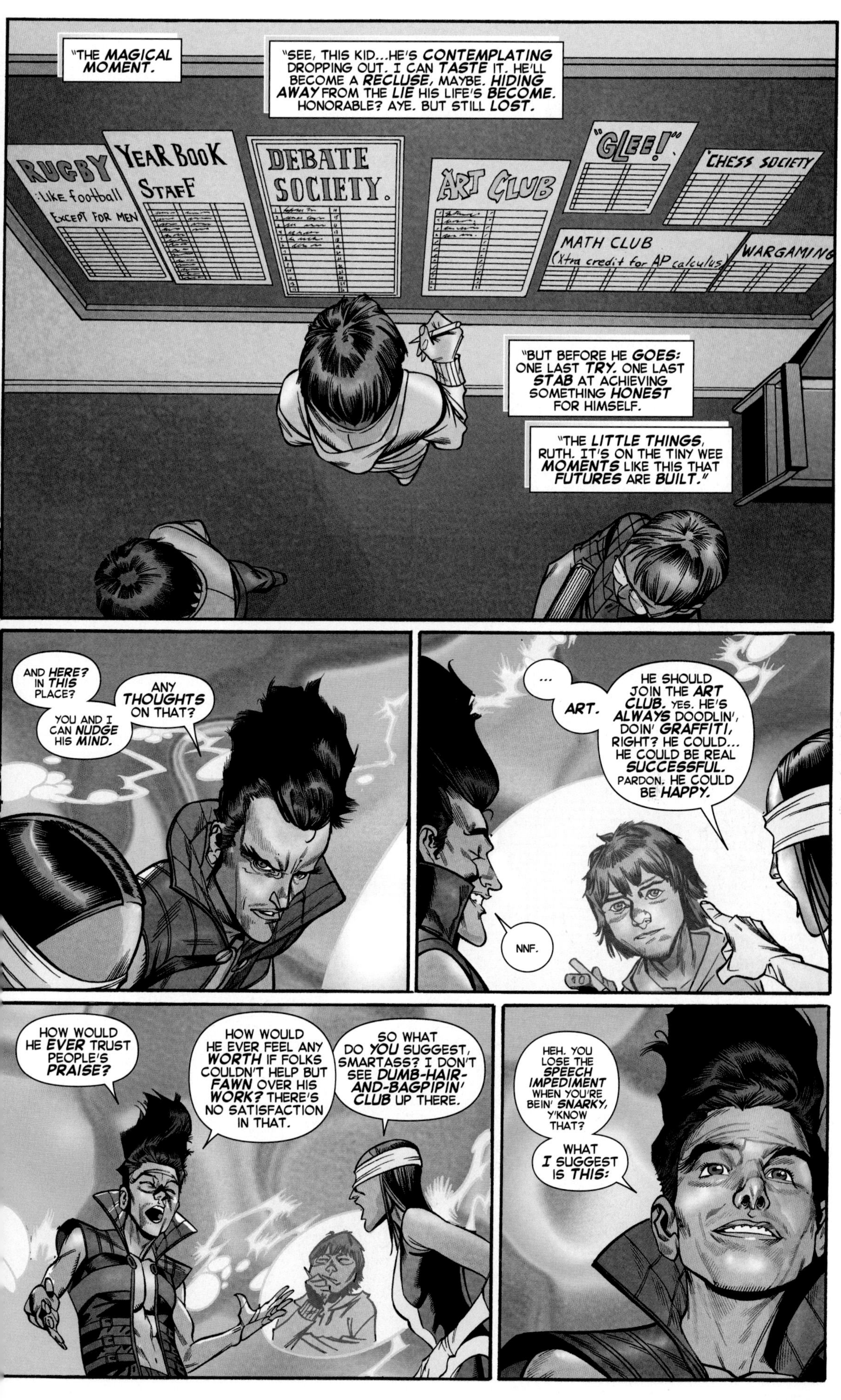
"THE MAGICAL MOMENT.
"SEE, THIS KID...HE'S CONTEMPLATING DROPPING OUT. I CAN TASTE IT. HE'LL BECOME A RECLUSE, MAYBE. HIDING AWAY FROM THE LIE HIS LIFE'S BECOME. HONORABLE? AYE. BUT STILL LOST.
RUGBY :Like football EXCEPT FOR MEN
YEAR BOOK STAFF
DEBATE SOCIETY.
ART CLUB
"GLEE!"
CHESS SOCIETY
MATH CLUB (Xtra credit for AP calculus)
WARGAMING
"BUT BEFORE HE GOES: ONE LAST TRY. ONE LAST STAB AT ACHIEVING SOMETHING HONEST FOR HIMSELF.
"THE LITTLE THINGS, RUTH. IT'S ON THE TINY WEE MOMENTS LIKE THIS THAT FUTURES ARE BUILT."
AND HERE? IN THIS PLACE?
YOU AND I CAN NUDGE HIS MIND.
ANY THOUGHTS ON THAT?
...
ART.
HE SHOULD JOIN THE ART CLUB. YES. HE'S ALWAYS DOODLIN', DOIN' GRAFFITI, RIGHT? HE COULD... HE COULD BE REAL SUCCESSFUL. PARDON. HE COULD BE HAPPY.
NNF.
HOW WOULD HE EVER TRUST PEOPLE'S PRAISE?
HOW WOULD HE EVER FEEL ANY WORTH IF FOLKS COULDN'T HELP BUT FAWN OVER HIS WORK? THERE'S NO SATISFACTION IN THAT.
SO WHAT DO YOU SUGGEST, SMARTASS? I DON'T SEE DUMB-HAIR-AND-BAGPIPIN' CLUB UP THERE.
HEH. YOU LOSE THE SPEECH IMPEDIMENT WHEN YOU'RE BEIN' SNARKY, Y'KNOW THAT?
WHAT I SUGGEST IS THIS:

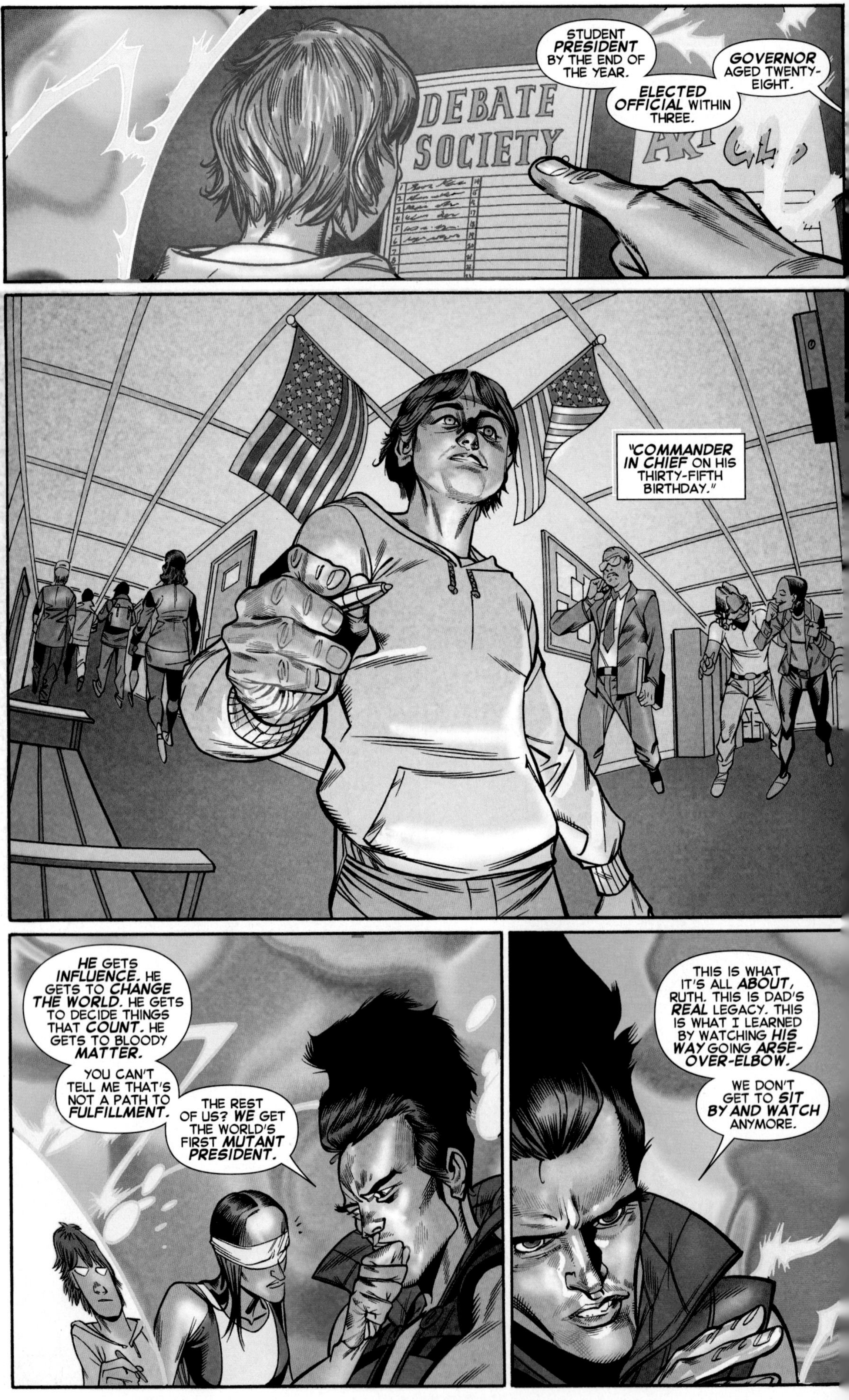

STUDENT PRESIDENT BY THE END OF THE YEAR.
ELECTED OFFICIAL WITHIN THREE.
GOVERNOR AGED TWENTY-EIGHT.
DEBATE SOCIETY
"COMMANDER IN CHIEF ON HIS THIRTY-FIFTH BIRTHDAY."
HE GETS INFLUENCE. HE GETS TO CHANGE THE WORLD. HE GETS TO DECIDE THINGS THAT COUNT. HE GETS TO BLOODY MATTER.
YOU CAN'T TELL ME THAT'S NOT A PATH TO FULFILLMENT.
THE REST OF US? WE GET THE WORLD'S FIRST MUTANT PRESIDENT.
THIS IS WHAT IT'S ALL ABOUT, RUTH. THIS IS DAD'S REAL LEGACY. THIS IS WHAT I LEARNED BY WATCHING HIS WAY GOING ARSE-OVER-ELBOW.
WE DON'T GET TO SIT BY AND WATCH ANYMORE.

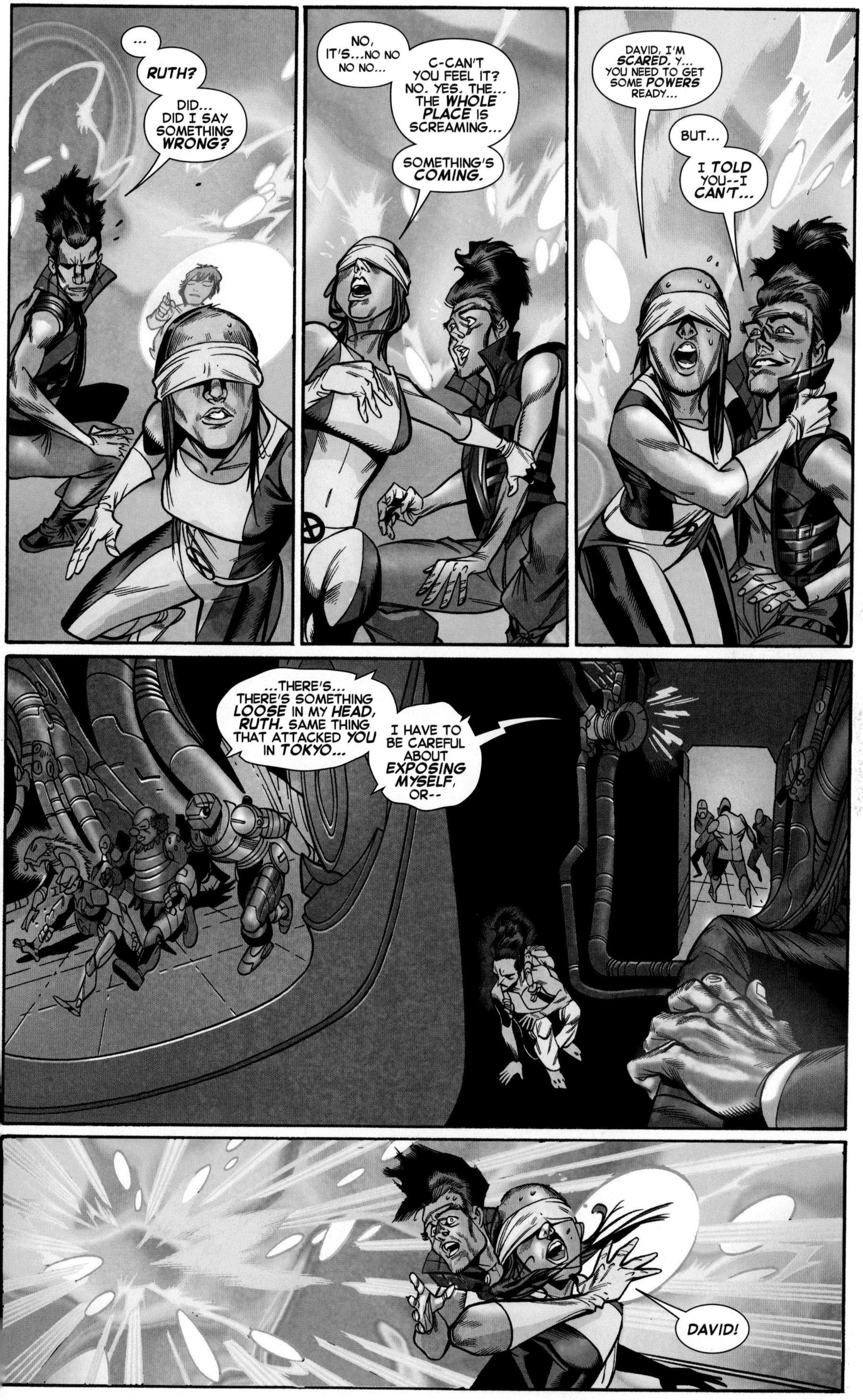
...
RUTH?
DID... DID I SAY SOMETHING WRONG?
NO, IT'S...NO NO NO NO...
C-CAN'T YOU FEEL IT? NO. YES. THE... THE WHOLE PLACE IS SCREAMING...
SOMETHING'S COMING.
DAVID, I'M SCARED. Y... YOU NEED TO GET SOME POWERS READY...
BUT...
I TOLD YOU--I CAN'T...
...THERE'S... THERE'S SOMETHING LOOSE IN MY HEAD, RUTH. SAME THING THAT ATTACKED YOU IN TOKYO...
I HAVE TO BE CAREFUL ABOUT EXPOSING MYSELF, OR--
DAVID!

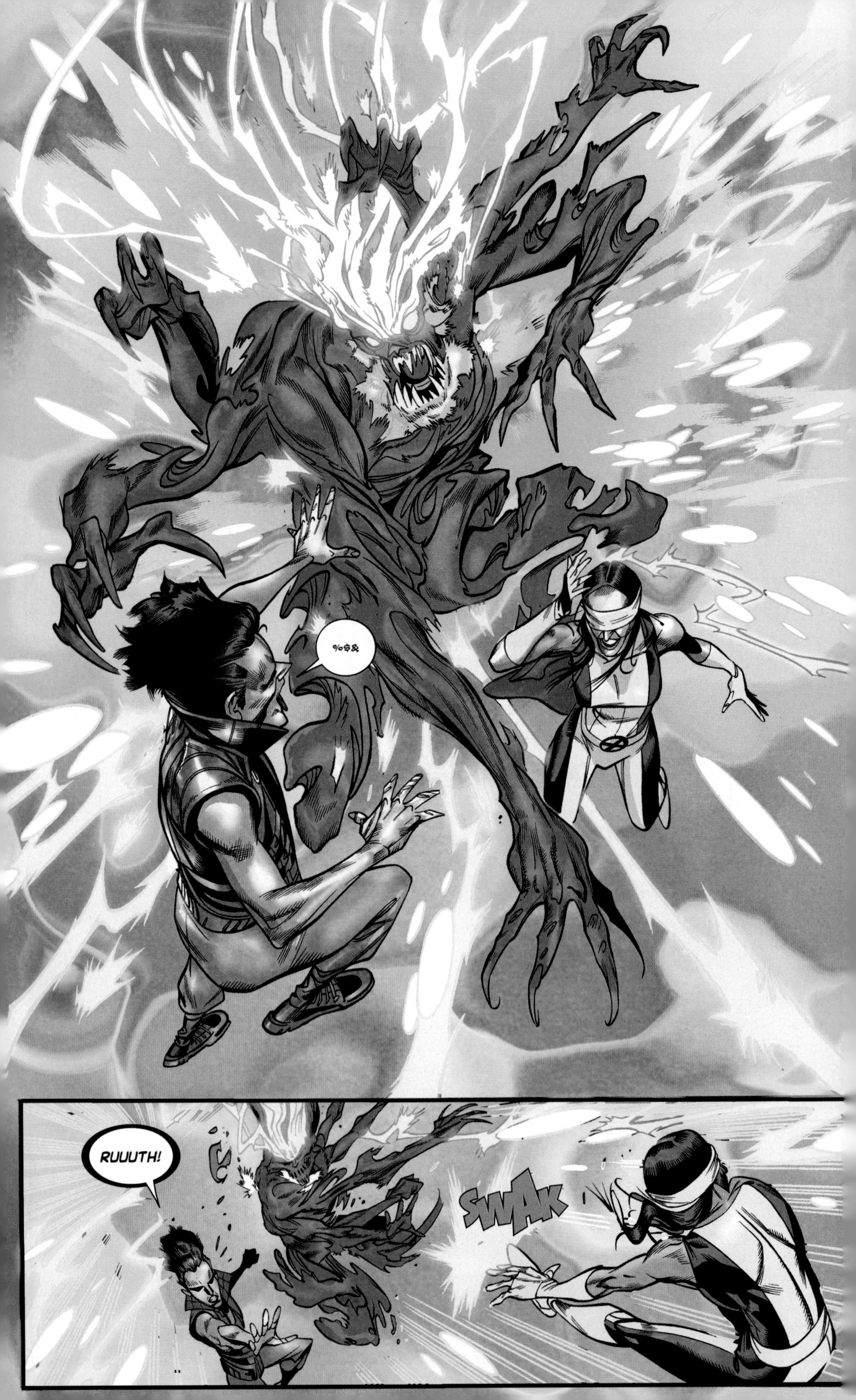
%$&
RUUUTH!
SWAK

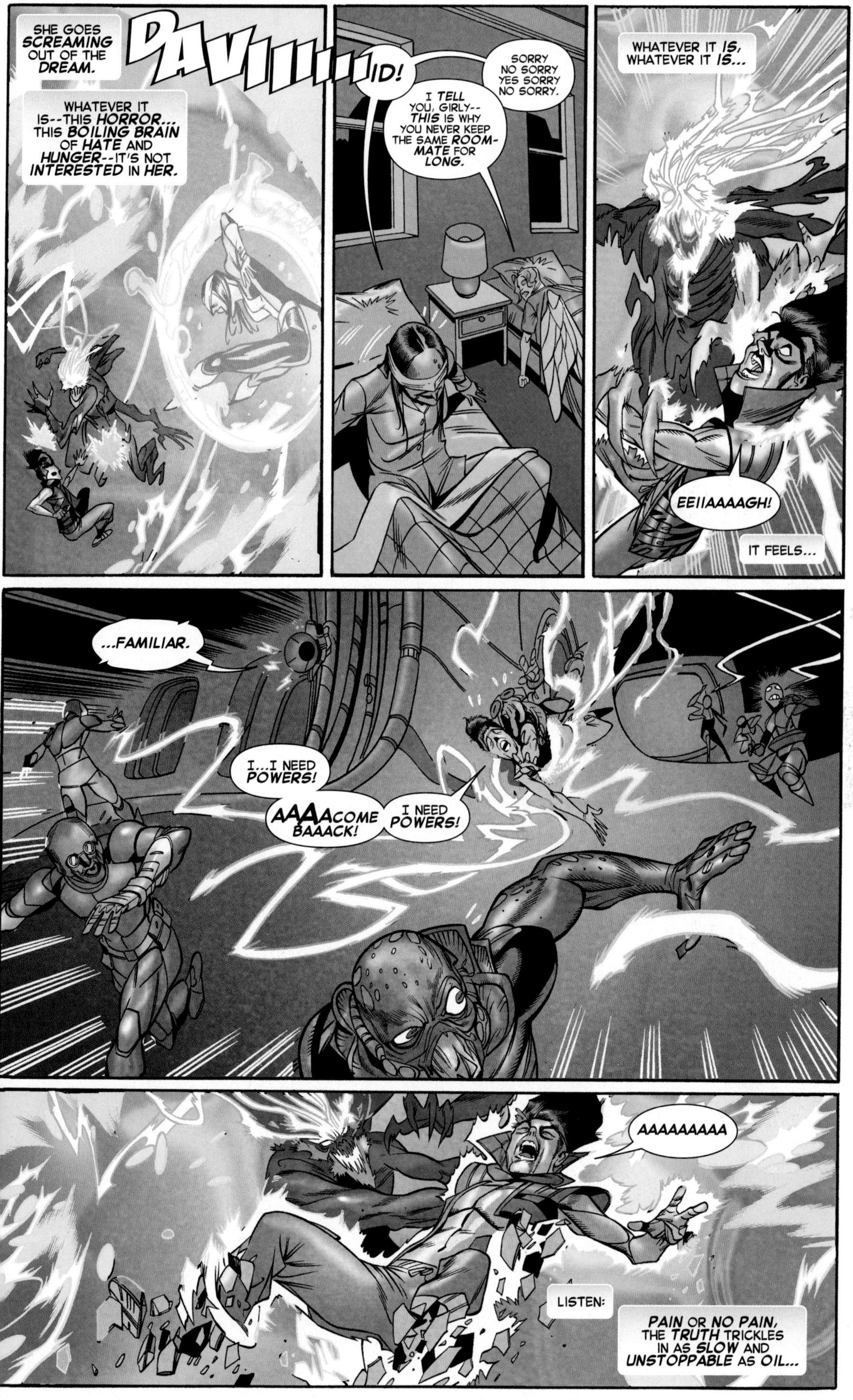
SHE GOES SCREAMING OUT OF THE DREAM.
DAVIIIIIIID!
WHATEVER IT IS--THIS HORROR... THIS BOILING BRAIN OF HATE AND HUNGER--IT'S NOT INTERESTED IN HER.
I TELL YOU, GIRLY-- THIS IS WHY YOU NEVER KEEP THE SAME ROOMMATE FOR LONG.
SORRY NO SORRY YES SORRY NO SORRY.
WHATEVER IT IS, WHATEVER IT IS...
EEIIAAAAGH!
IT FEELS...
...FAMILIAR.
I...I NEED POWERS!
AAAACOME BAAACK!
I NEED POWERS!
AAAAAAAAA
LISTEN:
PAIN OR NO PAIN, THE TRUTH TRICKLES IN AS SLOW AND UNSTOPPABLE AS OIL...

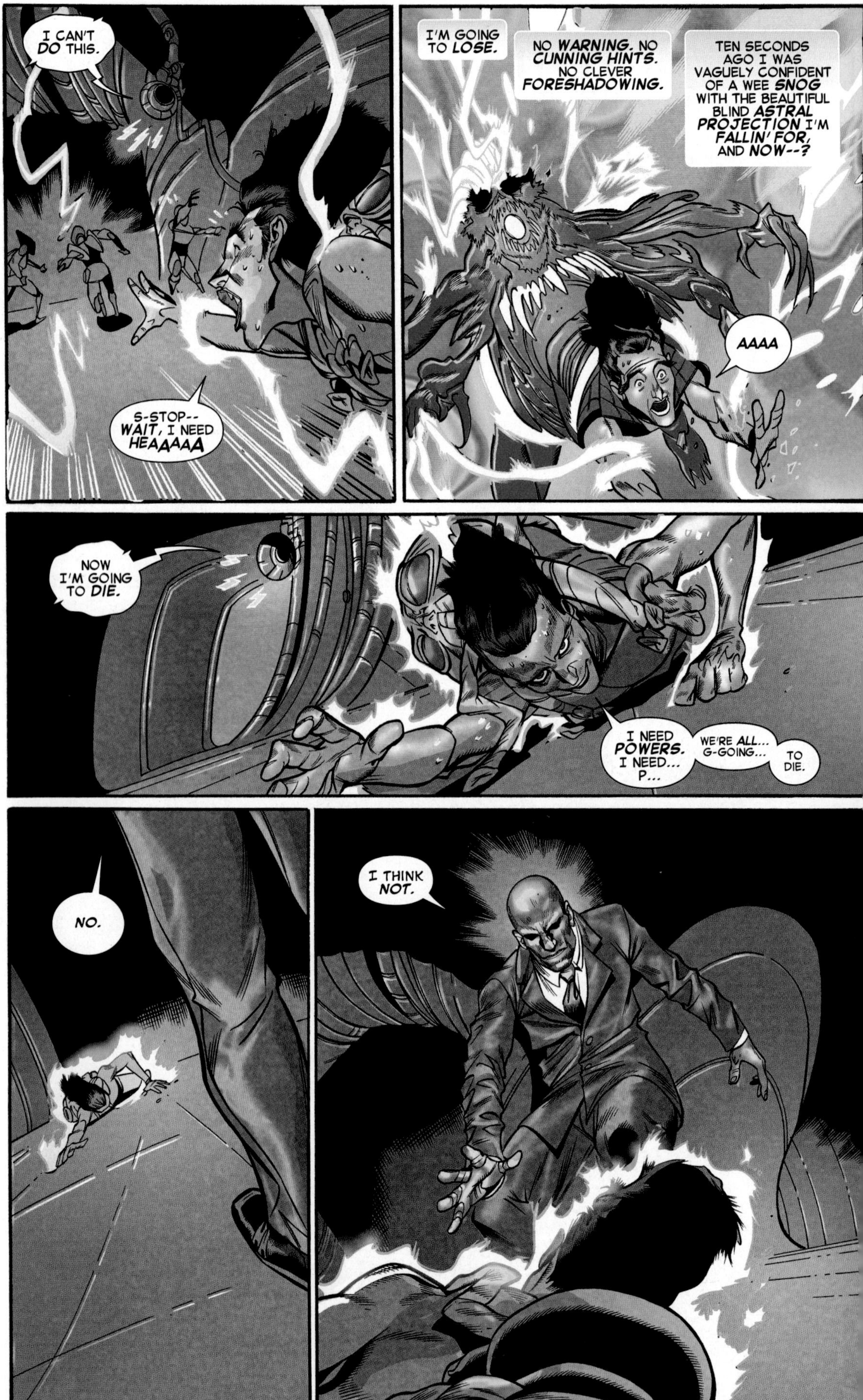
I CAN'T DO THIS.
S-STOP-- WAIT, I NEED HEAAAAA
I'M GOING TO LOSE.
NO WARNING. NO CUNNING HINTS. NO CLEVER FORESHADOWING.
TEN SECONDS AGO I WAS VAGUELY CONFIDENT OF A WEE SNOG WITH THE BEAUTIFUL BLIND ASTRAL PROJECTION I'M FALLIN' FOR, AND NOW--?
AAAA
NOW I'M GOING TO DIE.
I NEED POWERS. I NEED... P...
WE'RE ALL... G-GOING...
TO DIE.
NO.
I THINK NOT.

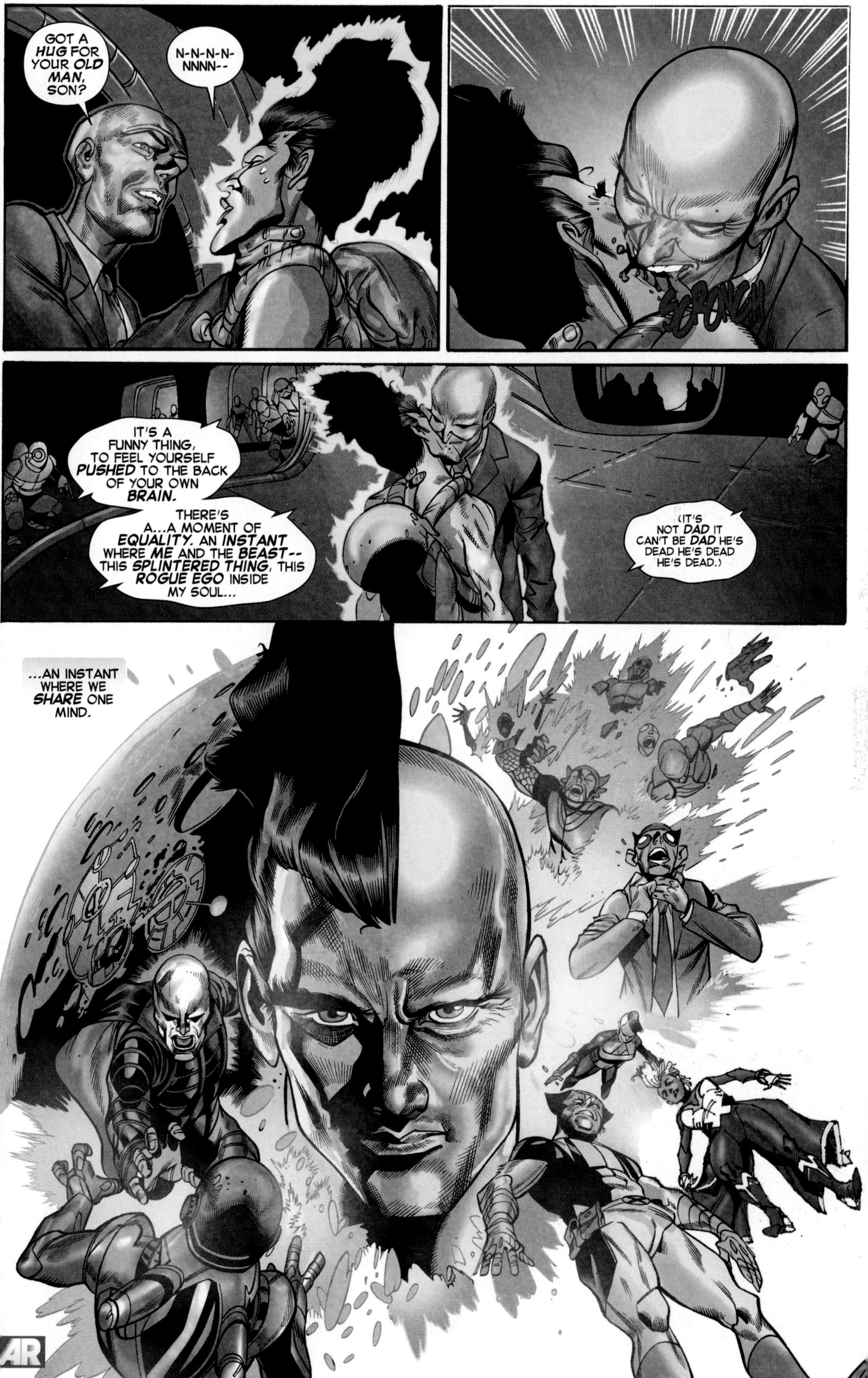
GOT A HUG FOR YOUR OLD MAN, SON?
N-N-N-N-NNNN--
SCRONCH
IT'S A FUNNY THING, TO FEEL YOURSELF PUSHED TO THE BACK OF YOUR OWN BRAIN.
THERE'S A...A MOMENT OF EQUALITY. AN INSTANT WHERE ME AND THE BEAST-- THIS SPLINTERED THING, THIS ROGUE EGO INSIDE MY SOUL...
(IT'S NOT DAD IT CAN'T BE DAD HE'S DEAD HE'S DEAD HE'S DEAD.)
...AN INSTANT WHERE WE SHARE ONE MIND.

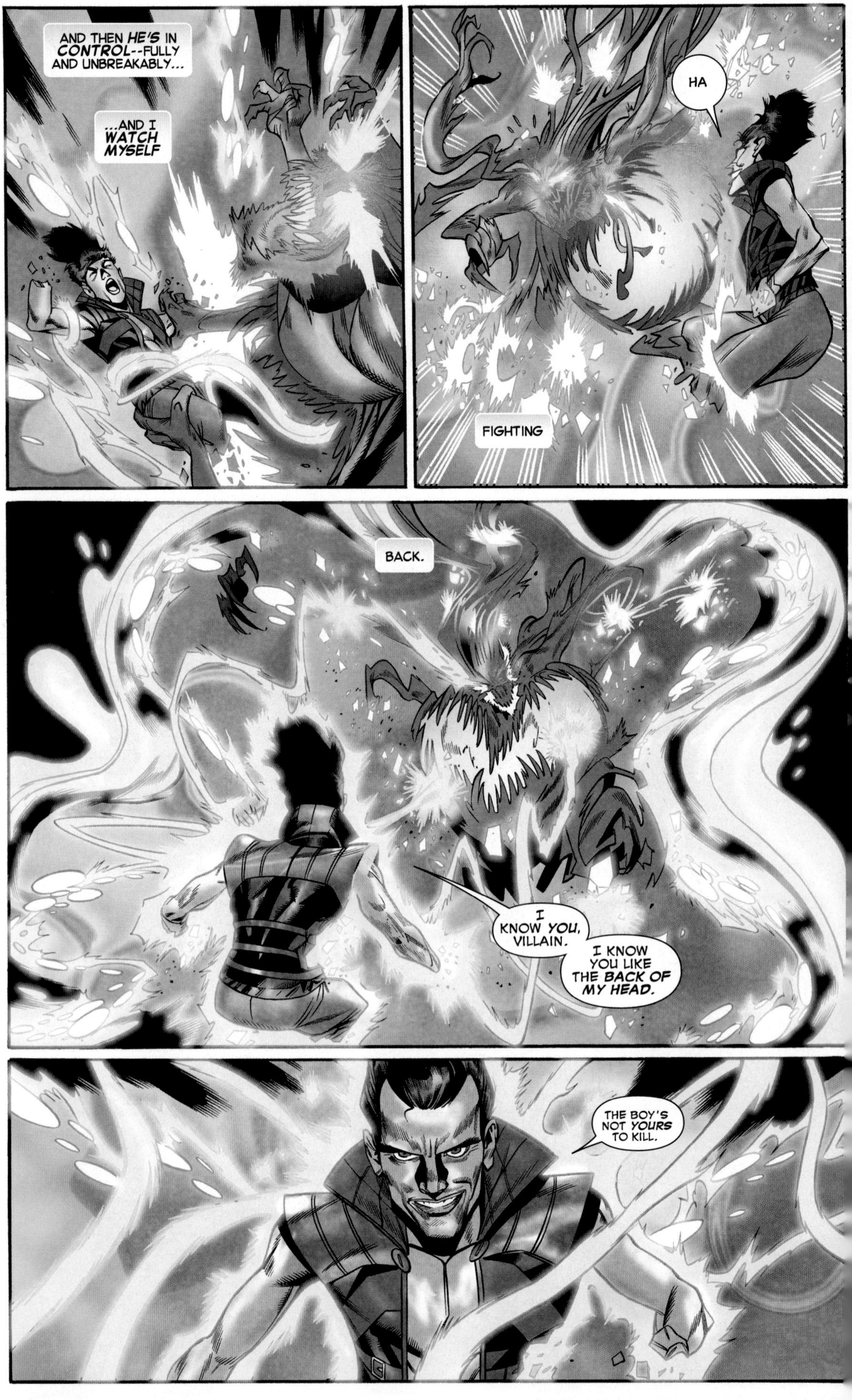
AND THEN HE'S IN CONTROL--FULLY AND UNBREAKABLY...
...AND I WATCH MYSELF
HA
FIGHTING
BACK.
I KNOW YOU, VILLAIN.
I KNOW YOU LIKE THE BACK OF MY HEAD.
THE BOY'S NOT YOURS TO KILL.

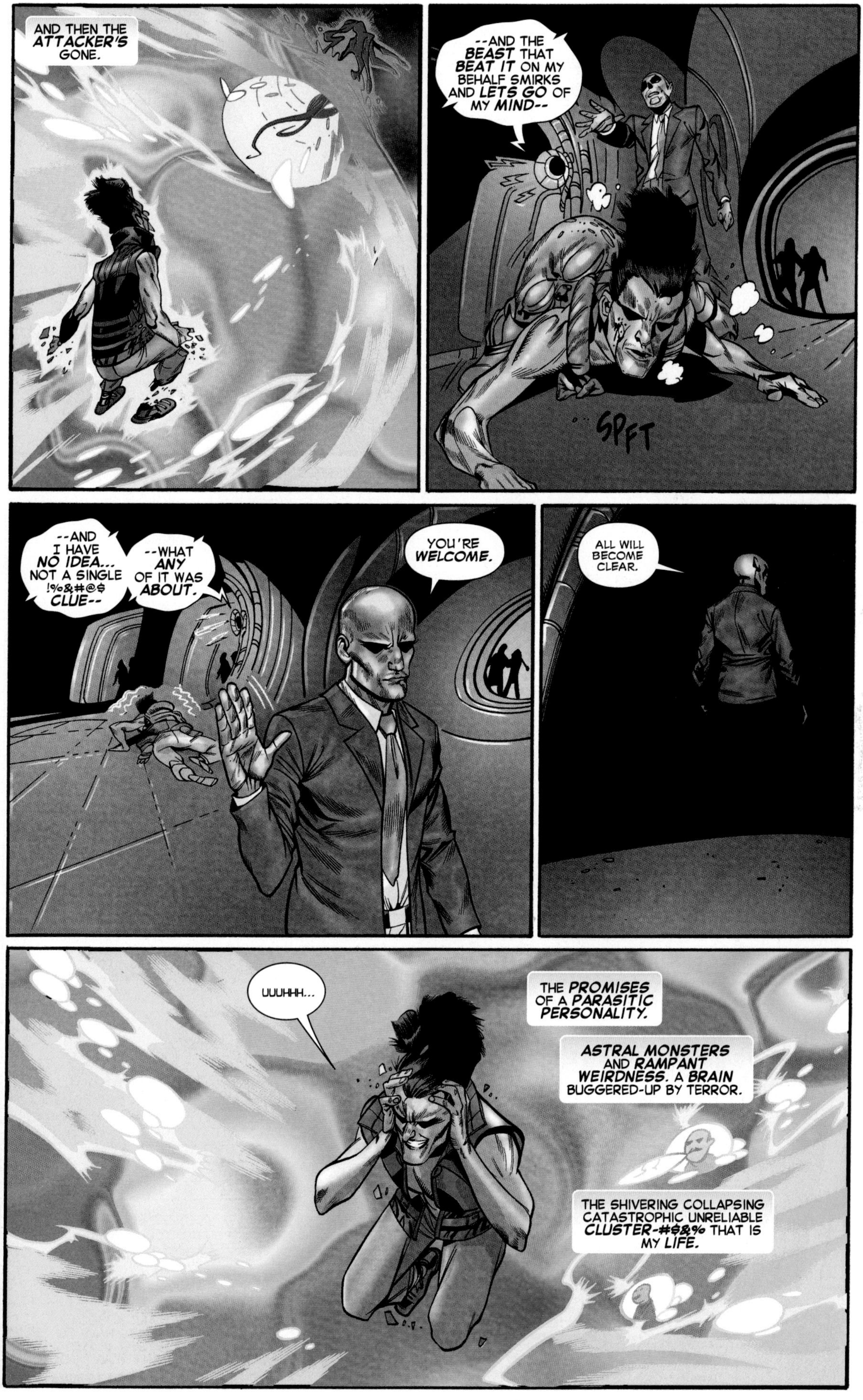
AND THEN THE ATTACKER'S GONE.
--AND THE BEAST THAT BEAT IT ON MY BEHALF SMIRKS AND LETS GO OF MY MIND--
SPFT
--AND I HAVE NO IDEA... NOT A SINGLE !%&#@$ CLUE--
--WHAT ANY OF IT WAS ABOUT.
YOU'RE WELCOME.
ALL WILL BECOME CLEAR.
UUUHHH...
THE PROMISES OF A PARASITIC PERSONALITY.
ASTRAL MONSTERS AND RAMPANT WEIRDNESS. A BRAIN BUGGERED-UP BY TERROR.
THE SHIVERING COLLAPSING CATASTROPHIC UNRELIABLE CLUSTER-#$&% THAT IS MY LIFE.

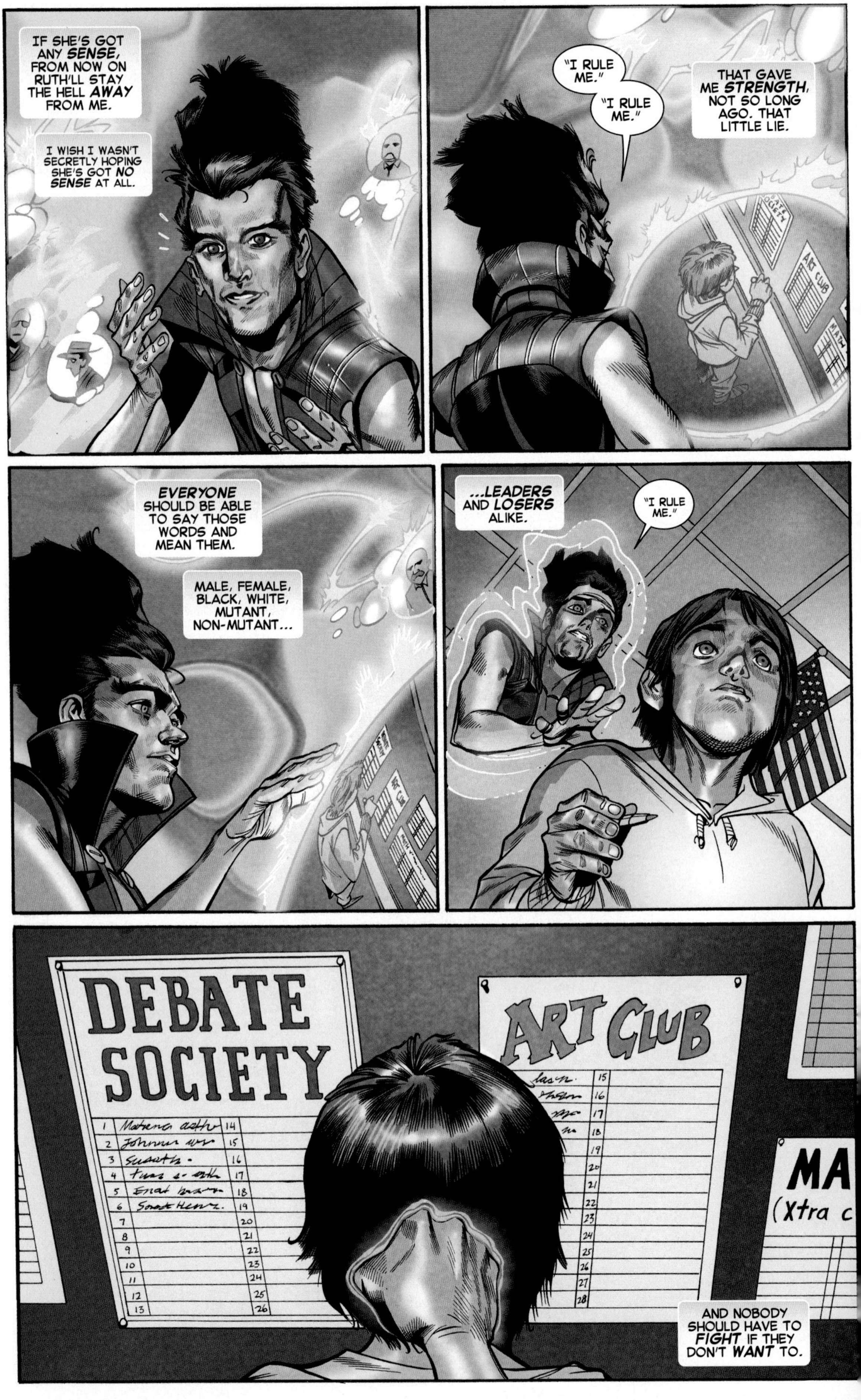
IF SHE'S GOT ANY SENSE, FROM NOW ON RUTH'LL STAY THE HELL AWAY FROM ME.
I WISH I WASN'T SECRETLY HOPING SHE'S GOT NO SENSE AT ALL.
"I RULE ME."
"I RULE ME."
THAT GAVE ME STRENGTH, NOT SO LONG AGO. THAT LITTLE LIE.
EVERYONE SHOULD BE ABLE TO SAY THOSE WORDS AND MEAN THEM.
MALE, FEMALE, BLACK, WHITE, MUTANT, NON-MUTANT...
...LEADERS AND LOSERS ALIKE.
"I RULE ME."
DEBATE SOCIETY
ART CLUB
MA
(Xtra c
AND NOBODY SHOULD HAVE TO FIGHT IF THEY DON'T WANT TO.

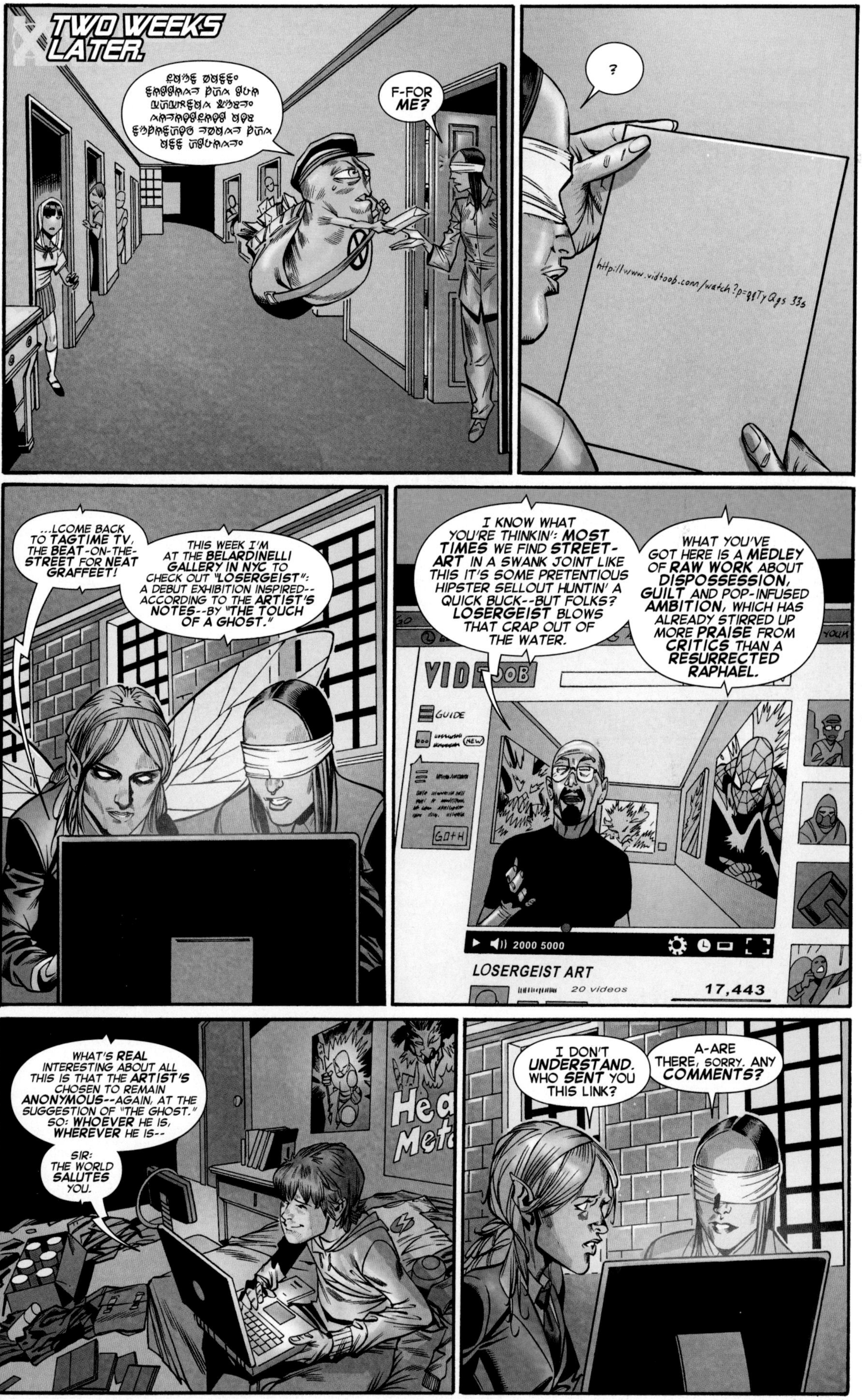
TWO WEEKS LATER.
F-FOR ME?
?
http://www.vidtoob.com/watch?p=g8TyQgs 33s
...LCOME BACK TO TAGTIME TV, THE BEAT-ON-THE-STREET FOR NEAT GRAFFEET!
THIS WEEK I'M AT THE BELARDINELLI GALLERY IN NYC TO CHECK OUT "LOSERGEIST": A DEBUT EXHIBITION INSPIRED--ACCORDING TO THE ARTIST'S NOTES--BY "THE TOUCH OF A GHOST."
I KNOW WHAT YOU'RE THINKIN': MOST TIMES WE FIND STREET-ART IN A SWANK JOINT LIKE THIS IT'S SOME PRETENTIOUS HIPSTER SELLOUT HUNTIN' A QUICK BUCK--BUT FOLKS? LOSERGEIST BLOWS THAT CRAP OUT OF THE WATER.
WHAT YOU'VE GOT HERE IS A MEDLEY OF RAW WORK ABOUT DISPOSSESSION, GUILT AND POP-INFUSED AMBITION, WHICH HAS ALREADY STIRRED UP MORE PRAISE FROM CRITICS THAN A RESURRECTED RAPHAEL.
VIDEOOB
GUIDE
NEW
GOTH
2000 5000
LOSERGEIST ART
20 videos
17,443
WHAT'S REAL INTERESTING ABOUT ALL THIS IS THAT THE ARTIST'S CHOSEN TO REMAIN ANONYMOUS--AGAIN, AT THE SUGGESTION OF "THE GHOST." SO: WHOEVER HE IS, WHEREVER HE IS--
SIR: THE WORLD SALUTES YOU.
I DON'T UNDERSTAND. WHO SENT YOU THIS LINK?
A-ARE THERE, SORRY. ANY COMMENTS?

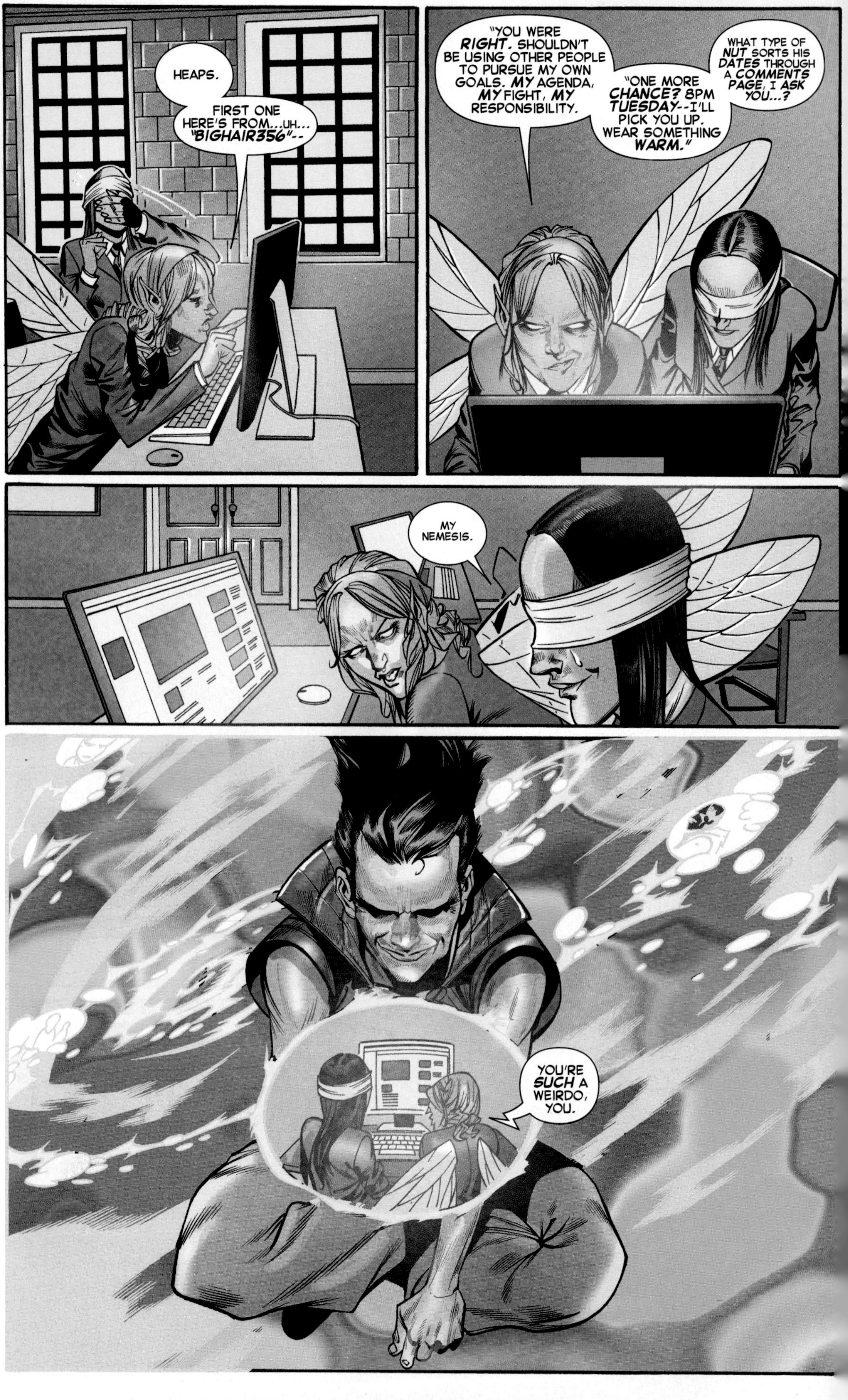
HEAPS.
FIRST ONE HERE'S FROM...UH... "BIGHAIR356"--
"YOU WERE RIGHT. SHOULDN'T BE USING OTHER PEOPLE TO PURSUE MY OWN GOALS. MY AGENDA, MY FIGHT, MY RESPONSIBILITY.
"ONE MORE CHANCE? 8PM TUESDAY--I'LL PICK YOU UP. WEAR SOMETHING WARM."
WHAT TYPE OF NUT SORTS HIS DATES THROUGH A COMMENTS PAGE, I ASK YOU...?
MY NEMESIS.
YOU'RE SUCH A WEIRDO, YOU.

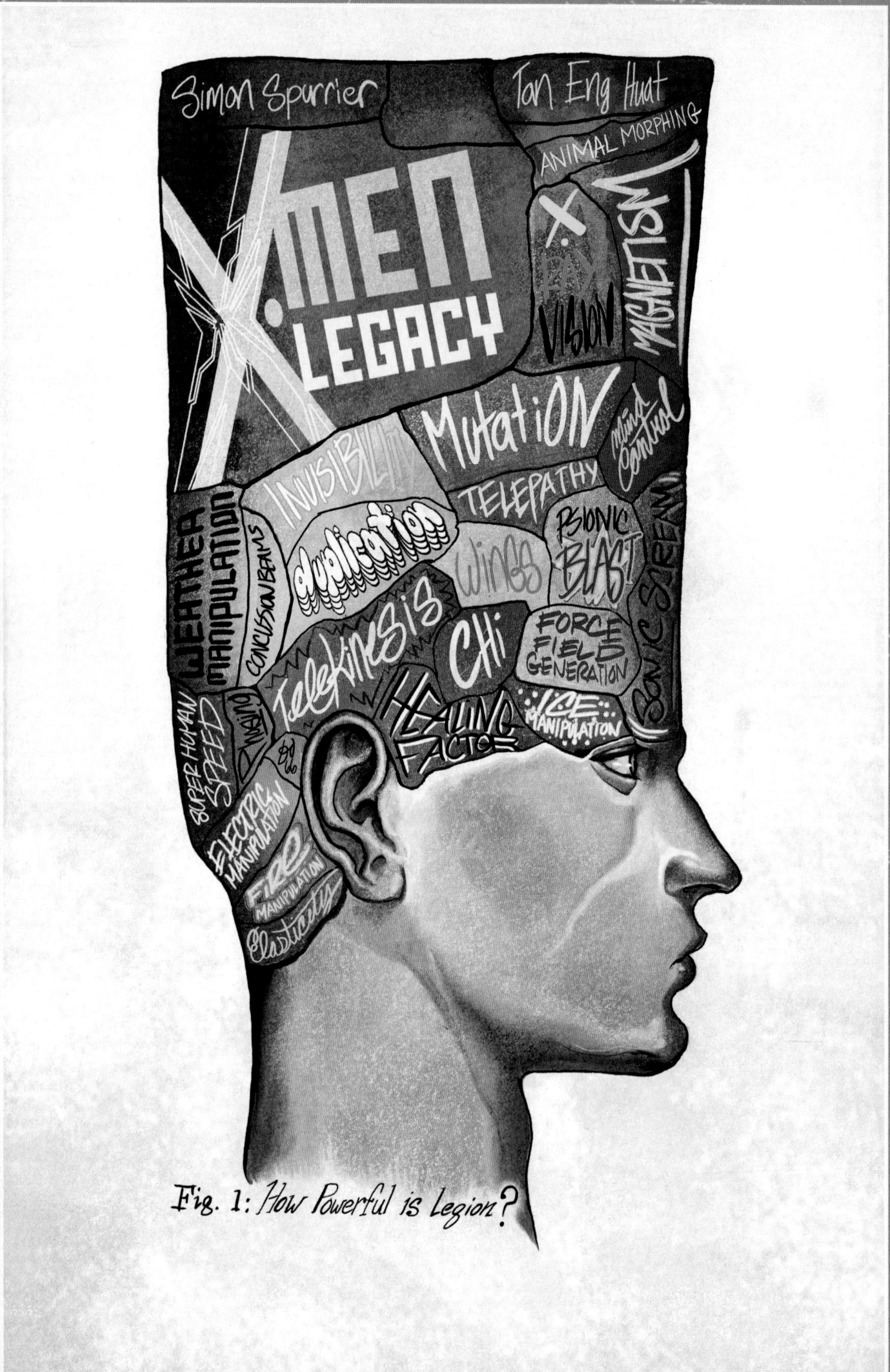
Simon Spurrier
Tan Eng Huat
X-MEN
LEGACY
ANIMAL MORPHING
VISION
MAGNETISM
MutatiON
Mind Control
TELEPATHY
WEATHER MANIPULATION
CONCUSSION BEAMS
duplication
WINGS
PSIONIC BLAST
SONIC SCREAM
Telekinesis
CHi
FORCE FIELD GENERATION
HEALING FACTOR
ICE MANIPULATION
SUPER HUMAN SPEED
ELECTRIC MANIPULATION
FIRE MANIPULATION
Elasticity
Fig. 1: How Powerful is Legion?

NINE

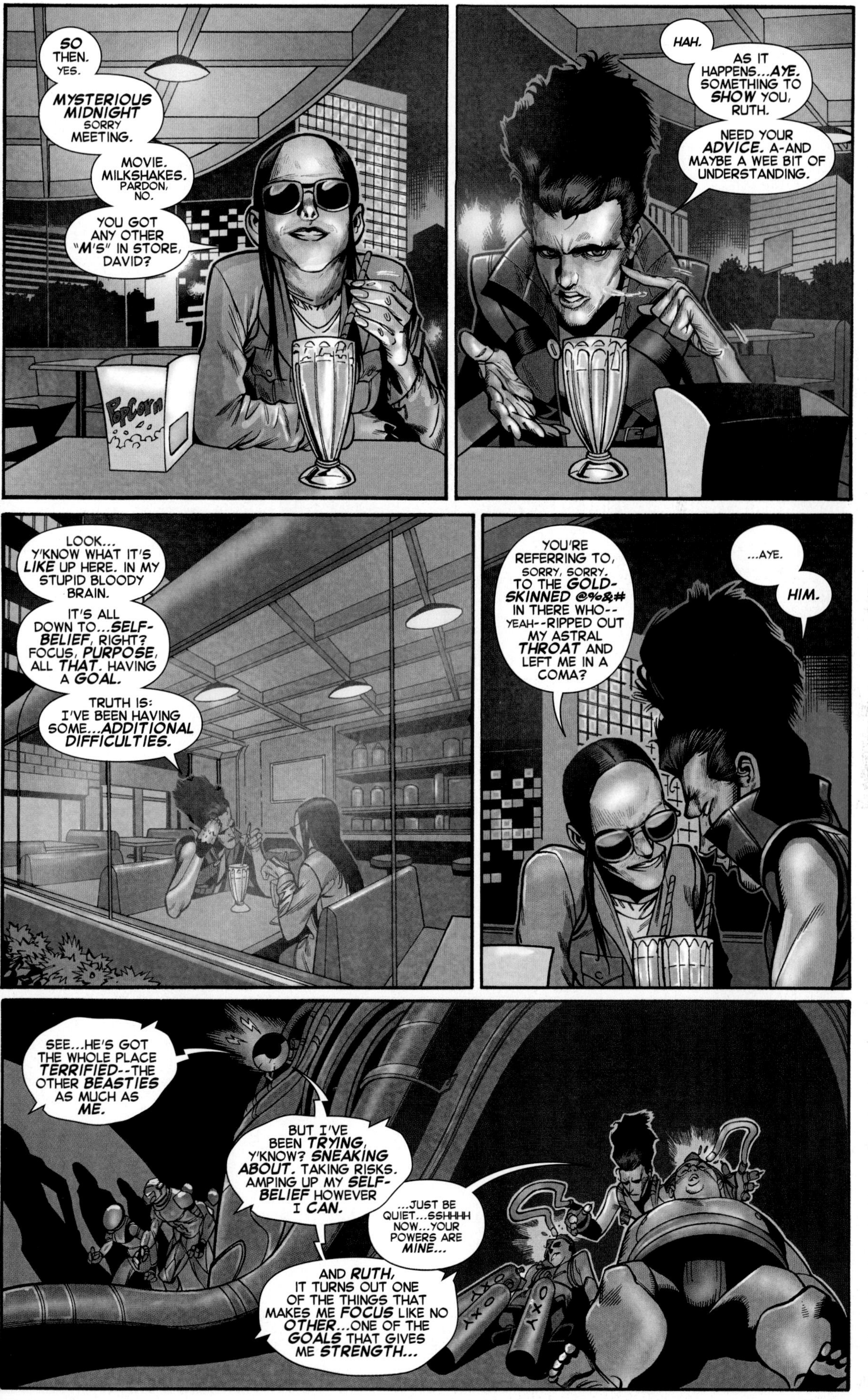
SO THEN. YES.
MYSTERIOUS MIDNIGHT SORRY MEETING.
MOVIE. MILKSHAKES. PARDON, NO.
YOU GOT ANY OTHER "M'S" IN STORE, DAVID?
HAH.
AS IT HAPPENS...AYE. SOMETHING TO SHOW YOU, RUTH.
NEED YOUR ADVICE. A-AND MAYBE A WEE BIT OF UNDERSTANDING.
LOOK... Y'KNOW WHAT IT'S LIKE UP HERE. IN MY STUPID BLOODY BRAIN.
IT'S ALL DOWN TO...SELF-BELIEF, RIGHT? FOCUS, PURPOSE, ALL THAT. HAVING A GOAL.
TRUTH IS: I'VE BEEN HAVING SOME...ADDITIONAL DIFFICULTIES.
YOU'RE REFERRING TO, SORRY, SORRY, TO THE GOLD-SKINNED @%&# IN THERE WHO--YEAH--RIPPED OUT MY ASTRAL THROAT AND LEFT ME IN A COMA?
...AYE.
HIM.
SEE...HE'S GOT THE WHOLE PLACE TERRIFIED--THE OTHER BEASTIES AS MUCH AS ME.
BUT I'VE BEEN TRYING, Y'KNOW? SNEAKING ABOUT. TAKING RISKS. AMPING UP MY SELF-BELIEF HOWEVER I CAN.
...JUST BE QUIET...SSHHHH NOW...YOUR POWERS ARE MINE...
AND RUTH, IT TURNS OUT ONE OF THE THINGS THAT MAKES ME FOCUS LIKE NO OTHER...ONE OF THE GOALS THAT GIVES ME STRENGTH...

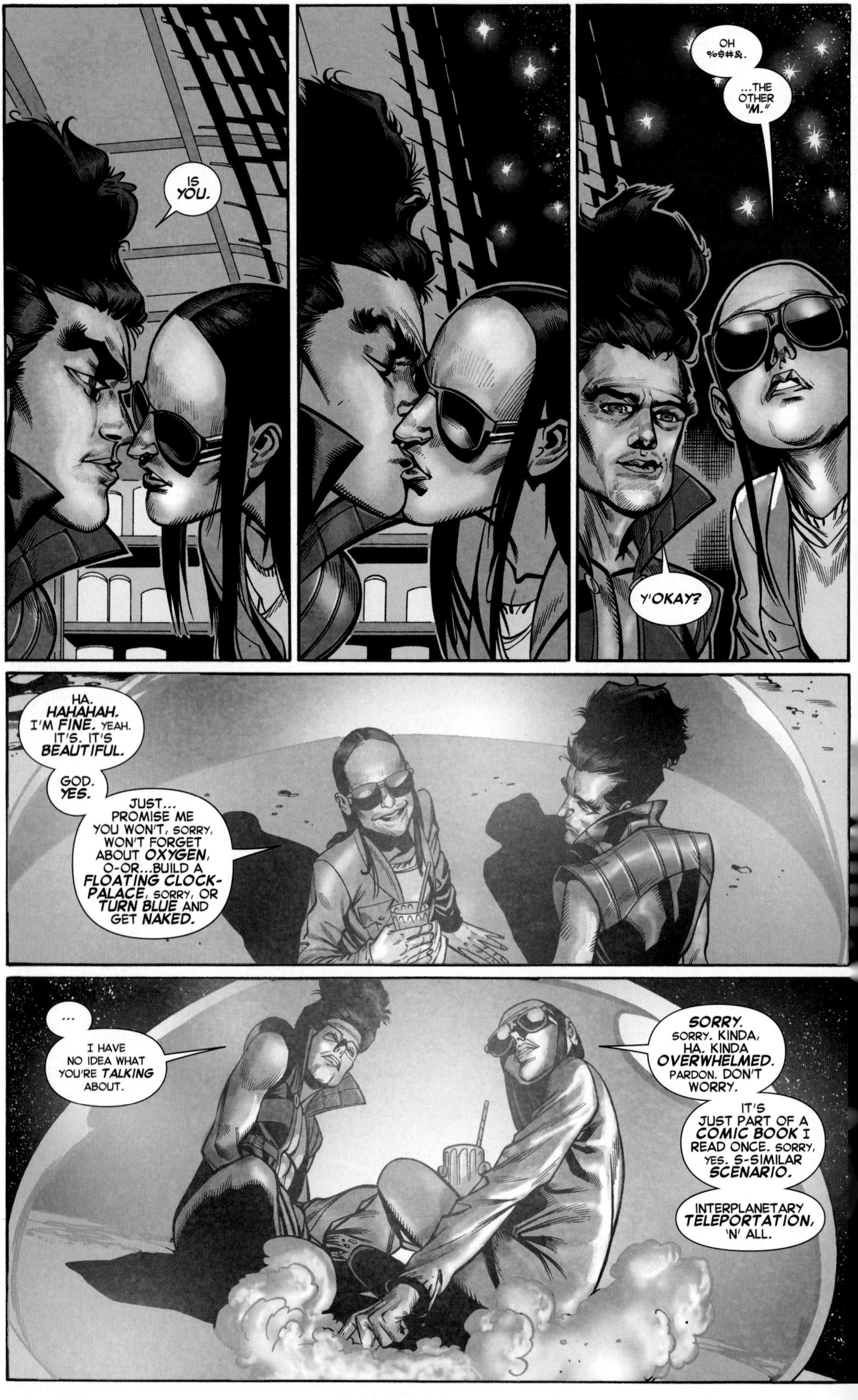
IS YOU.
OH %$#&.
...THE OTHER "M."
Y'OKAY?
HA. HAHAHAH. I'M FINE. YEAH. IT'S. IT'S BEAUTIFUL.
GOD. YES.
JUST... PROMISE ME YOU WON'T, SORRY, WON'T FORGET ABOUT OXYGEN, O-OR...BUILD A FLOATING CLOCK-PALACE, SORRY, OR TURN BLUE AND GET NAKED.
...
I HAVE NO IDEA WHAT YOU'RE TALKING ABOUT.
SORRY. SORRY. KINDA, HA. KINDA OVERWHELMED. PARDON. DON'T WORRY.
IT'S JUST PART OF A COMIC BOOK I READ ONCE. SORRY, YES. S-SIMILAR SCENARIO.
INTERPLANETARY TELEPORTATION, 'N' ALL.

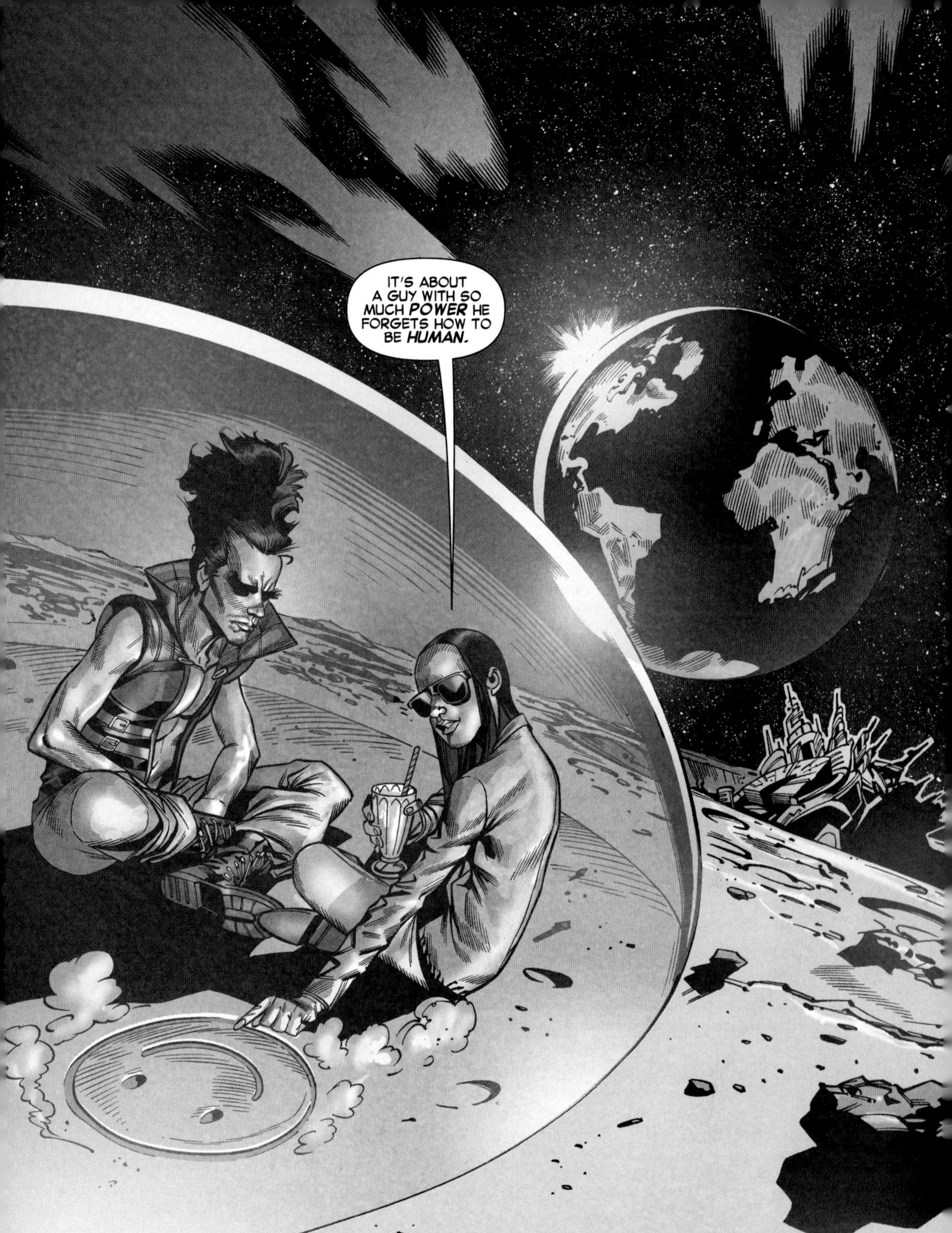

JUDGMENT OF DIANA

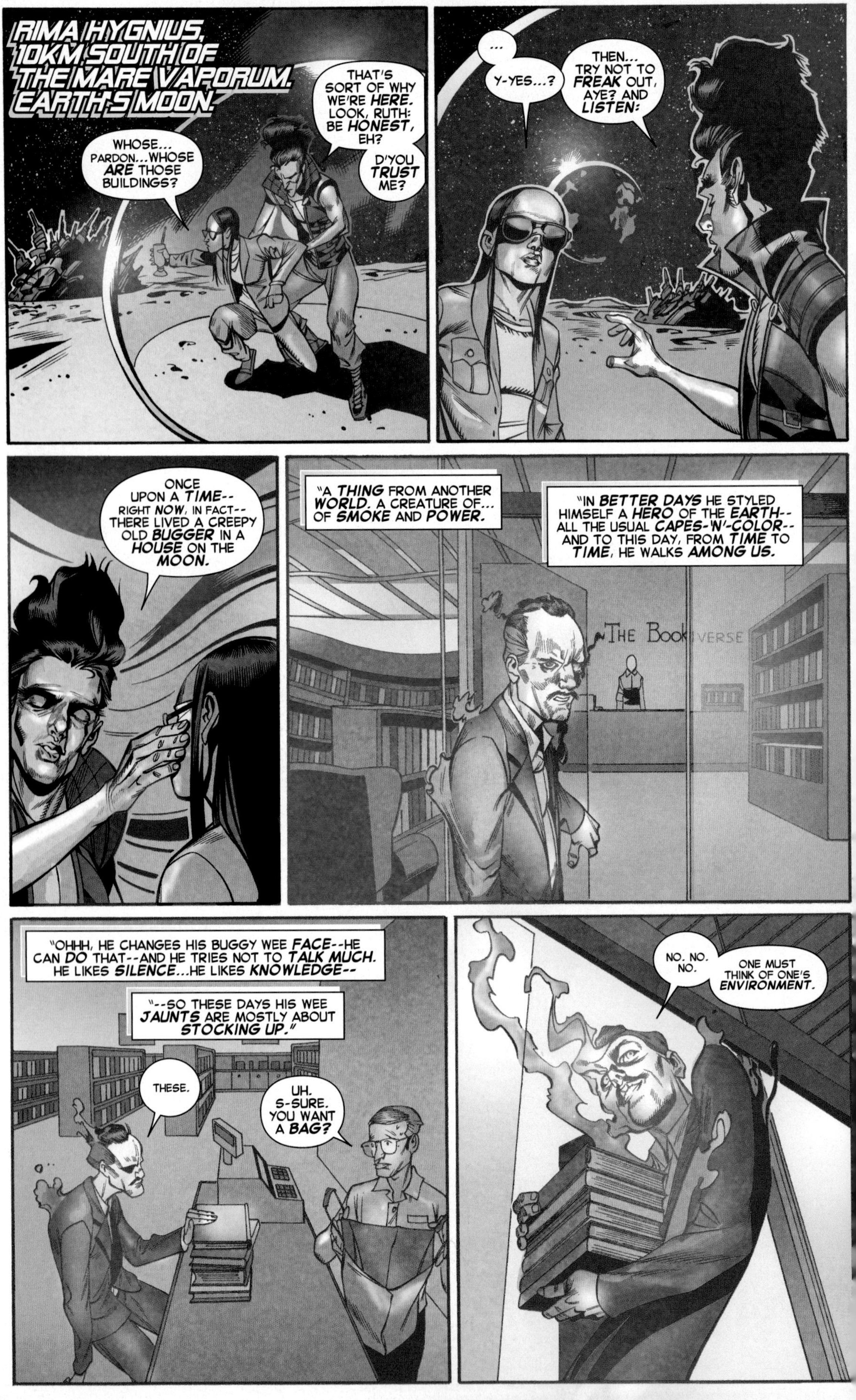
RIMA HYGNIUS, 10KM SOUTH OF THE MARE VAPORUM. EARTH'S MOON.
WHOSE... PARDON...WHOSE ARE THOSE BUILDINGS?
THAT'S SORT OF WHY WE'RE HERE. LOOK, RUTH: BE HONEST, EH?
D'YOU TRUST ME?
...
Y-YES...?
THEN... TRY NOT TO FREAK OUT, AYE? AND LISTEN:
ONCE UPON A TIME-- RIGHT NOW, IN FACT-- THERE LIVED A CREEPY OLD BUGGER IN A HOUSE ON THE MOON.
"A THING FROM ANOTHER WORLD. A CREATURE OF... OF SMOKE AND POWER.
"IN BETTER DAYS HE STYLED HIMSELF A HERO OF THE EARTH-- ALL THE USUAL CAPES-'N'-COLOR-- AND TO THIS DAY, FROM TIME TO TIME, HE WALKS AMONG US.
THE BOOKVERSE
"OHHH, HE CHANGES HIS BUGGY WEE FACE--HE CAN DO THAT--AND HE TRIES NOT TO TALK MUCH. HE LIKES SILENCE...HE LIKES KNOWLEDGE--
"--SO THESE DAYS HIS WEE JAUNTS ARE MOSTLY ABOUT STOCKING UP."
THESE.
UH. S-SURE. YOU WANT A BAG?
NO. NO. NO.
ONE MUST THINK OF ONE'S ENVIRONMENT.

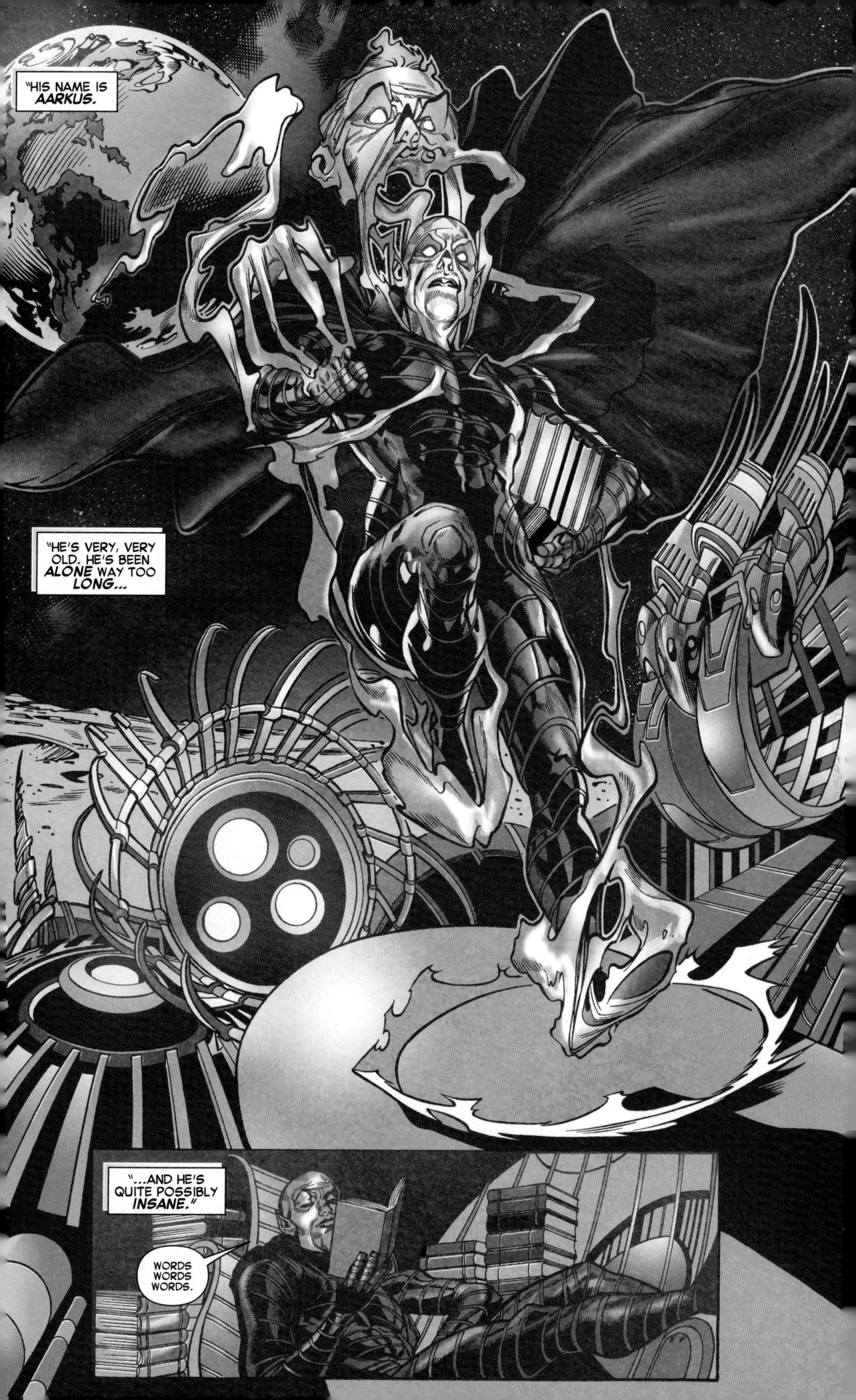
"HIS NAME IS AARKUS.
"HE'S VERY, VERY OLD. HE'S BEEN ALONE WAY TOO LONG...
"...AND HE'S QUITE POSSIBLY INSANE."
WORDS WORDS WORDS.

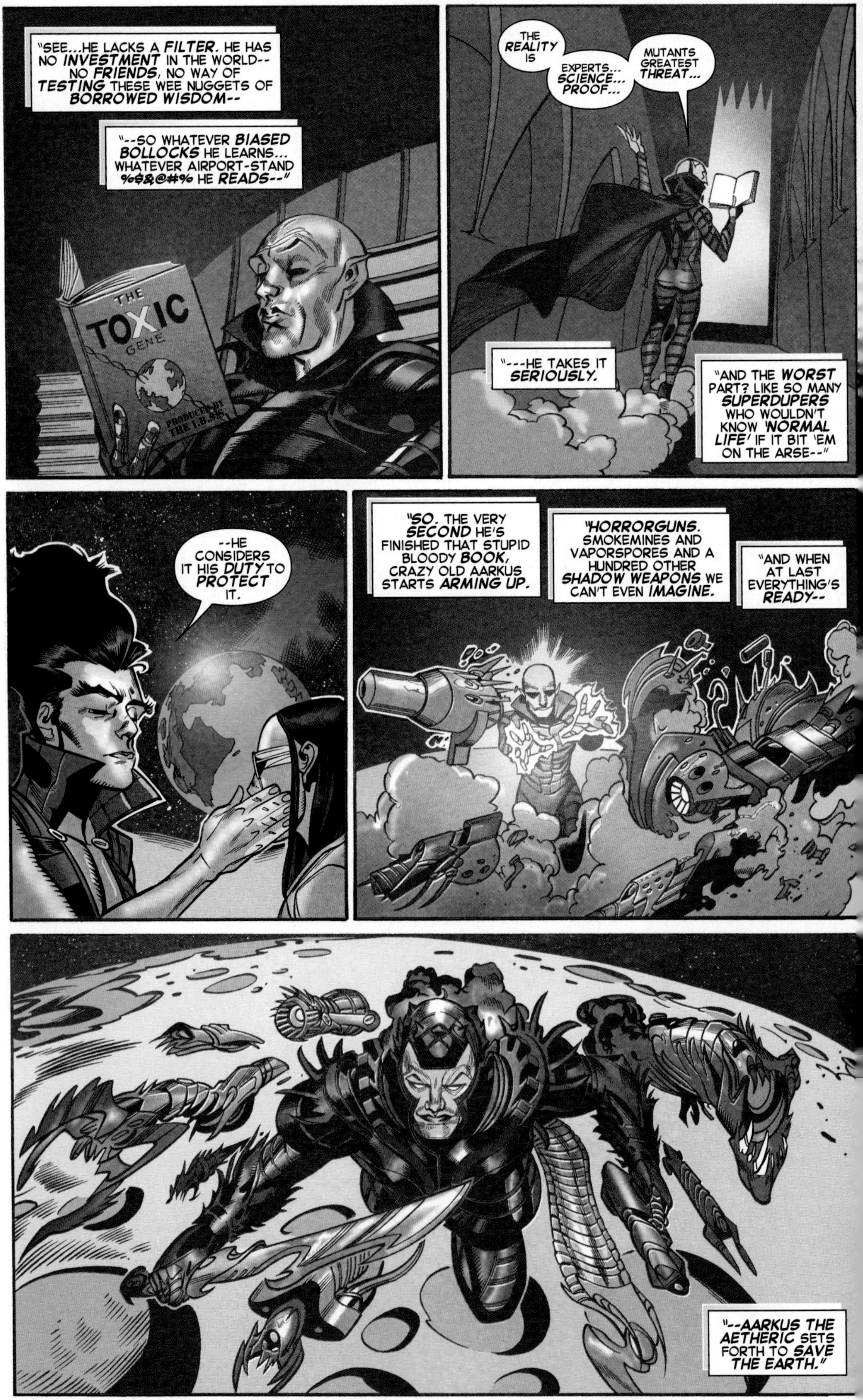

"SEE...HE LACKS A FILTER. HE HAS NO INVESTMENT IN THE WORLD-- NO FRIENDS, NO WAY OF TESTING THESE WEE NUGGETS OF BORROWED WISDOM--
"--SO WHATEVER BIASED BOLLOCKS HE LEARNS... WHATEVER AIRPORT-STAND %$&@#% HE READS--"
THE TOXIC GENE
PRODUCED BY THE I.B.S.S.
THE REALITY IS
EXPERTS... SCIENCE... PROOF...
MUTANTS GREATEST THREAT...
"---HE TAKES IT SERIOUSLY.
"AND THE WORST PART? LIKE SO MANY SUPERDUPERS WHO WOULDN'T KNOW 'NORMAL LIFE' IF IT BIT 'EM ON THE ARSE--"
--HE CONSIDERS IT HIS DUTY TO PROTECT IT.
"SO. THE VERY SECOND HE'S FINISHED THAT STUPID BLOODY BOOK, CRAZY OLD AARKUS STARTS ARMING UP.
"HORRORGUNS. SMOKEMINES AND VAPORSPORES AND A HUNDRED OTHER SHADOW WEAPONS WE CAN'T EVEN IMAGINE.
"AND WHEN AT LAST EVERYTHING'S READY--
"--AARKUS THE AETHERIC SETS FORTH TO SAVE THE EARTH."

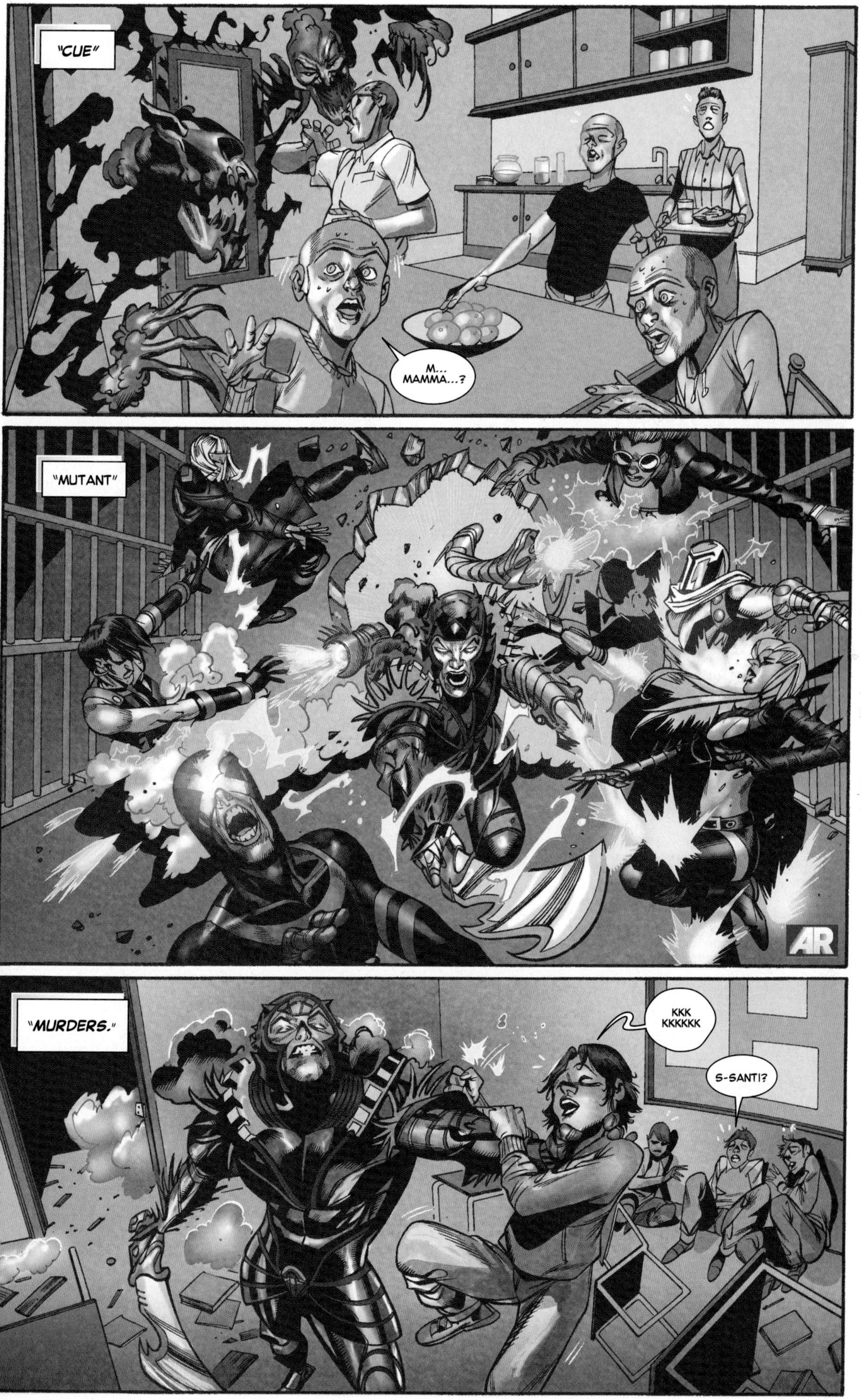
"CUE"
M... MAMMA...?
"MUTANT"
"MURDERS."
KKK KKKKKK
S-SANTI!?

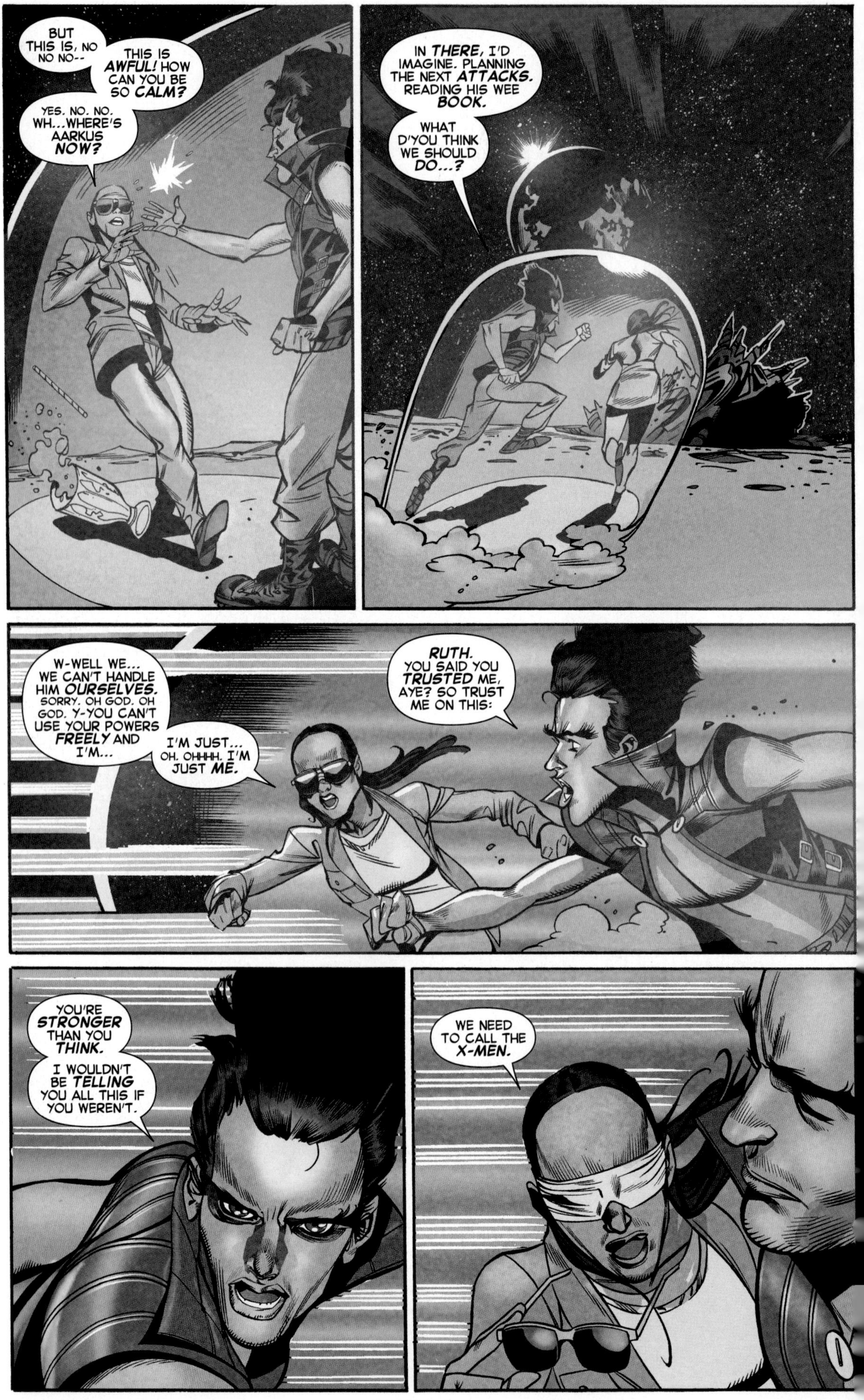
BUT THIS IS, NO NO NO--
THIS IS AWFUL! HOW CAN YOU BE SO CALM?
YES. NO. NO. WH...WHERE'S AARKUS NOW?
IN THERE, I'D IMAGINE. PLANNING THE NEXT ATTACKS. READING HIS WEE BOOK.
WHAT D'YOU THINK WE SHOULD DO...?
W-WELL WE... WE CAN'T HANDLE HIM OURSELVES. SORRY. OH GOD. OH GOD. Y-YOU CAN'T USE YOUR POWERS FREELY AND I'M...
I'M JUST... OH. OHHHH. I'M JUST ME.
RUTH. YOU SAID YOU TRUSTED ME, AYE? SO TRUST ME ON THIS:
YOU'RE STRONGER THAN YOU THINK.
I WOULDN'T BE TELLING YOU ALL THIS IF YOU WEREN'T.
WE NEED TO CALL THE X-MEN.

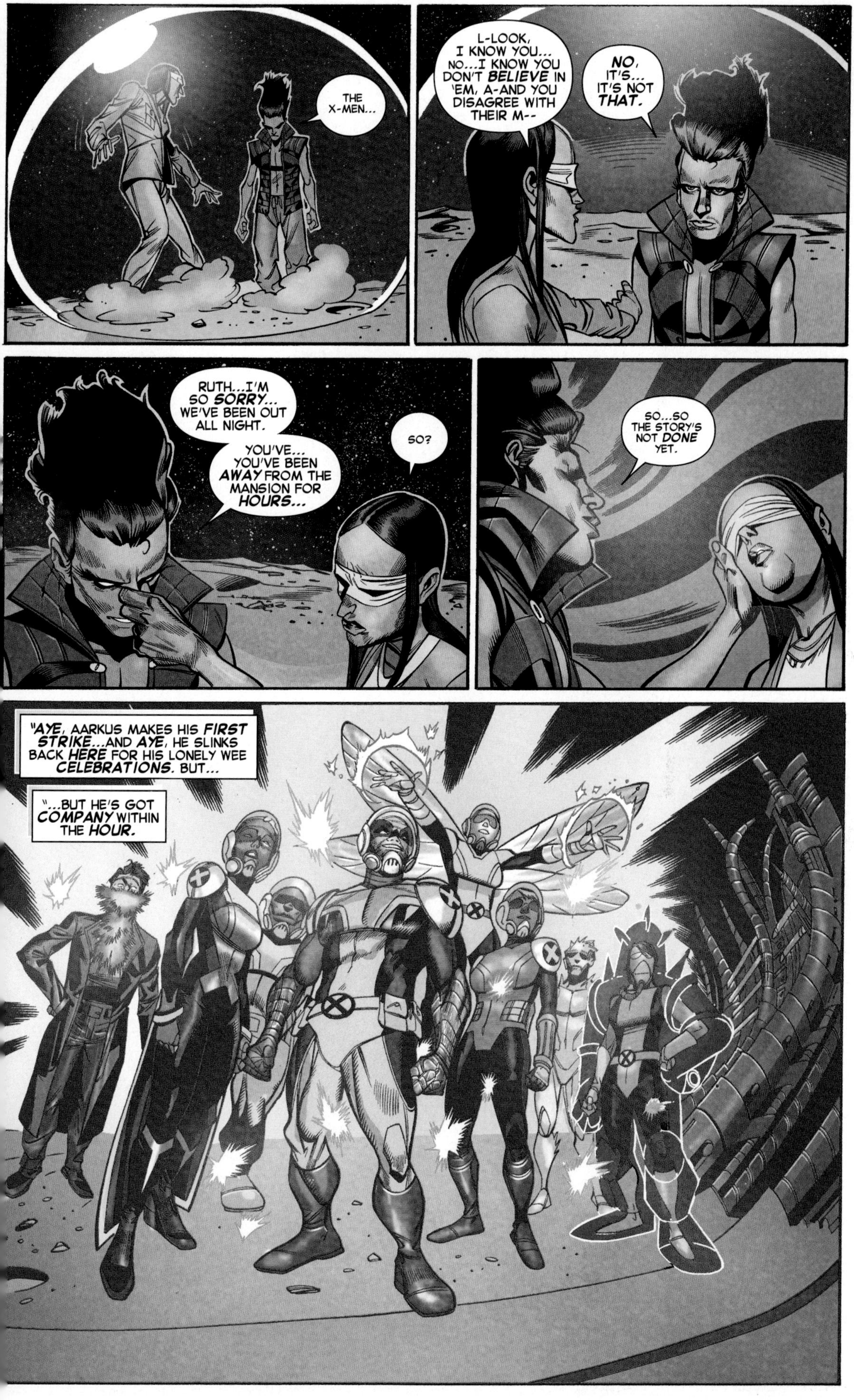
THE X-MEN...
L-LOOK, I KNOW YOU... NO...I KNOW YOU DON'T BELIEVE IN 'EM, A-AND YOU DISAGREE WITH THEIR M--
NO, IT'S... IT'S NOT THAT.
RUTH...I'M SO SORRY... WE'VE BEEN OUT ALL NIGHT.
YOU'VE... YOU'VE BEEN AWAY FROM THE MANSION FOR HOURS...
SO?
SO...SO THE STORY'S NOT DONE YET.
"AYE, AARKUS MAKES HIS FIRST STRIKE...AND AYE, HE SLINKS BACK HERE FOR HIS LONELY WEE CELEBRATIONS. BUT...
"...BUT HE'S GOT COMPANY WITHIN THE HOUR.

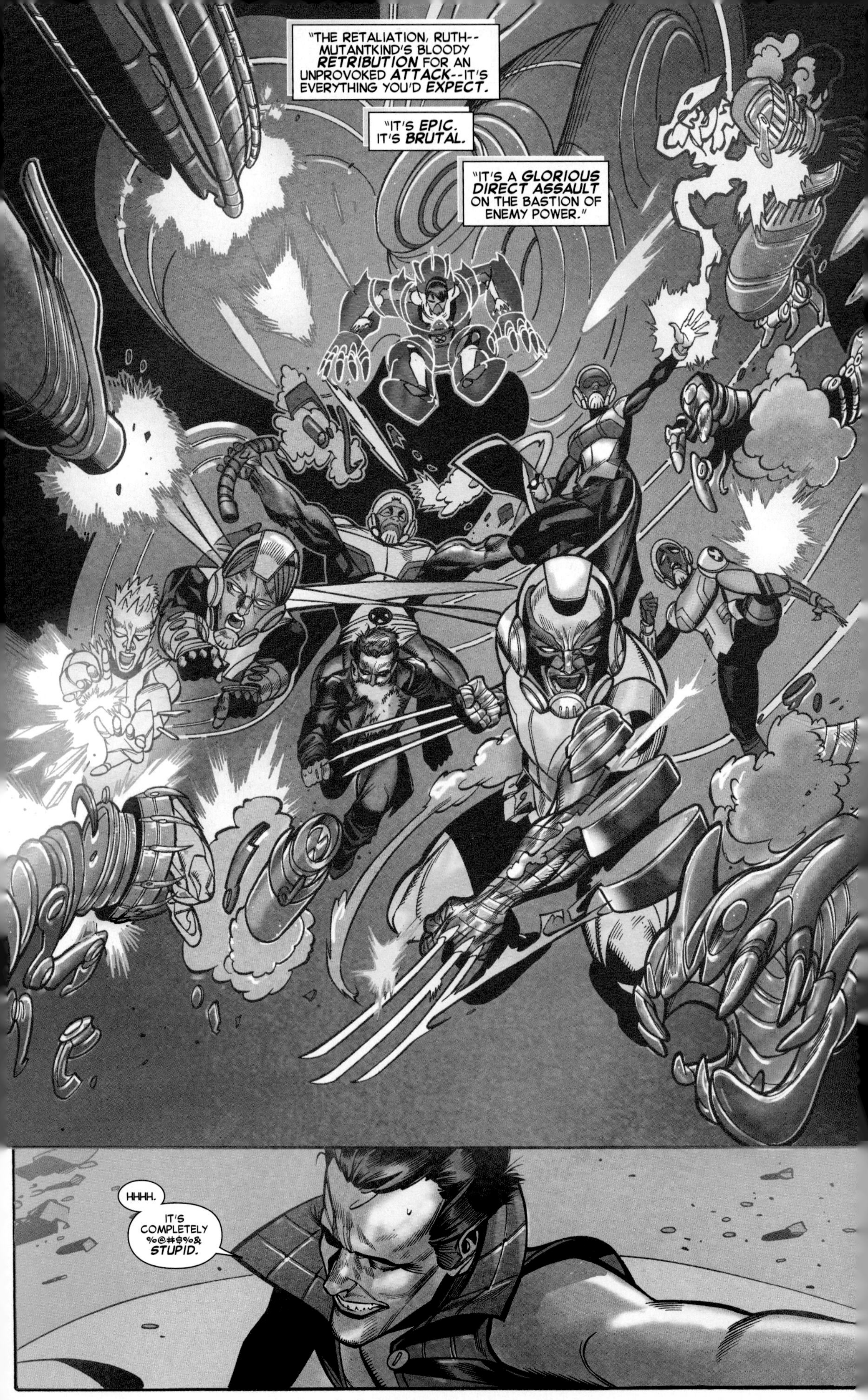
"THE RETALIATION, RUTH--MUTANTKIND'S BLOODY RETRIBUTION FOR AN UNPROVOKED ATTACK--IT'S EVERYTHING YOU'D EXPECT.
"IT'S EPIC. IT'S BRUTAL.
"IT'S A GLORIOUS DIRECT ASSAULT ON THE BASTION OF ENEMY POWER."
HHHH.
IT'S COMPLETELY %@#$%& STUPID.

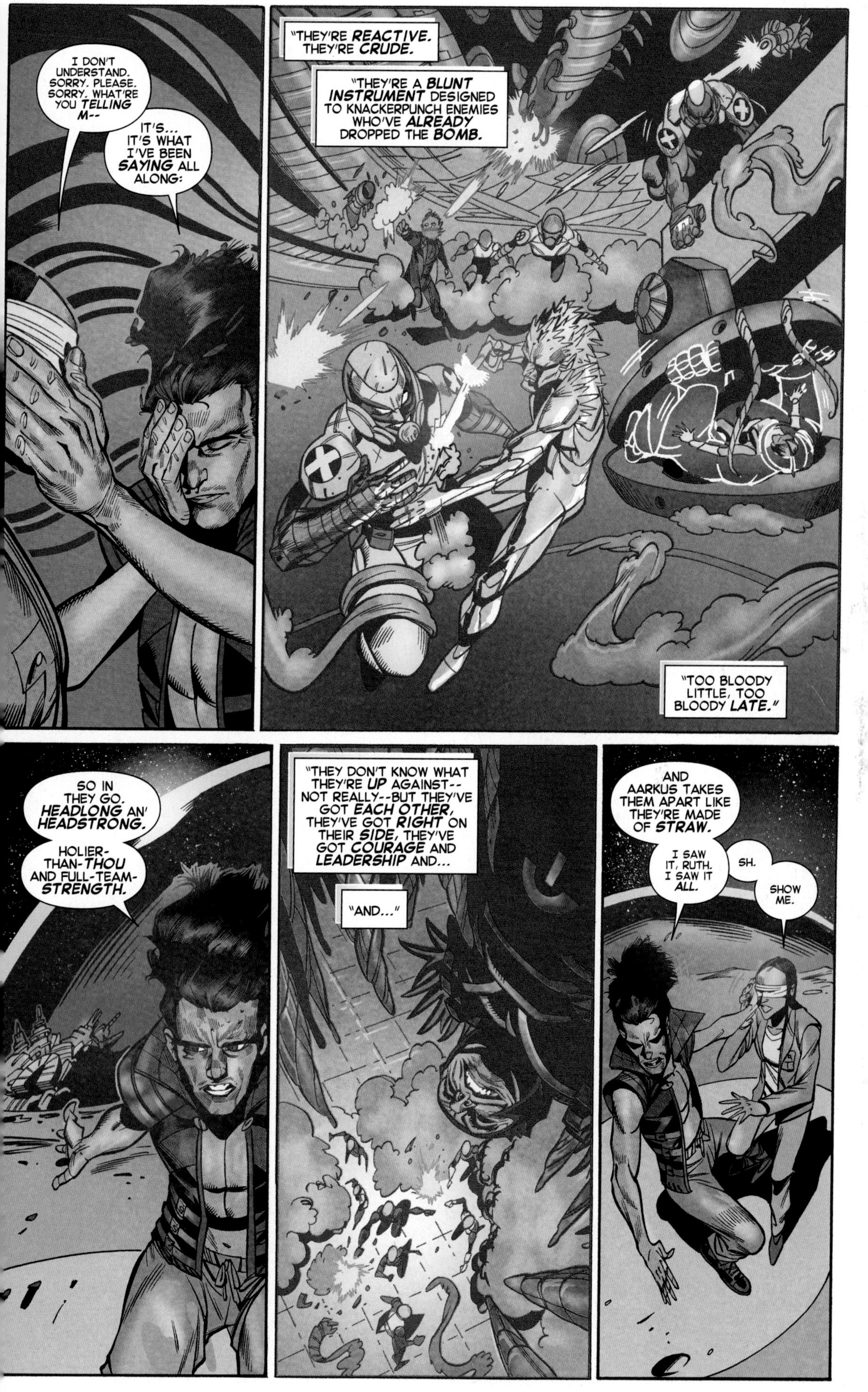
I DON'T UNDERSTAND. SORRY. PLEASE. SORRY. WHAT'RE YOU TELLING M--
IT'S... IT'S WHAT I'VE BEEN SAYING ALL ALONG:
"THEY'RE REACTIVE. THEY'RE CRUDE.
"THEY'RE A BLUNT INSTRUMENT DESIGNED TO KNACKERPUNCH ENEMIES WHO'VE ALREADY DROPPED THE BOMB.
"TOO BLOODY LITTLE, TOO BLOODY LATE."
SO IN THEY GO. HEADLONG AN' HEADSTRONG.
HOLIER-THAN-THOU AND FULL-TEAM-STRENGTH.
"THEY DON'T KNOW WHAT THEY'RE UP AGAINST--NOT REALLY--BUT THEY'VE GOT EACH OTHER, THEY'VE GOT RIGHT ON THEIR SIDE, THEY'VE GOT COURAGE AND LEADERSHIP AND...
"AND..."
AND AARKUS TAKES THEM APART LIKE THEY'RE MADE OF STRAW.
I SAW IT, RUTH. I SAW IT ALL.
SH.
SHOW ME.

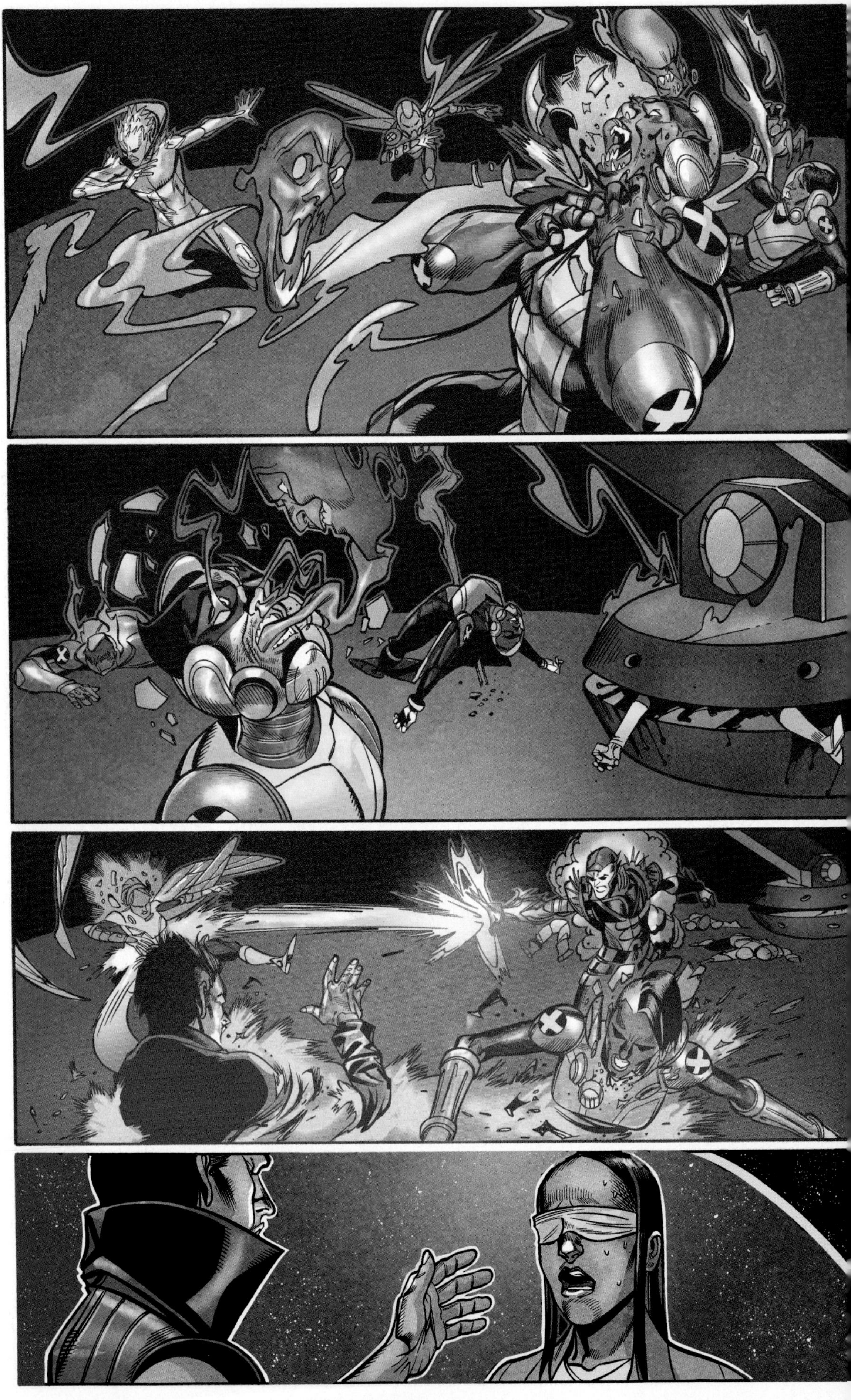

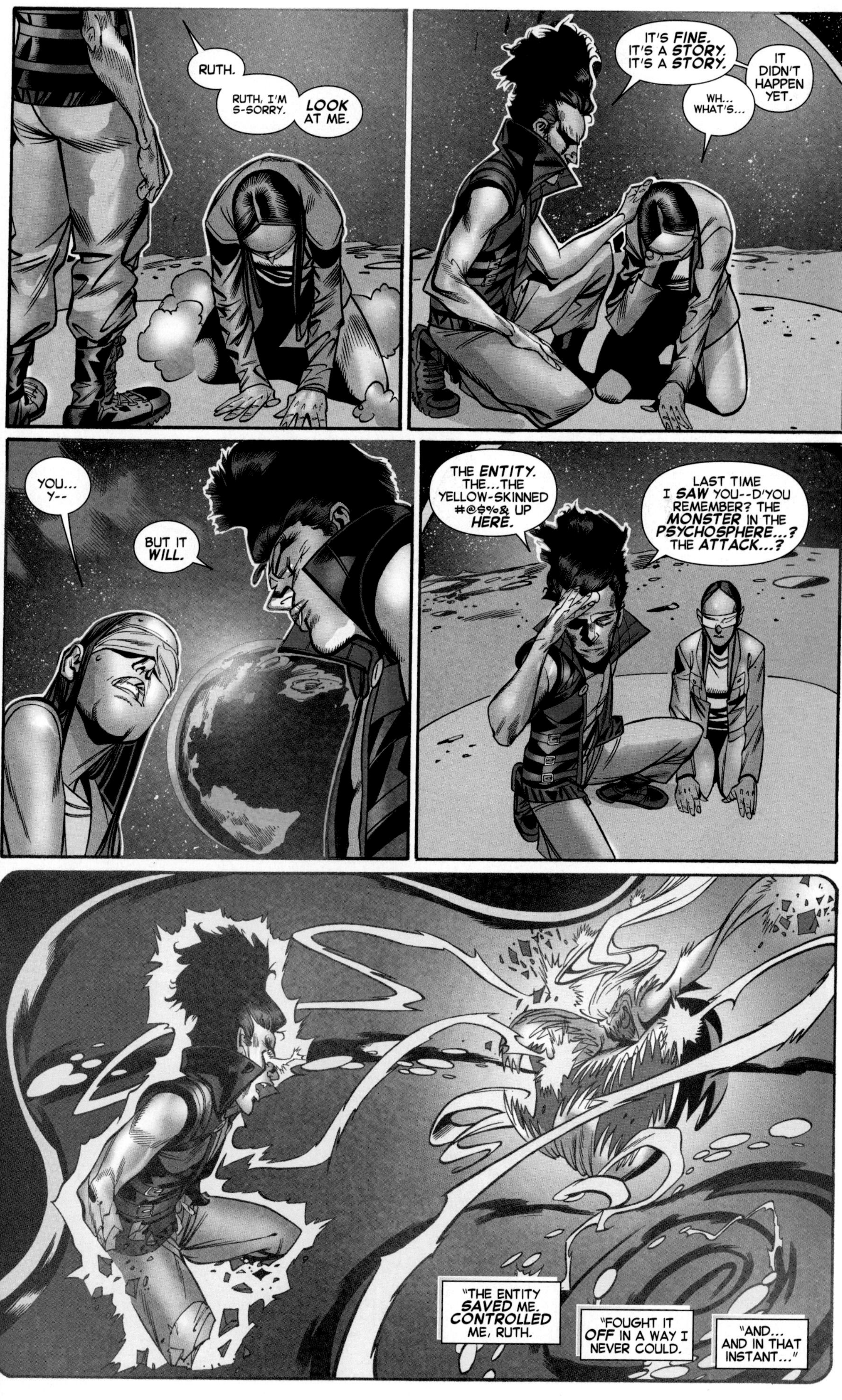

RUTH.
RUTH, I'M S-SORRY. LOOK AT ME.
IT'S FINE. IT'S A STORY. IT'S A STORY.
WH... WHAT'S...
IT DIDN'T HAPPEN YET.
YOU... Y--
BUT IT WILL.
THE ENTITY. THE...THE YELLOW-SKINNED #@$%& UP HERE.
LAST TIME I SAW YOU--D'YOU REMEMBER? THE MONSTER IN THE PSYCHOSPHERE...? THE ATTACK...?
"THE ENTITY SAVED ME. CONTROLLED ME, RUTH.
"FOUGHT IT OFF IN A WAY I NEVER COULD.
"AND... AND IN THAT INSTANT..."

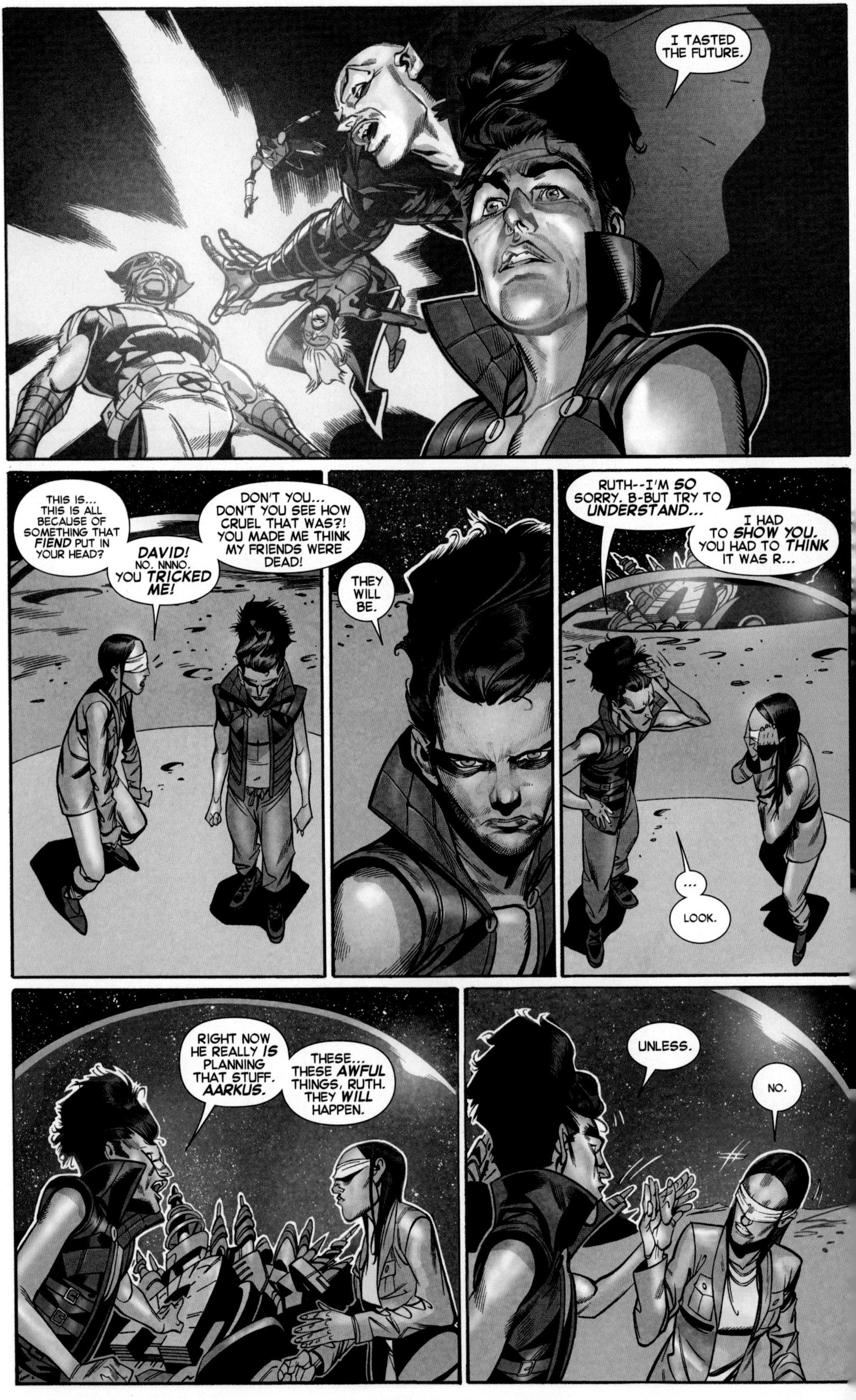
I TASTED THE FUTURE.
THIS IS... THIS IS ALL BECAUSE OF SOMETHING THAT FIEND PUT IN YOUR HEAD?
DAVID! NO. NNNO. YOU TRICKED ME!
DON'T YOU... DON'T YOU SEE HOW CRUEL THAT WAS?! YOU MADE ME THINK MY FRIENDS WERE DEAD!
THEY WILL BE.
RUTH--I'M SO SORRY. B-BUT TRY TO UNDERSTAND...
I HAD TO SHOW YOU. YOU HAD TO THINK IT WAS R...
...
LOOK.
RIGHT NOW HE REALLY IS PLANNING THAT STUFF. AARKUS.
THESE... THESE AWFUL THINGS, RUTH. THEY WILL HAPPEN.
UNLESS.
NO.

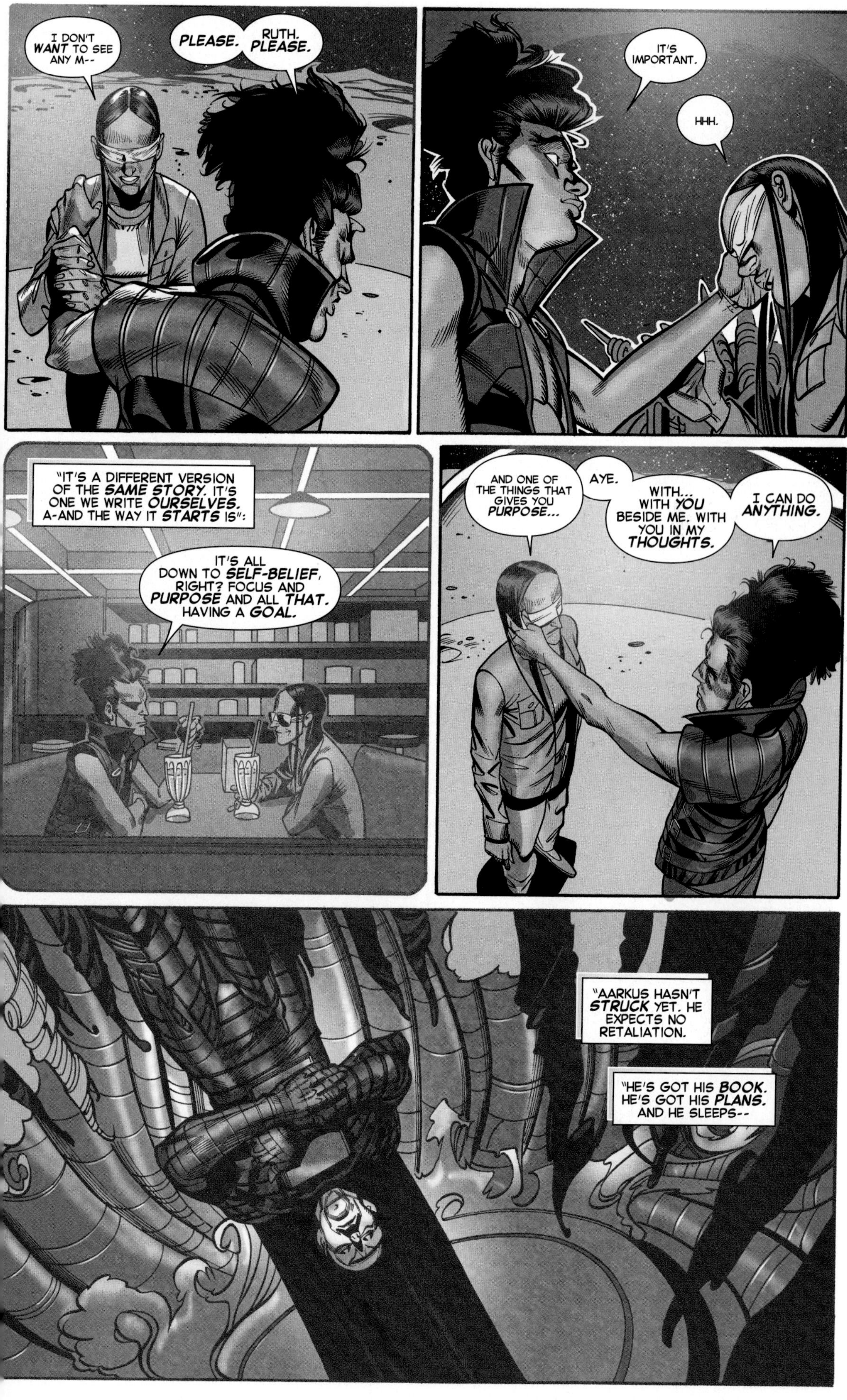
I DON'T WANT TO SEE ANY M--
PLEASE.
RUTH. PLEASE.
IT'S IMPORTANT.
HHH.
"IT'S A DIFFERENT VERSION OF THE SAME STORY. IT'S ONE WE WRITE OURSELVES. A-AND THE WAY IT STARTS IS":
IT'S ALL DOWN TO SELF-BELIEF, RIGHT? FOCUS AND PURPOSE AND ALL THAT. HAVING A GOAL.
AND ONE OF THE THINGS THAT GIVES YOU PURPOSE...
AYE.
WITH... WITH YOU BESIDE ME. WITH YOU IN MY THOUGHTS.
I CAN DO ANYTHING.
"AARKUS HASN'T STRUCK YET. HE EXPECTS NO RETALIATION.
"HE'S GOT HIS BOOK. HE'S GOT HIS PLANS. AND HE SLEEPS--

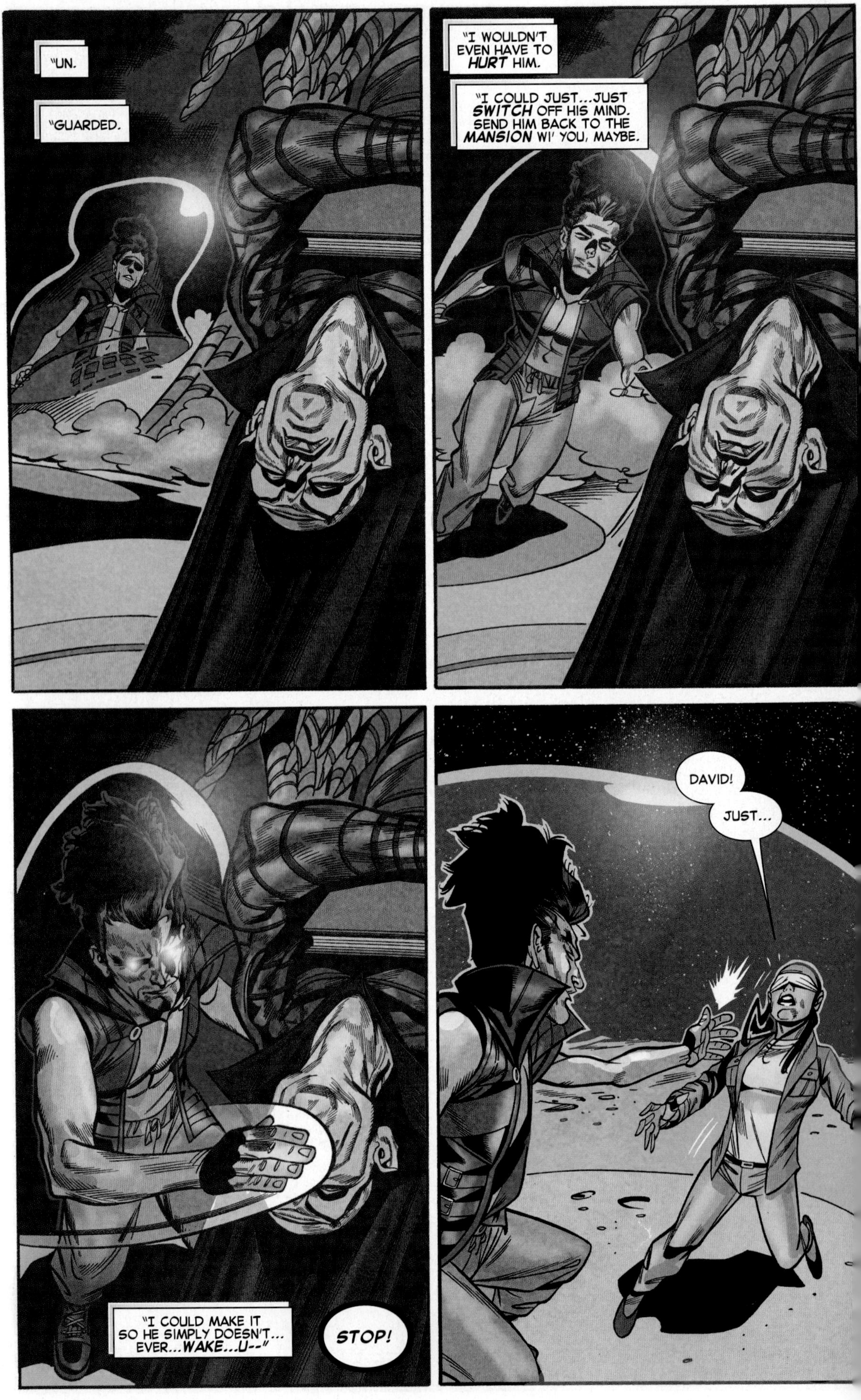
"UN.
"GUARDED.
"I WOULDN'T EVEN HAVE TO HURT HIM.
"I COULD JUST...JUST SWITCH OFF HIS MIND. SEND HIM BACK TO THE MANSION WI' YOU, MAYBE.
"I COULD MAKE IT SO HE SIMPLY DOESN'T... EVER...WAKE...U--"
STOP!
DAVID!
JUST...

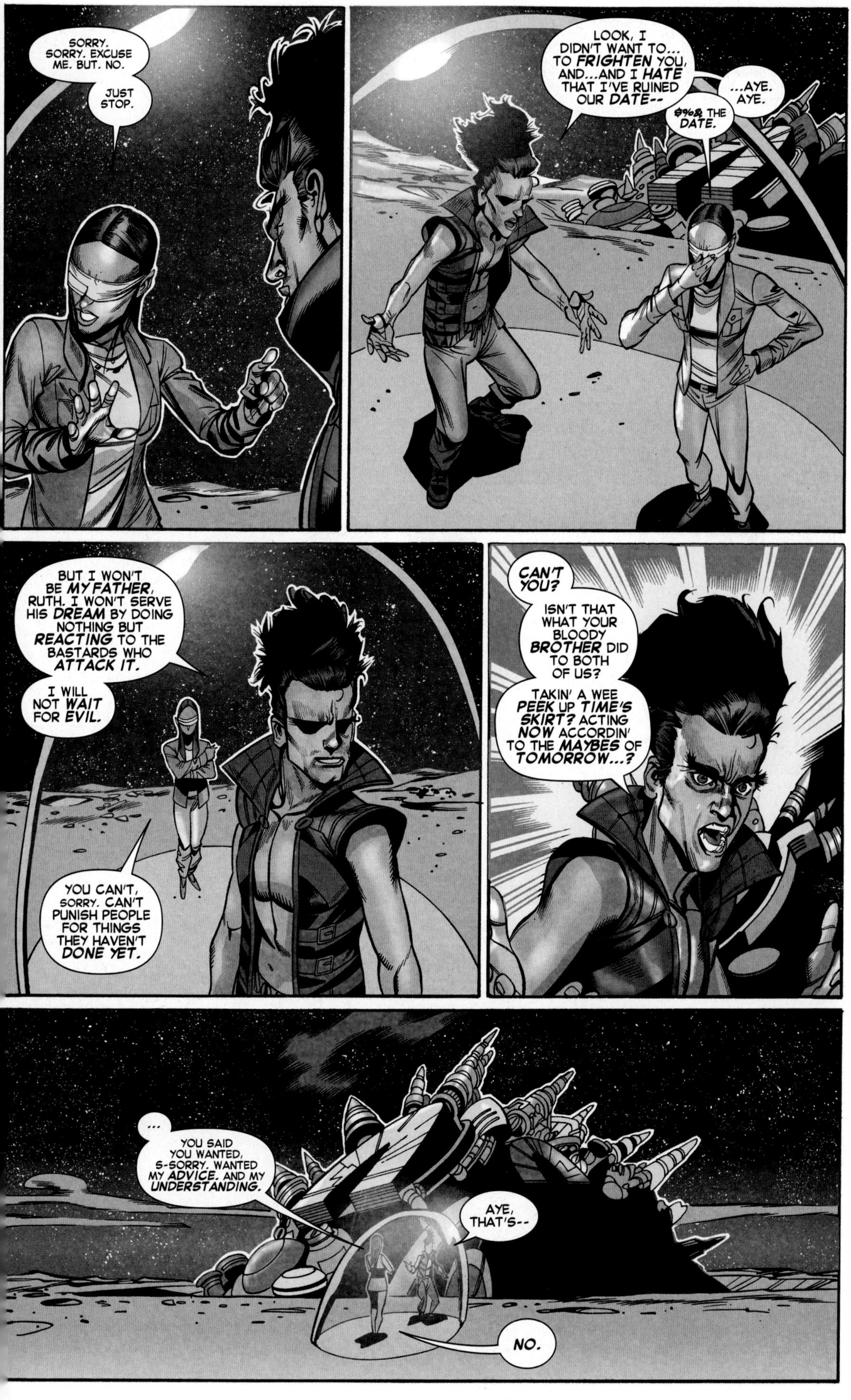
SORRY. SORRY. EXCUSE ME. BUT. NO.
JUST STOP.
LOOK, I DIDN'T WANT TO... TO FRIGHTEN YOU, AND...AND I HATE THAT I'VE RUINED OUR DATE--
...AYE. AYE.
$%&, THE DATE.
BUT I WON'T BE MY FATHER, RUTH. I WON'T SERVE HIS DREAM BY DOING NOTHING BUT REACTING TO THE BASTARDS WHO ATTACK IT.
I WILL NOT WAIT FOR EVIL.
YOU CAN'T, SORRY. CAN'T PUNISH PEOPLE FOR THINGS THEY HAVEN'T DONE YET.
CAN'T YOU?
ISN'T THAT WHAT YOUR BLOODY BROTHER DID TO BOTH OF US?
TAKIN' A WEE PEEK UP TIME'S SKIRT? ACTING NOW ACCORDIN' TO THE MAYBES OF TOMORROW...?
...
YOU SAID YOU WANTED, S-SORRY. WANTED MY ADVICE. AND MY UNDERSTANDING.
AYE, THAT'S--
NO.

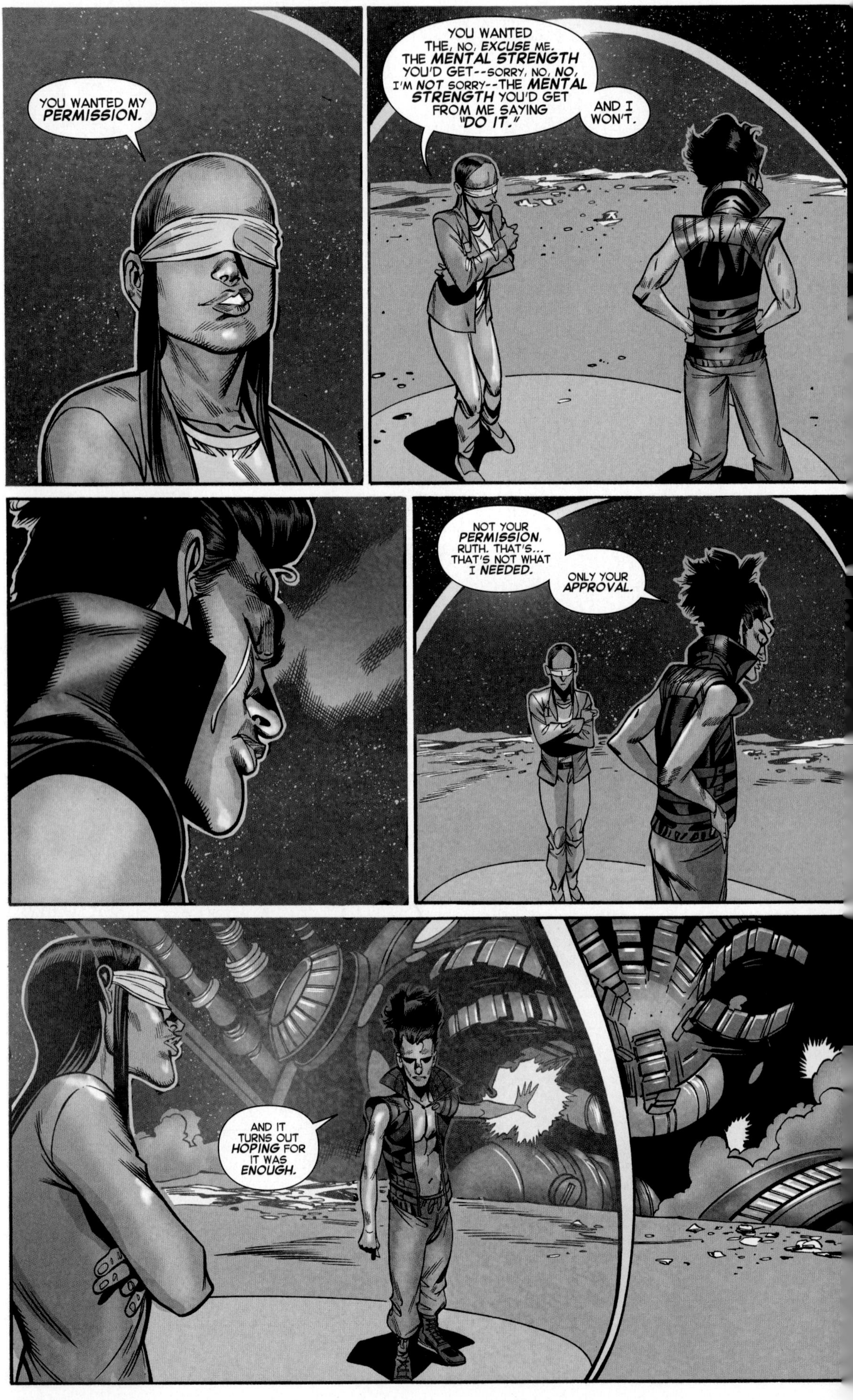
YOU WANTED MY PERMISSION.
YOU WANTED THE, NO, EXCUSE ME. THE MENTAL STRENGTH YOU'D GET--SORRY, NO, NO, I'M NOT SORRY--THE MENTAL STRENGTH YOU'D GET FROM ME SAYING "DO IT."
AND I WON'T.
NOT YOUR PERMISSION, RUTH. THAT'S... THAT'S NOT WHAT I NEEDED.
ONLY YOUR APPROVAL.
AND IT TURNS OUT HOPING FOR IT WAS ENOUGH.

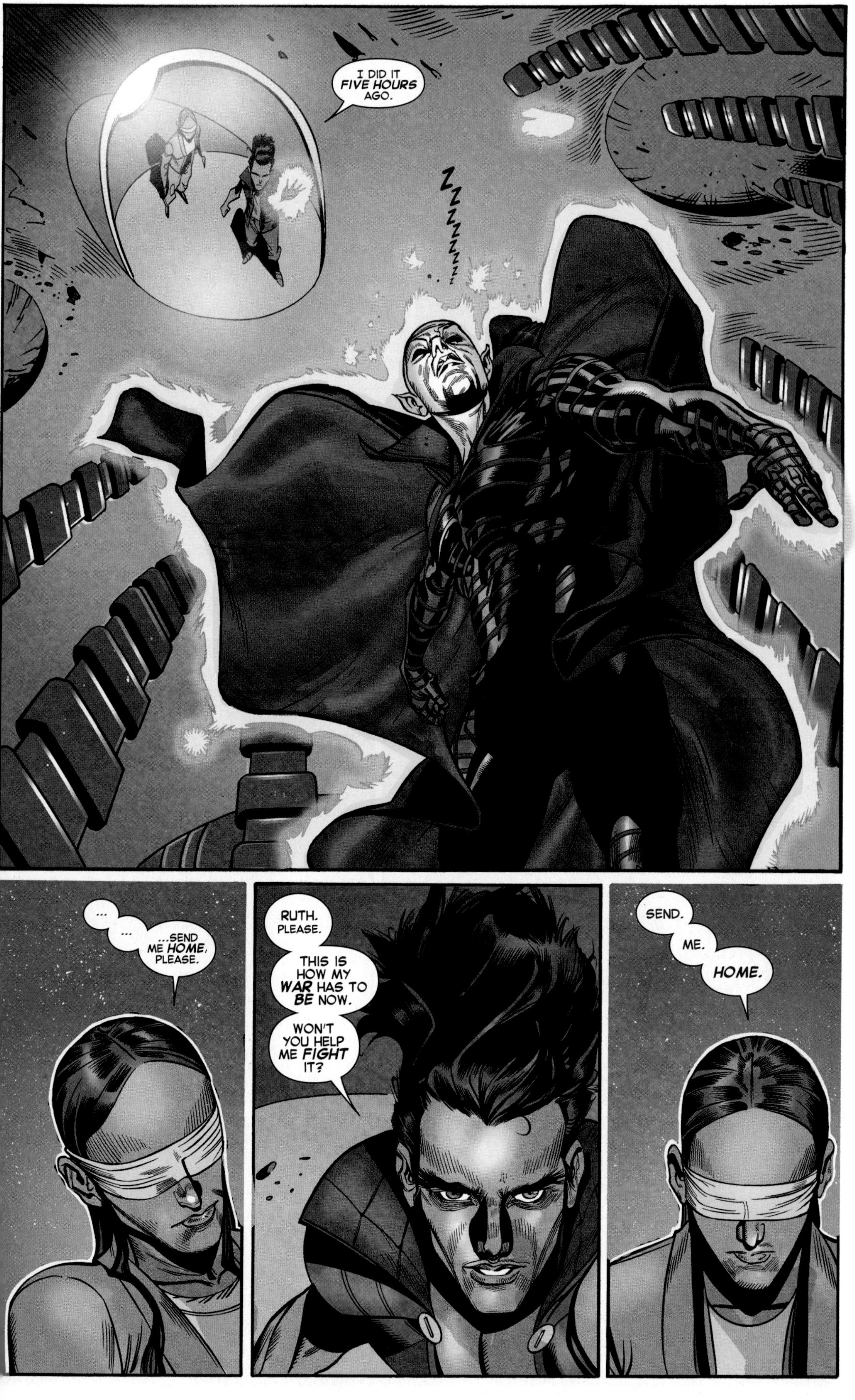
I DID IT FIVE HOURS AGO.
ZZZZZZZZ
...
...
...SEND ME HOME, PLEASE.
RUTH. PLEASE.
THIS IS HOW MY WAR HAS TO BE NOW.
WON'T YOU HELP ME FIGHT IT?
SEND.
ME.
HOME.

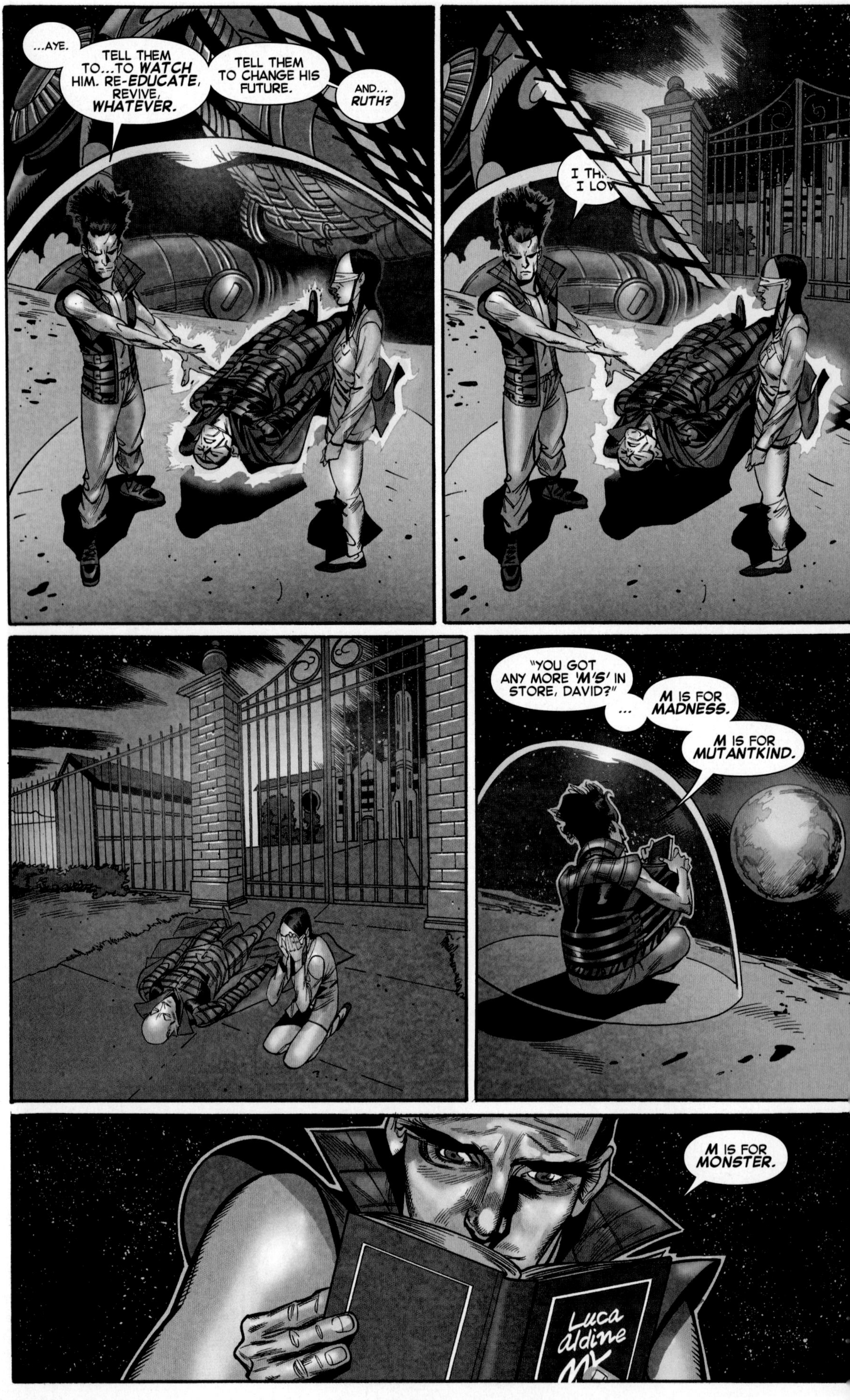
...AYE.
TELL THEM TO...TO WATCH HIM. RE-EDUCATE, REVIVE, WHATEVER.
TELL THEM TO CHANGE HIS FUTURE.
AND... RUTH?
I TH I LOV
"YOU GOT ANY MORE 'M'S' IN STORE, DAVID?"
... M IS FOR MADNESS.
M IS FOR MUTANTKIND.
M IS FOR MONSTER.
Luca aldine

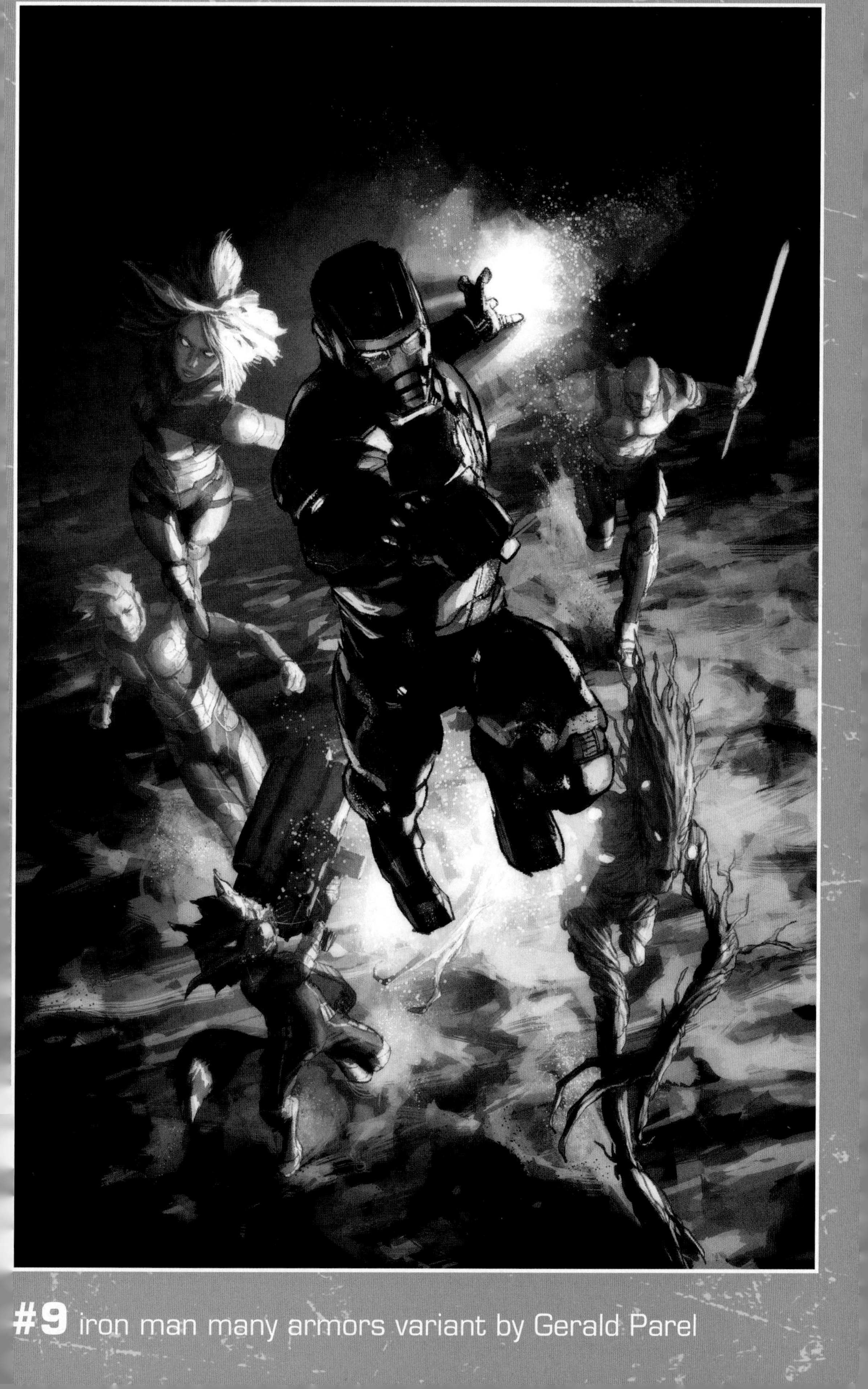

#9 iron man many armors variant by Gerald Parel

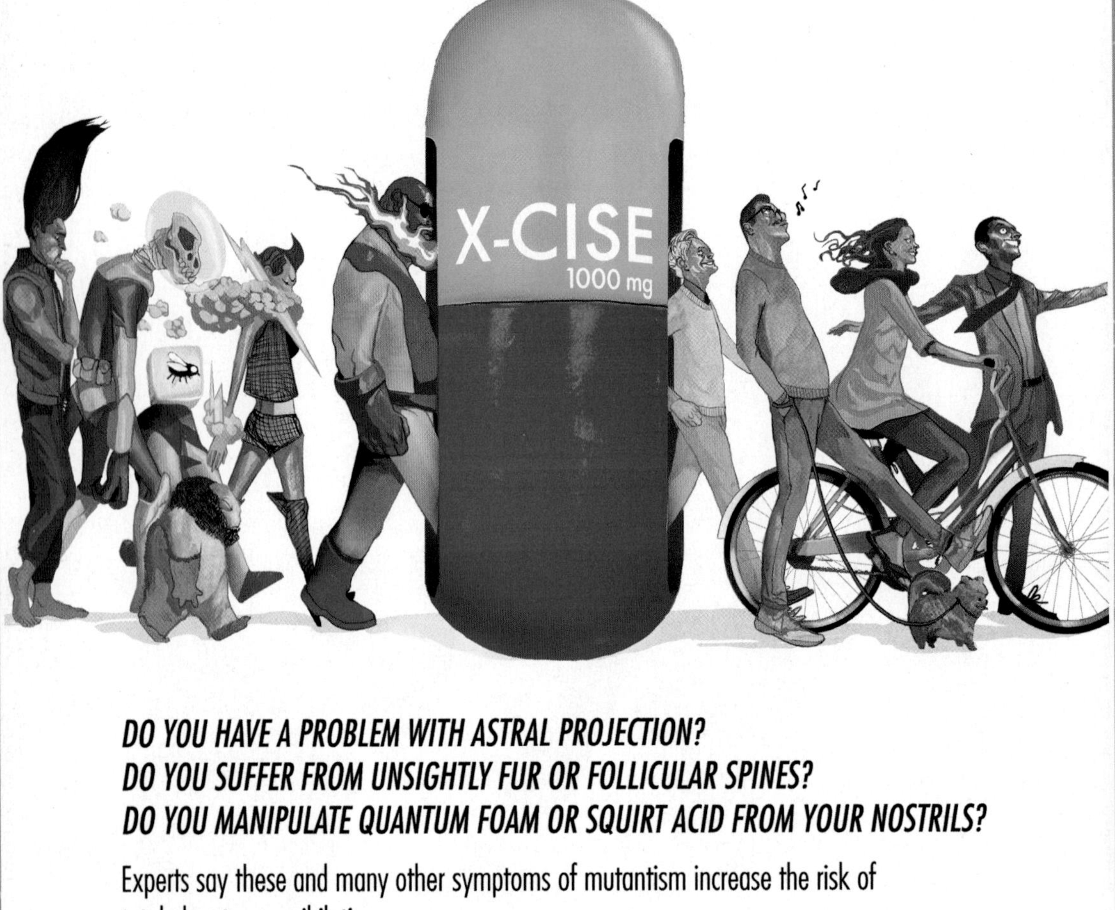

X-CISE
1000 mg

DO YOU HAVE A PROBLEM WITH ASTRAL PROJECTION?
DO YOU SUFFER FROM UNSIGHTLY FUR OR FOLLICULAR SPINES?
DO YOU MANIPULATE QUANTUM FOAM OR SQUIRT ACID FROM YOUR NOSTRILS?

Experts say these and many other symptoms of mutantism increase the risk of total planetary annihilation.

THINK LIFE. THINK HUMAN. THINK *X-CISE* DD68

* may cause severe and irreparable brain damage I·B·S·S LABORATORIES inx.

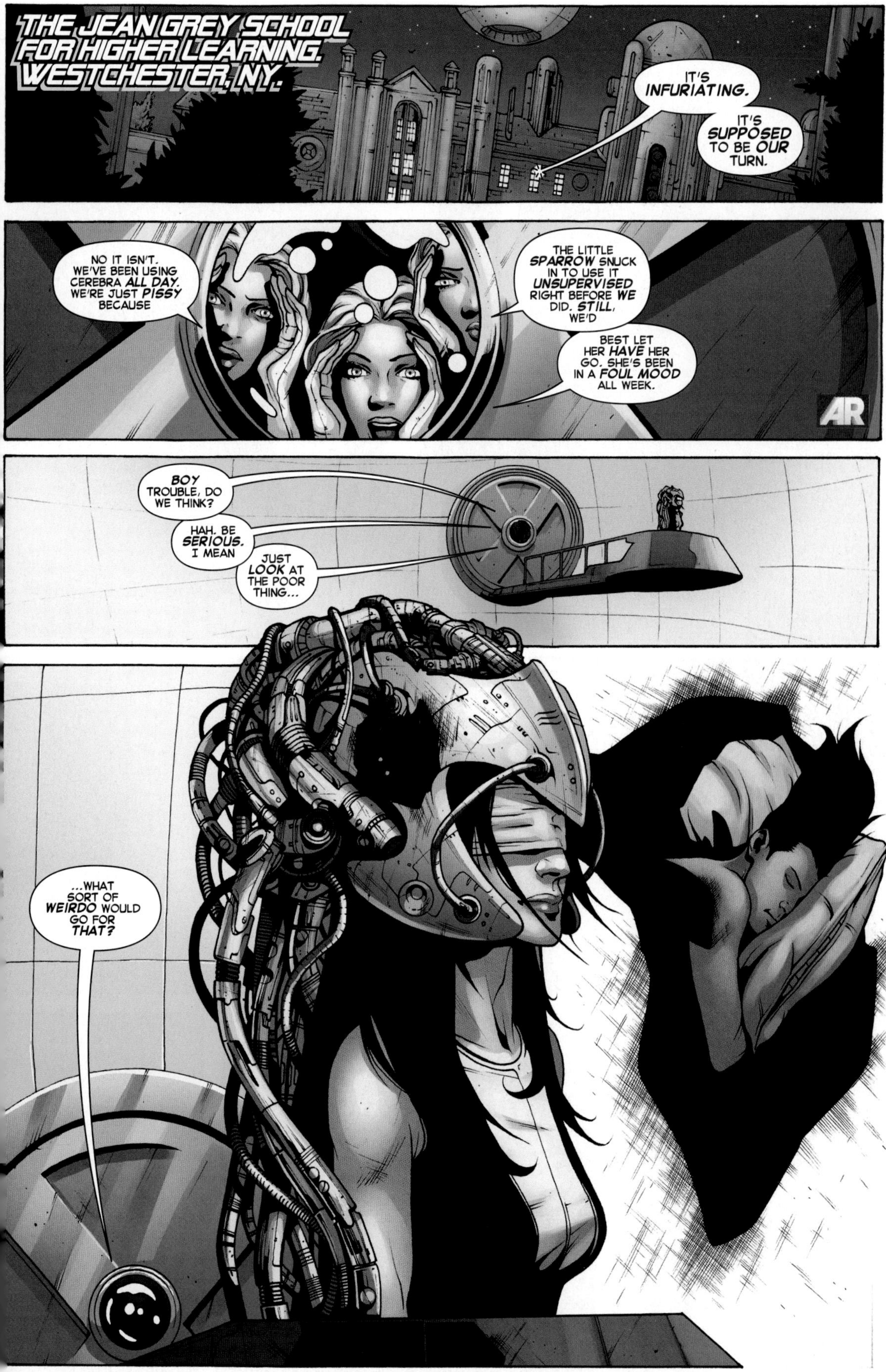
THE JEAN GREY SCHOOL FOR HIGHER LEARNING. WESTCHESTER, NY.
IT'S INFURIATING.
IT'S SUPPOSED TO BE OUR TURN.
NO IT ISN'T. WE'VE BEEN USING CEREBRA ALL DAY. WE'RE JUST PISSY BECAUSE
THE LITTLE SPARROW SNUCK IN TO USE IT UNSUPERVISED RIGHT BEFORE WE DID. STILL, WE'D
BEST LET HER HAVE HER GO. SHE'S BEEN IN A FOUL MOOD ALL WEEK.
AR
BOY TROUBLE, DO WE THINK?
HAH. BE SERIOUS. I MEAN
JUST LOOK AT THE POOR THING...
...WHAT SORT OF WEIRDO WOULD GO FOR THAT?

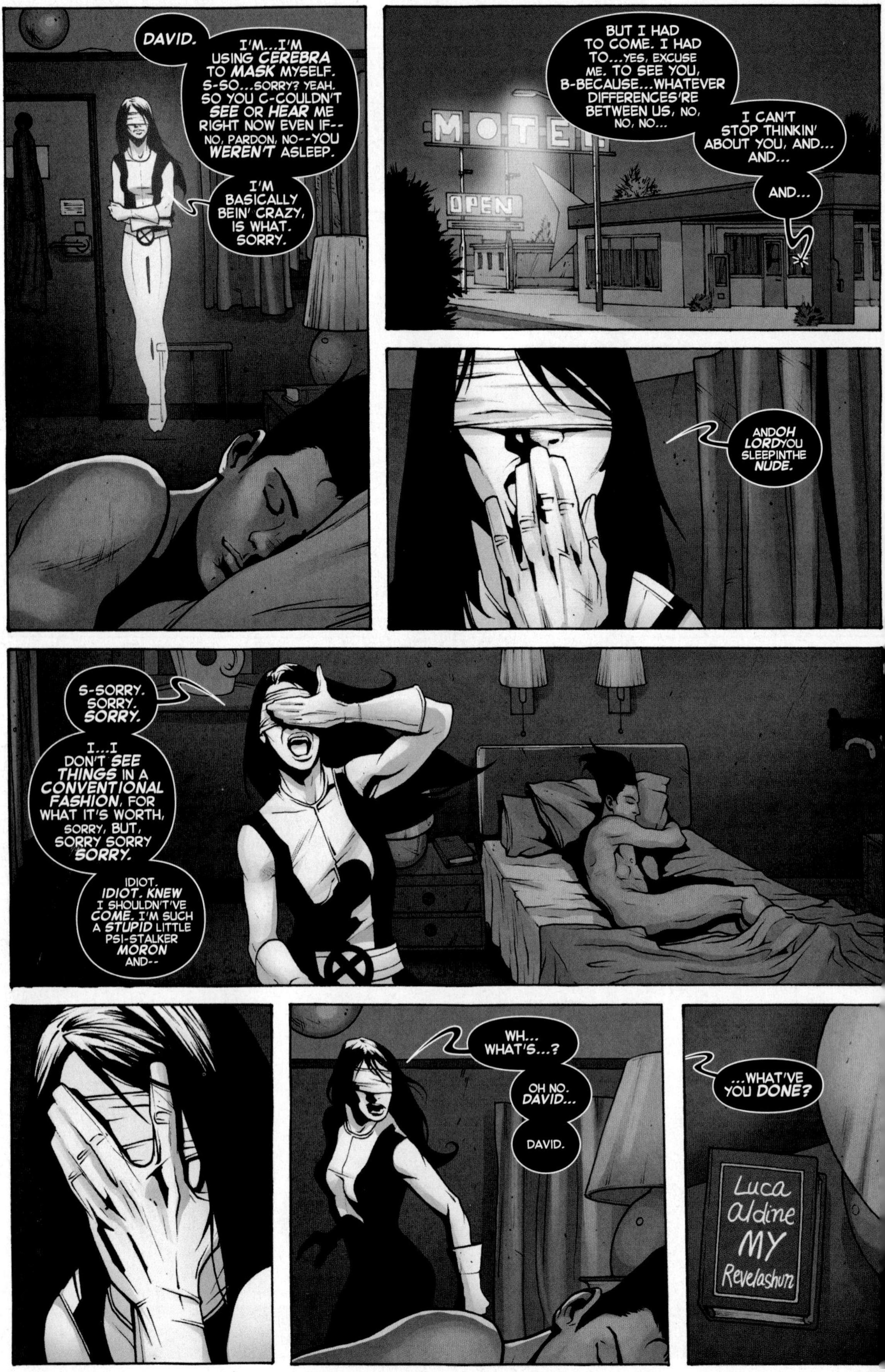
DAVID.
I'M...I'M USING CEREBRA TO MASK MYSELF. S-SO...SORRY? YEAH. SO YOU C-COULDN'T SEE OR HEAR ME RIGHT NOW EVEN IF--NO, PARDON, NO--YOU WEREN'T ASLEEP.
I'M BASICALLY BEIN' CRAZY, IS WHAT. SORRY.
BUT I HAD TO COME. I HAD TO...YES, EXCUSE ME. TO SEE YOU, B-BECAUSE...WHATEVER DIFFERENCES'RE BETWEEN US, NO, NO, NO...
MOTEL
OPEN
I CAN'T STOP THINKIN' ABOUT YOU, AND... AND...
AND...
ANDOH LORDYOU SLEEPINTHE NUDE.
S-SORRY. SORRY. SORRY.
I...I DON'T SEE THINGS IN A CONVENTIONAL FASHION, FOR WHAT IT'S WORTH, SORRY, BUT, SORRY SORRY SORRY.
IDIOT. IDIOT. KNEW I SHOULDN'T'VE COME. I'M SUCH A STUPID LITTLE PSI-STALKER MORON AND--
WH... WHAT'S...?
OH NO. DAVID...
DAVID.
...WHAT'VE YOU DONE?
Luca aldine MY Revelashun

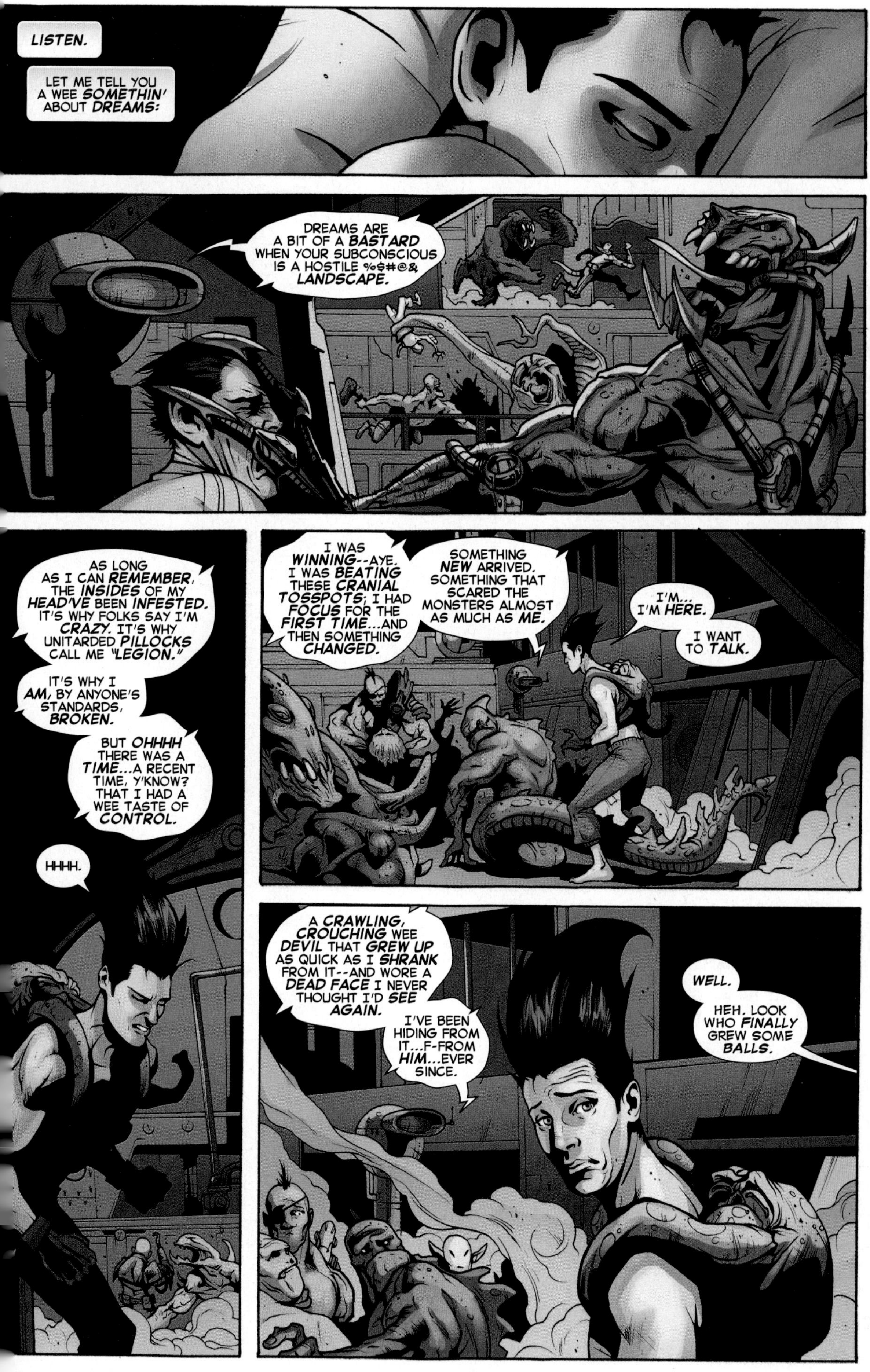
LISTEN.
LET ME TELL YOU A WEE SOMETHIN' ABOUT DREAMS:
DREAMS ARE A BIT OF A BASTARD WHEN YOUR SUBCONSCIOUS IS A HOSTILE %$#@& LANDSCAPE.
AS LONG AS I CAN REMEMBER, THE INSIDES OF MY HEAD'VE BEEN INFESTED. IT'S WHY FOLKS SAY I'M CRAZY. IT'S WHY UNITARDED PILLOCKS CALL ME "LEGION."
IT'S WHY I AM, BY ANYONE'S STANDARDS, BROKEN.
BUT OHHHH THERE WAS A TIME...A RECENT TIME, Y'KNOW? THAT I HAD A WEE TASTE OF CONTROL.
HHHH.
I WAS WINNING--AYE. I WAS BEATING THESE CRANIAL TOSSPOTS; I HAD FOCUS FOR THE FIRST TIME...AND THEN SOMETHING CHANGED.
SOMETHING NEW ARRIVED. SOMETHING THAT SCARED THE MONSTERS ALMOST AS MUCH AS ME.
I'M... I'M HERE.
I WANT TO TALK.
A CRAWLING, CROUCHING WEE DEVIL THAT GREW UP AS QUICK AS I SHRANK FROM IT--AND WORE A DEAD FACE I NEVER THOUGHT I'D SEE AGAIN.
I'VE BEEN HIDING FROM IT...F-FROM HIM...EVER SINCE.
WELL.
HEH. LOOK WHO FINALLY GREW SOME BALLS.

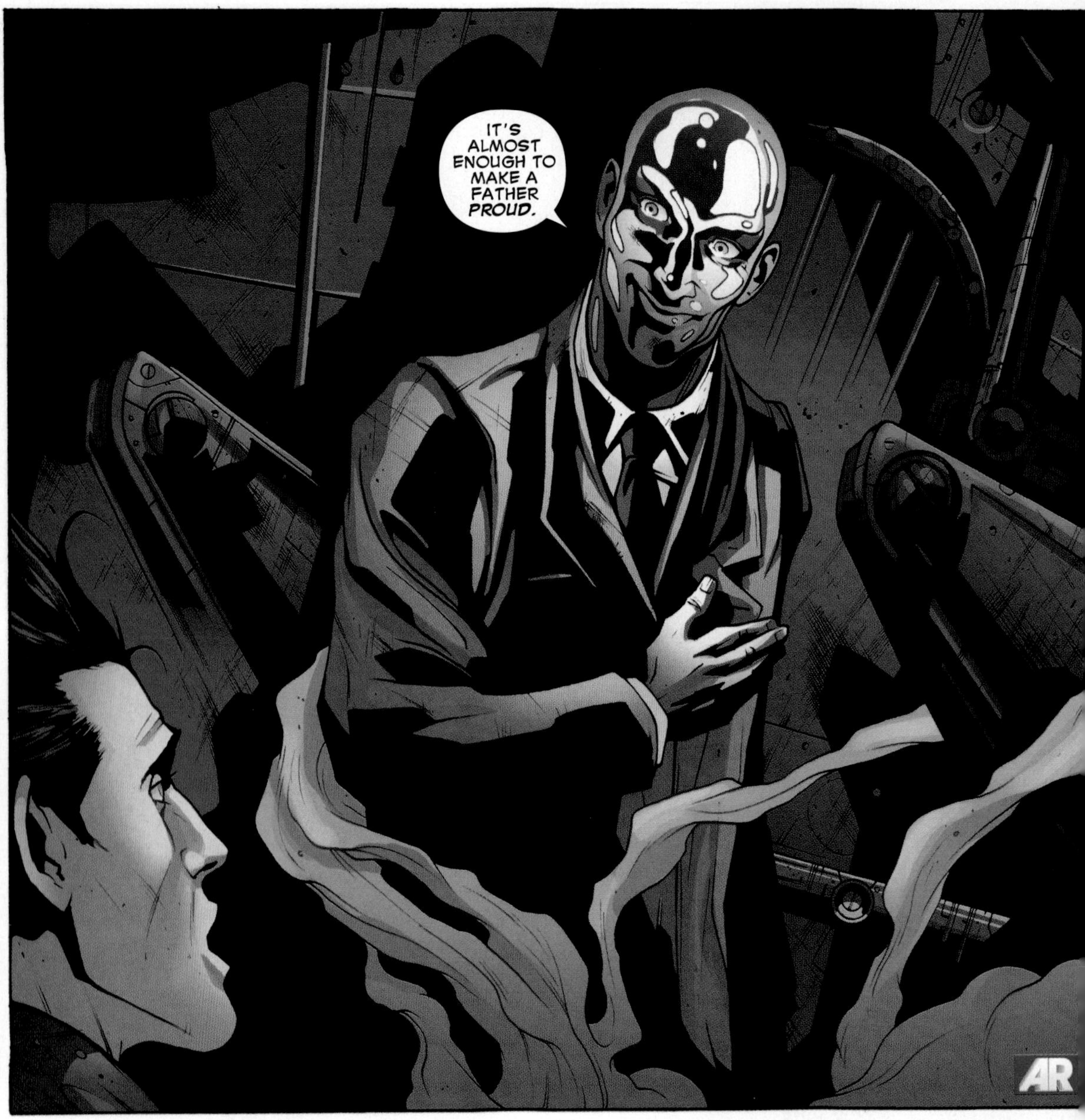
IT'S ALMOST ENOUGH TO MAKE A FATHER PROUD.

INVASIVE EXOTIC PART ONE

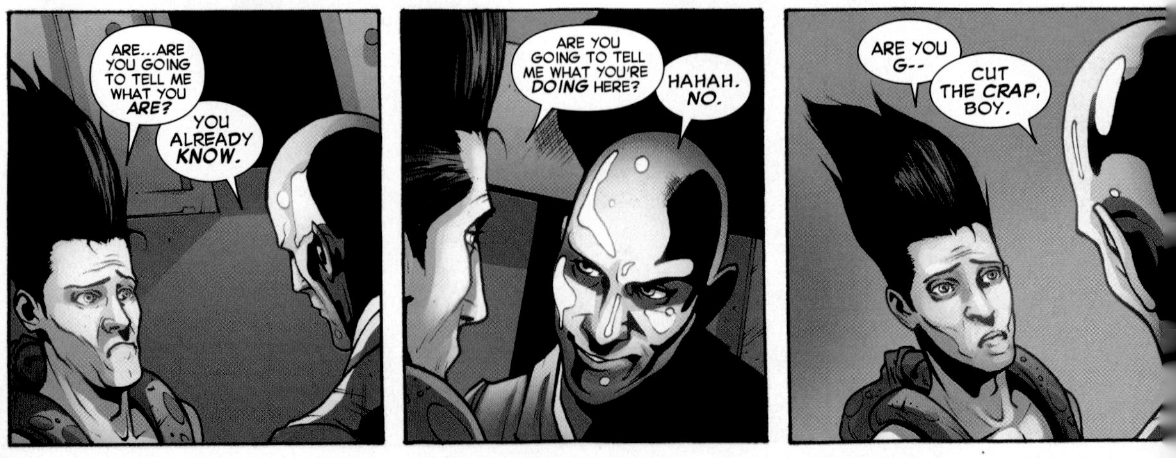
ARE...ARE YOU GOING TO TELL ME WHAT YOU ARE?
YOU ALREADY KNOW.
ARE YOU GOING TO TELL ME WHAT YOU'RE DOING HERE?
HAHAH. NO.
ARE YOU G--
CUT THE CRAP, BOY.

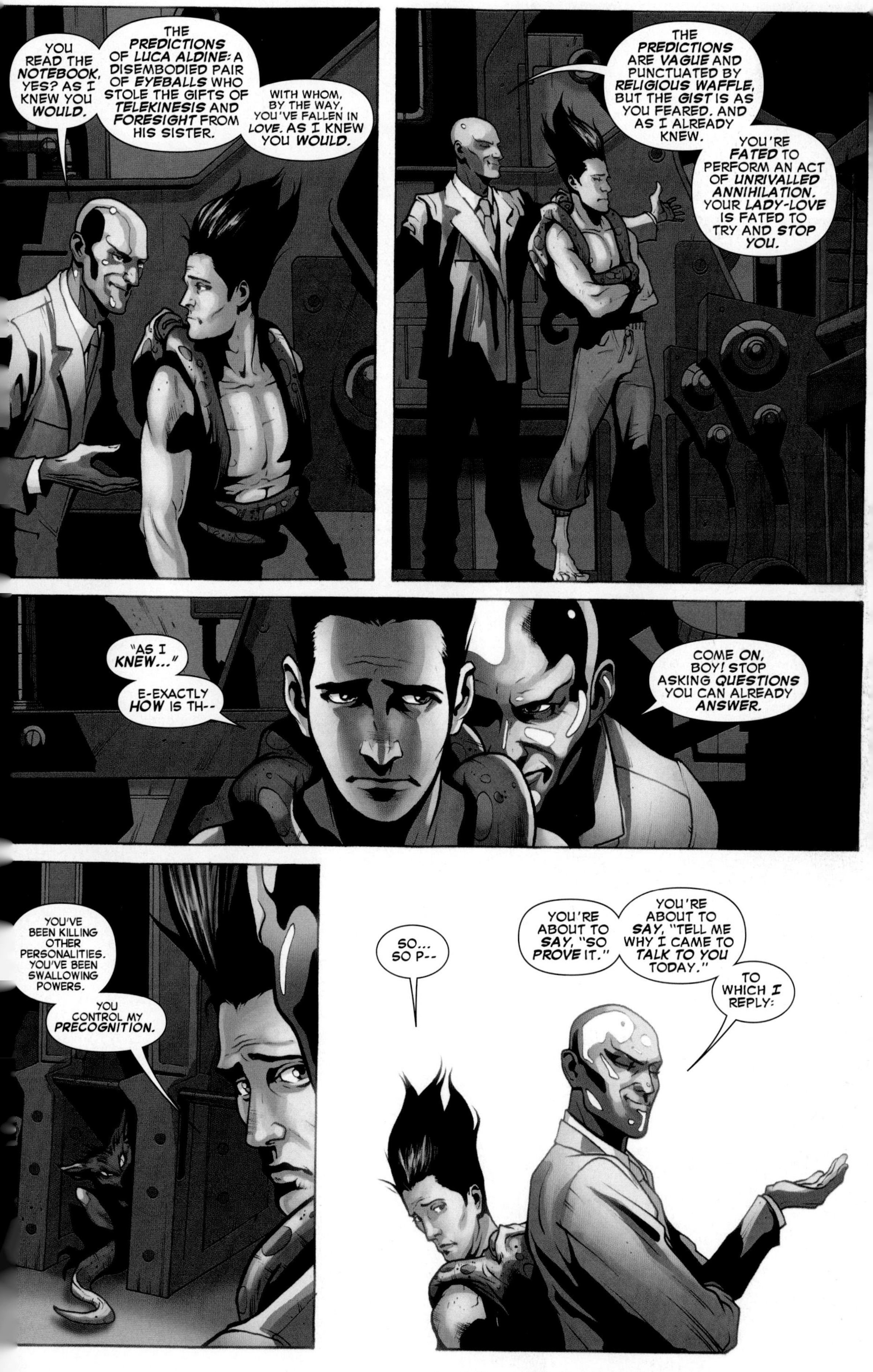
YOU READ THE NOTEBOOK, YES? AS I KNEW YOU WOULD.
THE PREDICTIONS OF LUCA ALDINE: A DISEMBODIED PAIR OF EYEBALLS WHO STOLE THE GIFTS OF TELEKINESIS AND FORESIGHT FROM HIS SISTER.
WITH WHOM, BY THE WAY, YOU'VE FALLEN IN LOVE. AS I KNEW YOU WOULD.
THE PREDICTIONS ARE VAGUE AND PUNCTUATED BY RELIGIOUS WAFFLE, BUT THE GIST IS AS YOU FEARED. AND AS I ALREADY KNEW.
YOU'RE FATED TO PERFORM AN ACT OF UNRIVALLED ANNIHILATION. YOUR LADY-LOVE IS FATED TO TRY AND STOP YOU.
"AS I KNEW..."
E-EXACTLY HOW IS TH--
COME ON, BOY! STOP ASKING QUESTIONS YOU CAN ALREADY ANSWER.
YOU'VE BEEN KILLING OTHER PERSONALITIES. YOU'VE BEEN SWALLOWING POWERS.
YOU CONTROL MY PRECOGNITION.
SO... SO P--
YOU'RE ABOUT TO SAY, "SO PROVE IT."
YOU'RE ABOUT TO SAY, "TELL ME WHY I CAME TO TALK TO YOU TODAY."
TO WHICH I REPLY:

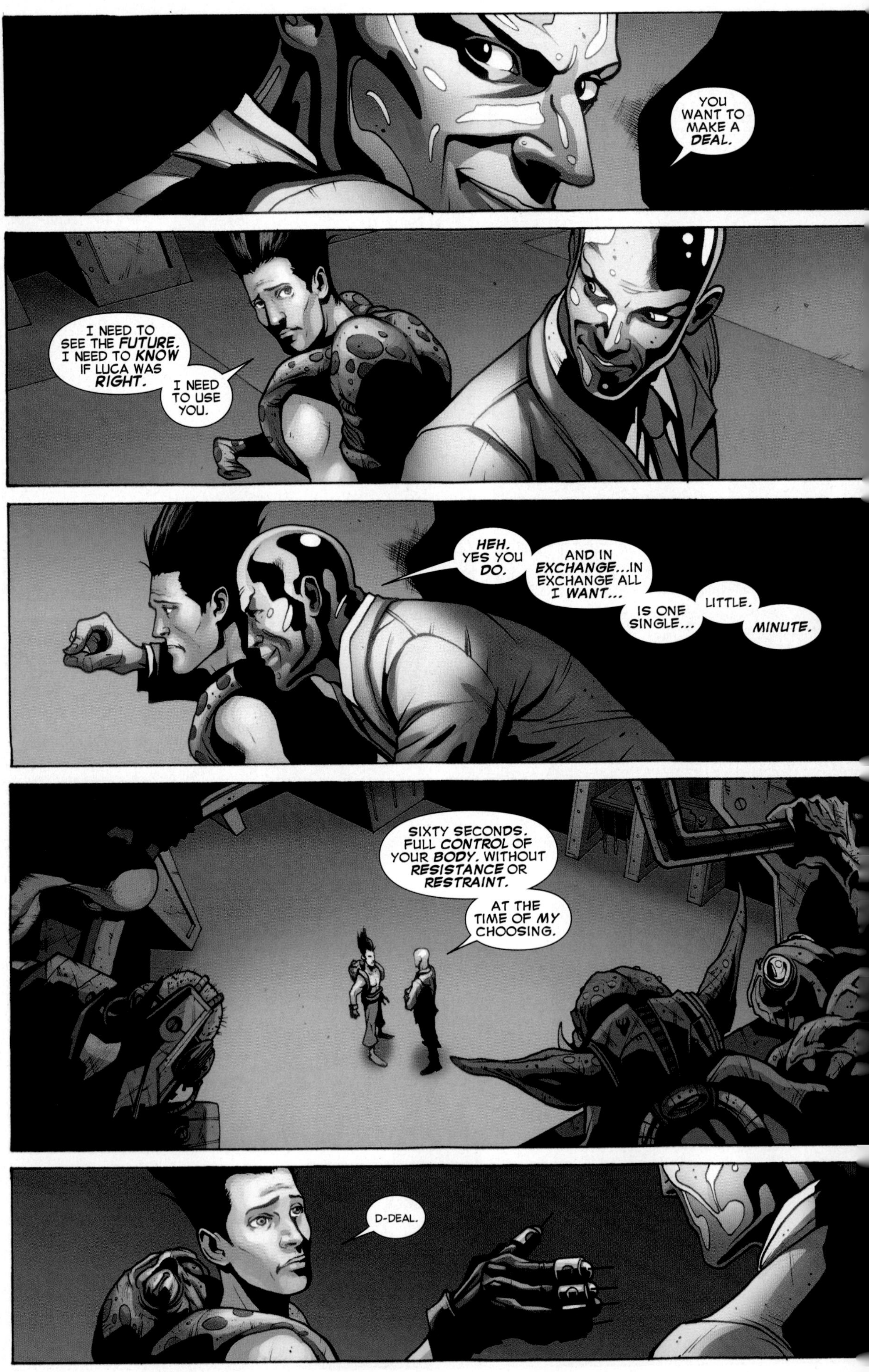
YOU WANT TO MAKE A DEAL.
I NEED TO SEE THE FUTURE. I NEED TO KNOW IF LUCA WAS RIGHT.
I NEED TO USE YOU.
HEH. YES YOU DO.
AND IN EXCHANGE...IN EXCHANGE ALL I WANT...
IS ONE SINGLE...
LITTLE.
MINUTE.
SIXTY SECONDS. FULL CONTROL OF YOUR BODY. WITHOUT RESISTANCE OR RESTRAINT.
AT THE TIME OF MY CHOOSING.
D-DEAL.

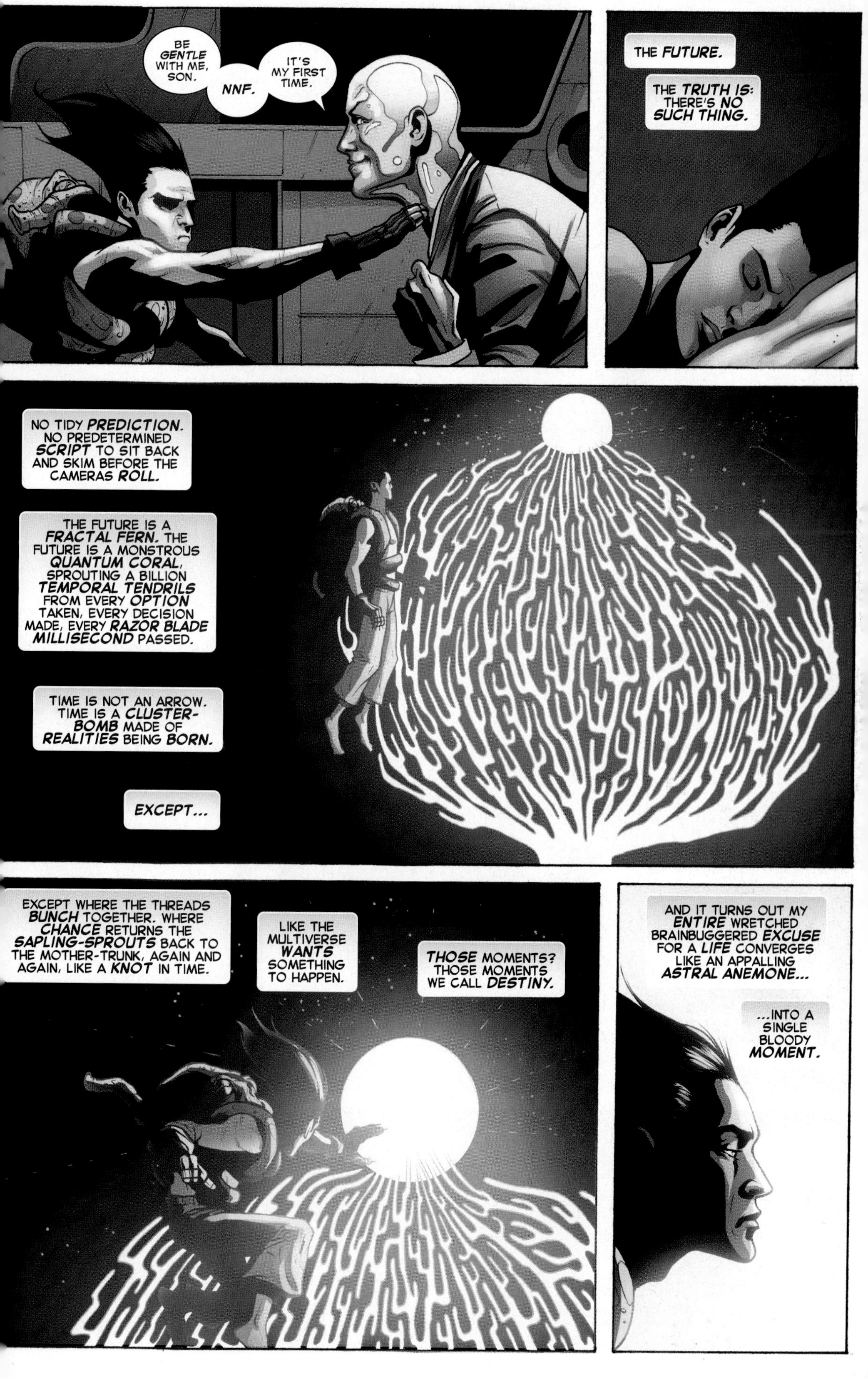
BE GENTLE WITH ME, SON.
NNF.
IT'S MY FIRST TIME.
THE FUTURE.
THE TRUTH IS: THERE'S NO SUCH THING.
NO TIDY PREDICTION. NO PREDETERMINED SCRIPT TO SIT BACK AND SKIM BEFORE THE CAMERAS ROLL.
THE FUTURE IS A FRACTAL FERN. THE FUTURE IS A MONSTROUS QUANTUM CORAL, SPROUTING A BILLION TEMPORAL TENDRILS FROM EVERY OPTION TAKEN, EVERY DECISION MADE, EVERY RAZOR BLADE MILLISECOND PASSED.
TIME IS NOT AN ARROW. TIME IS A CLUSTER-BOMB MADE OF REALITIES BEING BORN.
EXCEPT...
EXCEPT WHERE THE THREADS BUNCH TOGETHER. WHERE CHANCE RETURNS THE SAPLING-SPROUTS BACK TO THE MOTHER-TRUNK, AGAIN AND AGAIN, LIKE A KNOT IN TIME.
LIKE THE MULTIVERSE WANTS SOMETHING TO HAPPEN.
THOSE MOMENTS? THOSE MOMENTS WE CALL DESTINY.
AND IT TURNS OUT MY ENTIRE WRETCHED BRAINBUGGERED EXCUSE FOR A LIFE CONVERGES LIKE AN APPALLING ASTRAL ANEMONE...
...INTO A SINGLE BLOODY MOMENT.

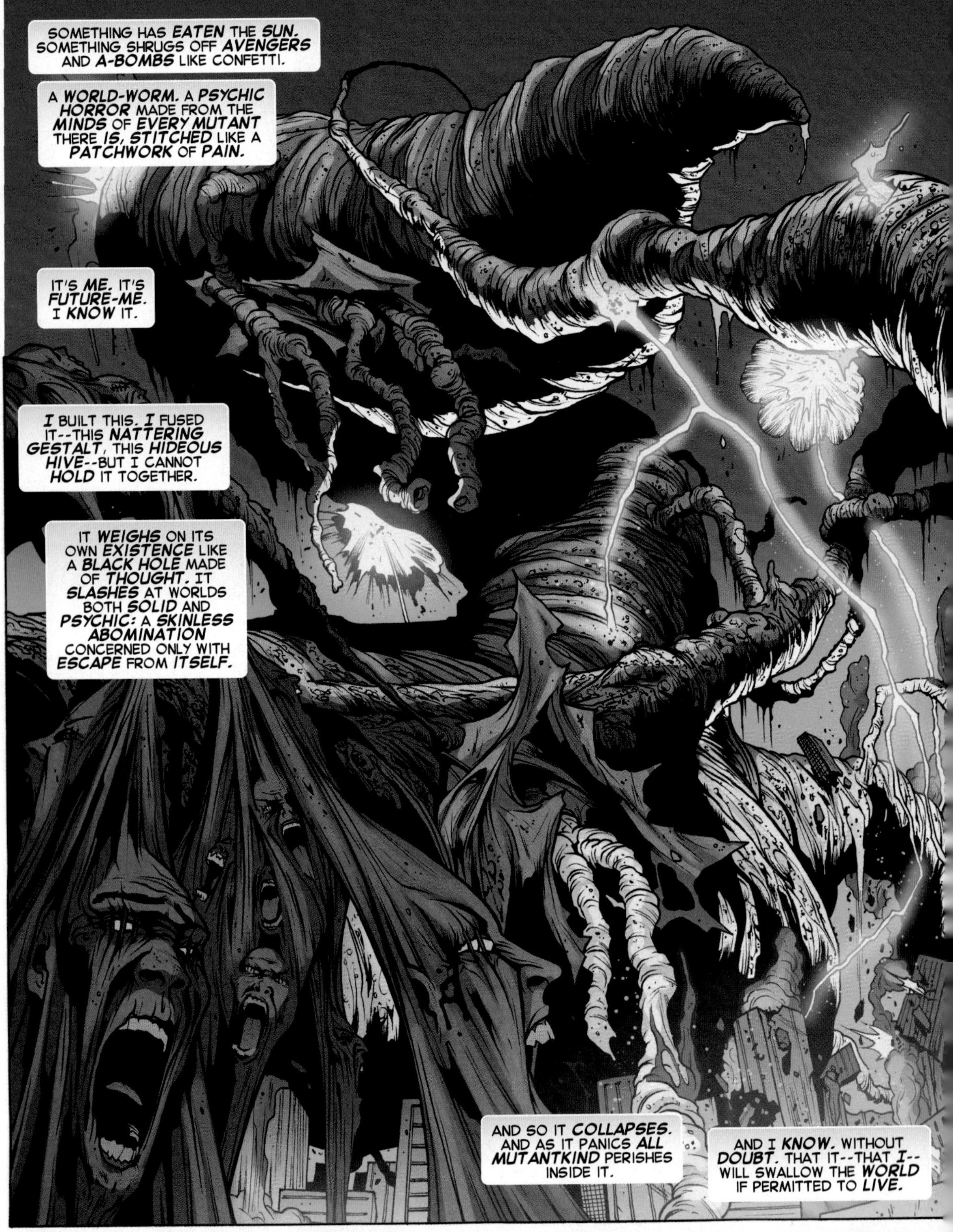
SOMETHING HAS EATEN THE SUN. SOMETHING SHRUGS OFF AVENGERS AND A-BOMBS LIKE CONFETTI.
A WORLD-WORM. A PSYCHIC HORROR MADE FROM THE MINDS OF EVERY MUTANT THERE IS, STITCHED LIKE A PATCHWORK OF PAIN.
IT'S ME. IT'S FUTURE-ME. I KNOW IT.
I BUILT THIS. I FUSED IT--THIS NATTERING GESTALT, THIS HIDEOUS HIVE--BUT I CANNOT HOLD IT TOGETHER.
IT WEIGHS ON ITS OWN EXISTENCE LIKE A BLACK HOLE MADE OF THOUGHT. IT SLASHES AT WORLDS BOTH SOLID AND PSYCHIC: A SKINLESS ABOMINATION CONCERNED ONLY WITH ESCAPE FROM ITSELF.
AND SO IT COLLAPSES. AND AS IT PANICS ALL MUTANTKIND PERISHES INSIDE IT.
AND I KNOW. WITHOUT DOUBT. THAT IT--THAT I--WILL SWALLOW THE WORLD IF PERMITTED TO LIVE.
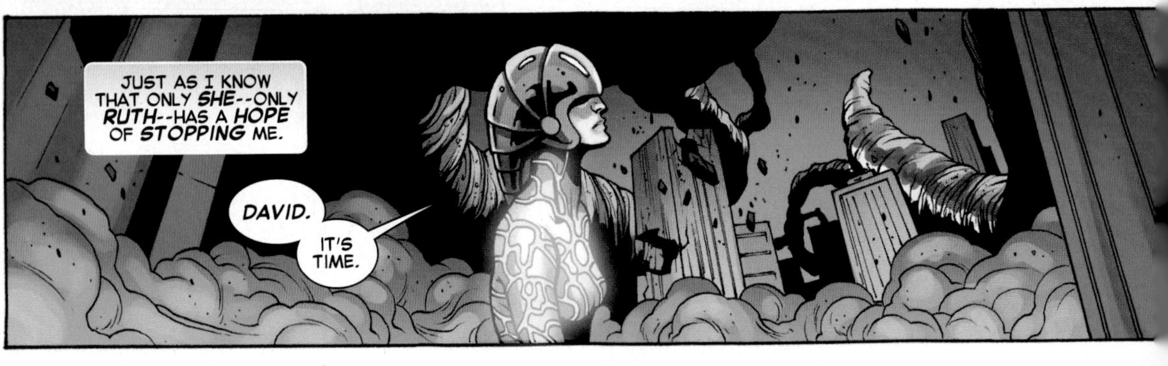
JUST AS I KNOW THAT ONLY SHE--ONLY RUTH--HAS A HOPE OF STOPPING ME.
DAVID.
IT'S TIME.

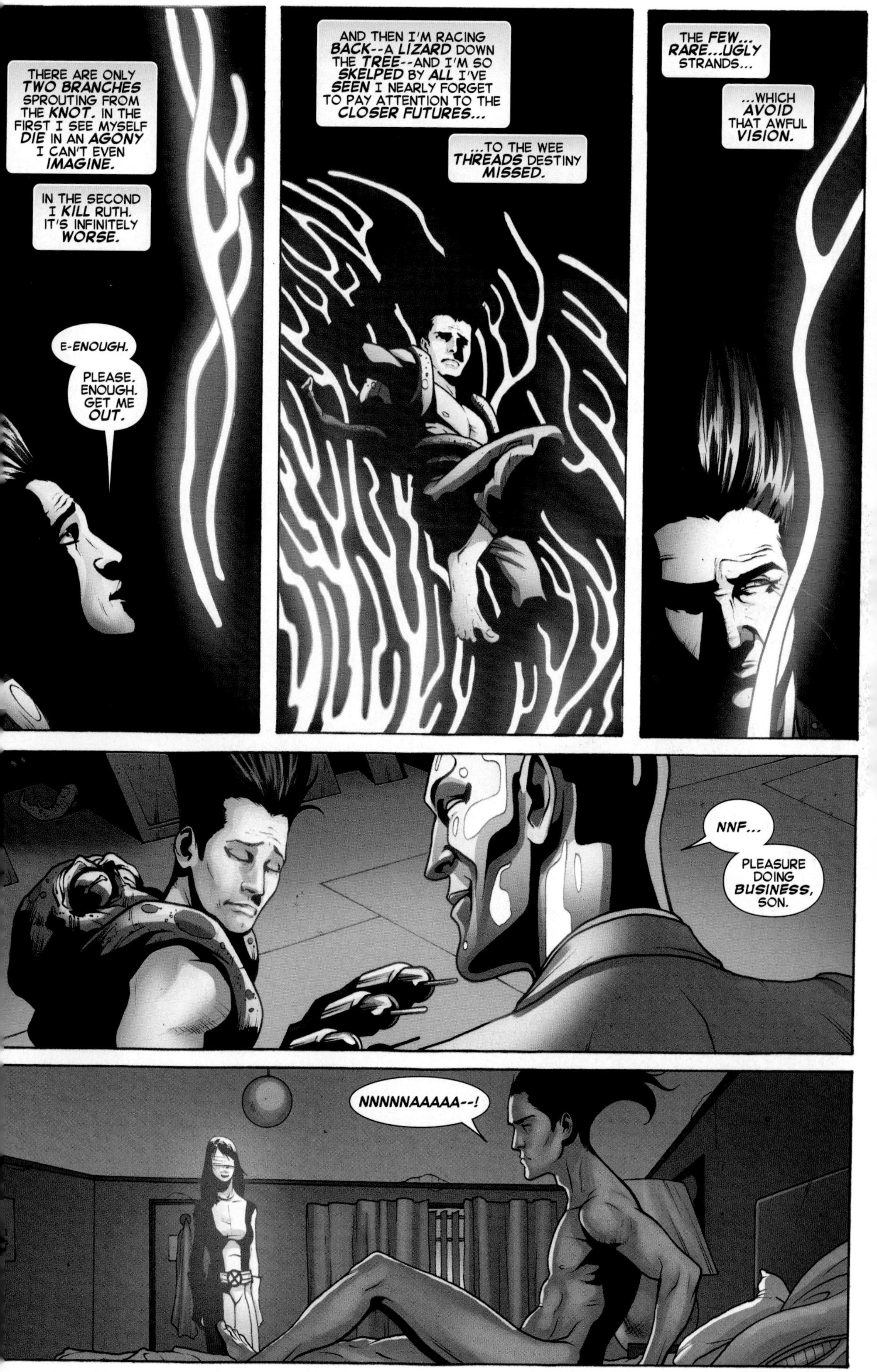
THERE ARE ONLY TWO BRANCHES SPROUTING FROM THE KNOT. IN THE FIRST I SEE MYSELF DIE IN AN AGONY I CAN'T EVEN IMAGINE.
IN THE SECOND I KILL RUTH. IT'S INFINITELY WORSE.
E-ENOUGH.
PLEASE. ENOUGH. GET ME OUT.
AND THEN I'M RACING BACK--A LIZARD DOWN THE TREE--AND I'M SO SKELPED BY ALL I'VE SEEN I NEARLY FORGET TO PAY ATTENTION TO THE CLOSER FUTURES...
...TO THE WEE THREADS DESTINY MISSED.
THE FEW... RARE...UGLY STRANDS...
...WHICH AVOID THAT AWFUL VISION.
NNF...
PLEASURE DOING BUSINESS, SON.
NNNNNAAAAA--!

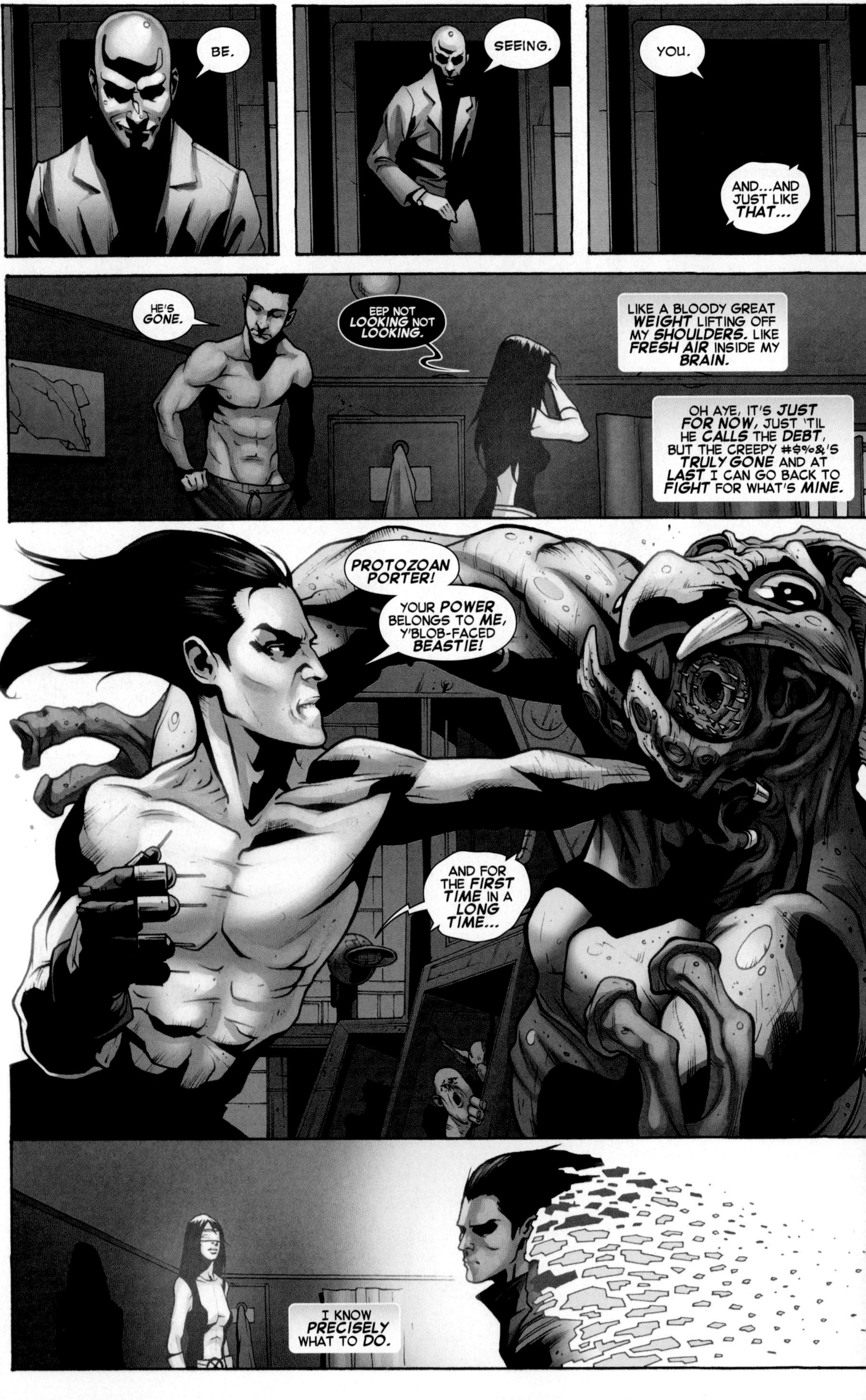
BE.
SEEING.
YOU.
AND...AND JUST LIKE THAT...
HE'S GONE.
EEP NOT LOOKING NOT LOOKING.
LIKE A BLOODY GREAT WEIGHT LIFTING OFF MY SHOULDERS. LIKE FRESH AIR INSIDE MY BRAIN.
OH AYE, IT'S JUST FOR NOW, JUST 'TIL HE CALLS THE DEBT, BUT THE CREEPY #$%&'S TRULY GONE AND AT LAST I CAN GO BACK TO FIGHT FOR WHAT'S MINE.
PROTOZOAN PORTER!
YOUR POWER BELONGS TO ME, Y'BLOB-FACED BEASTIE!
AND FOR THE FIRST TIME IN A LONG TIME...
I KNOW PRECISELY WHAT TO DO.

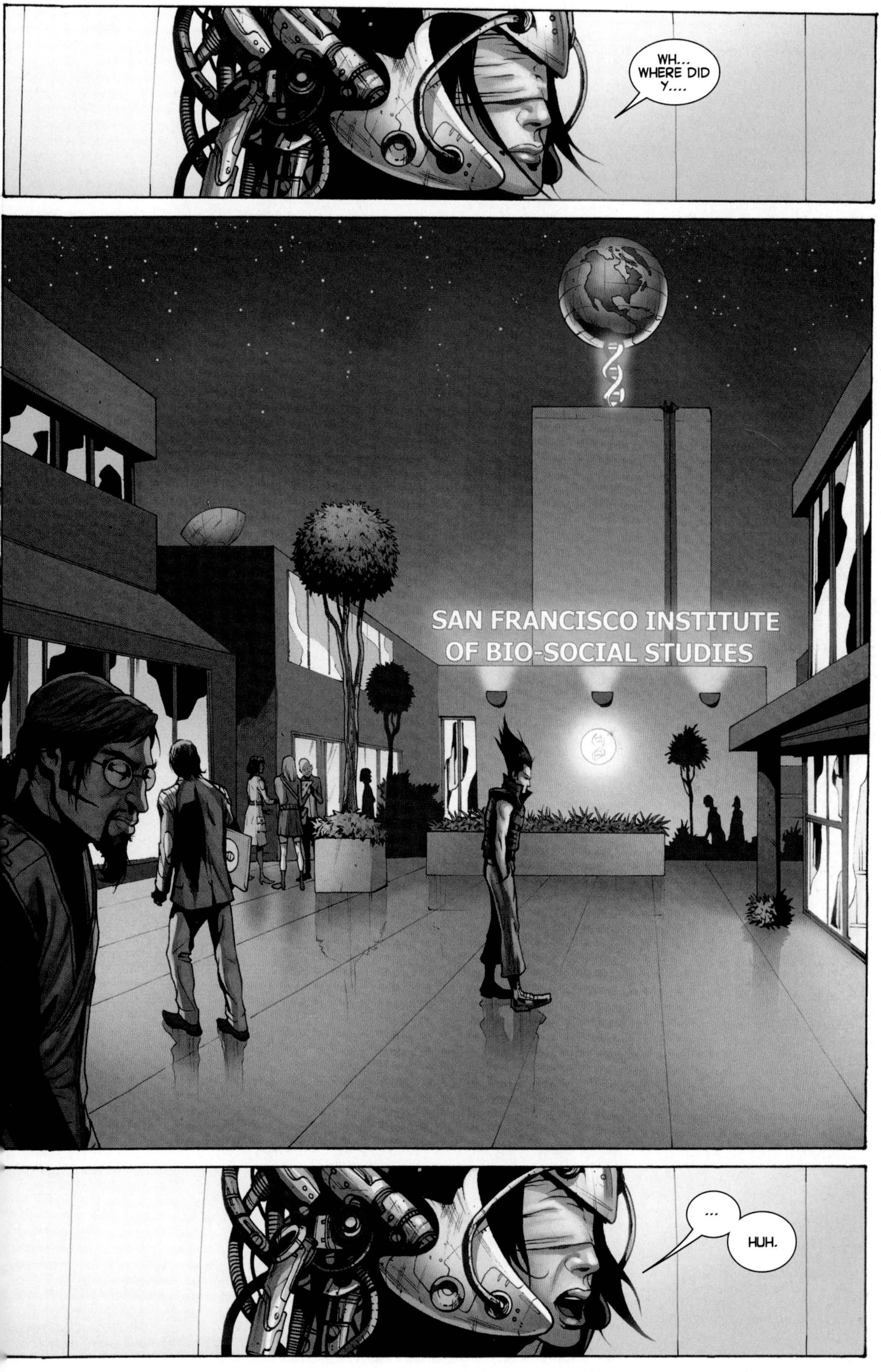
WH...
WHERE DID
Y....
SAN FRANCISCO INSTITUTE
OF BIO-SOCIAL STUDIES
...
HUH.

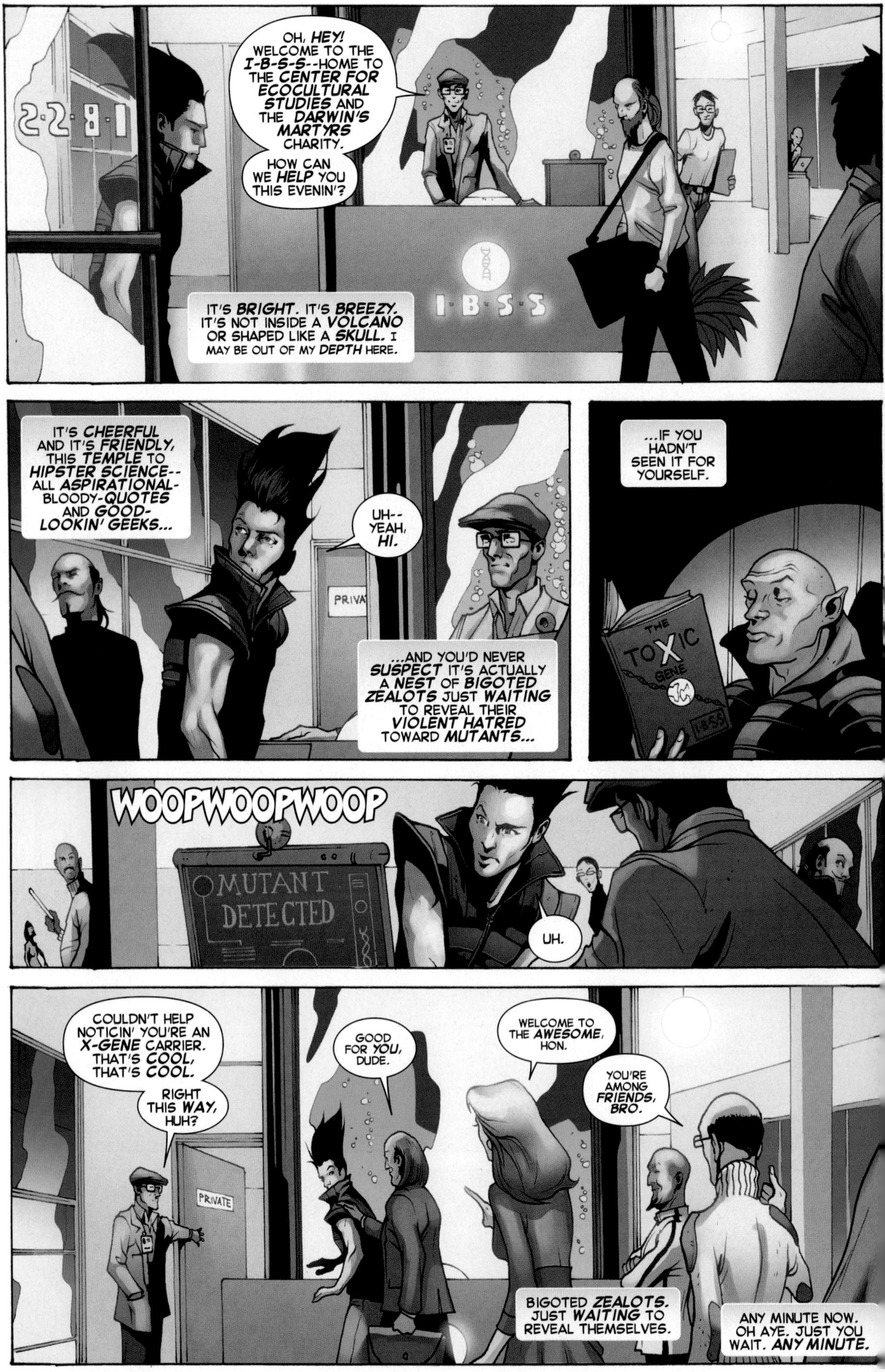
OH, HEY! WELCOME TO THE I-B-S-S--HOME TO THE CENTER FOR ECOCULTURAL STUDIES AND THE DARWIN'S MARTYRS CHARITY.
HOW CAN WE HELP YOU THIS EVENIN'?
2281
I B S S
IT'S BRIGHT. IT'S BREEZY. IT'S NOT INSIDE A VOLCANO OR SHAPED LIKE A SKULL. I MAY BE OUT OF MY DEPTH HERE.
IT'S CHEERFUL AND IT'S FRIENDLY, THIS TEMPLE TO HIPSTER SCIENCE--ALL ASPIRATIONAL-BLOODY-QUOTES AND GOOD-LOOKIN' GEEKS...
UH--YEAH, HI.
PRIVAT
...AND YOU'D NEVER SUSPECT IT'S ACTUALLY A NEST OF BIGOTED ZEALOTS JUST WAITING TO REVEAL THEIR VIOLENT HATRED TOWARD MUTANTS...
...IF YOU HADN'T SEEN IT FOR YOURSELF.
THE TOXIC GENE
IBSS
WOOPWOOPWOOP
MUTANT DETECTED
UH.
COULDN'T HELP NOTICIN' YOU'RE AN X-GENE CARRIER. THAT'S COOL, THAT'S COOL.
RIGHT THIS WAY, HUH?
PRIVATE
GOOD FOR YOU, DUDE.
WELCOME TO THE AWESOME, HON.
YOU'RE AMONG FRIENDS, BRO.
BIGOTED ZEALOTS. JUST WAITING TO REVEAL THEMSELVES.
ANY MINUTE NOW. OH AYE. JUST YOU WAIT. ANY MINUTE.

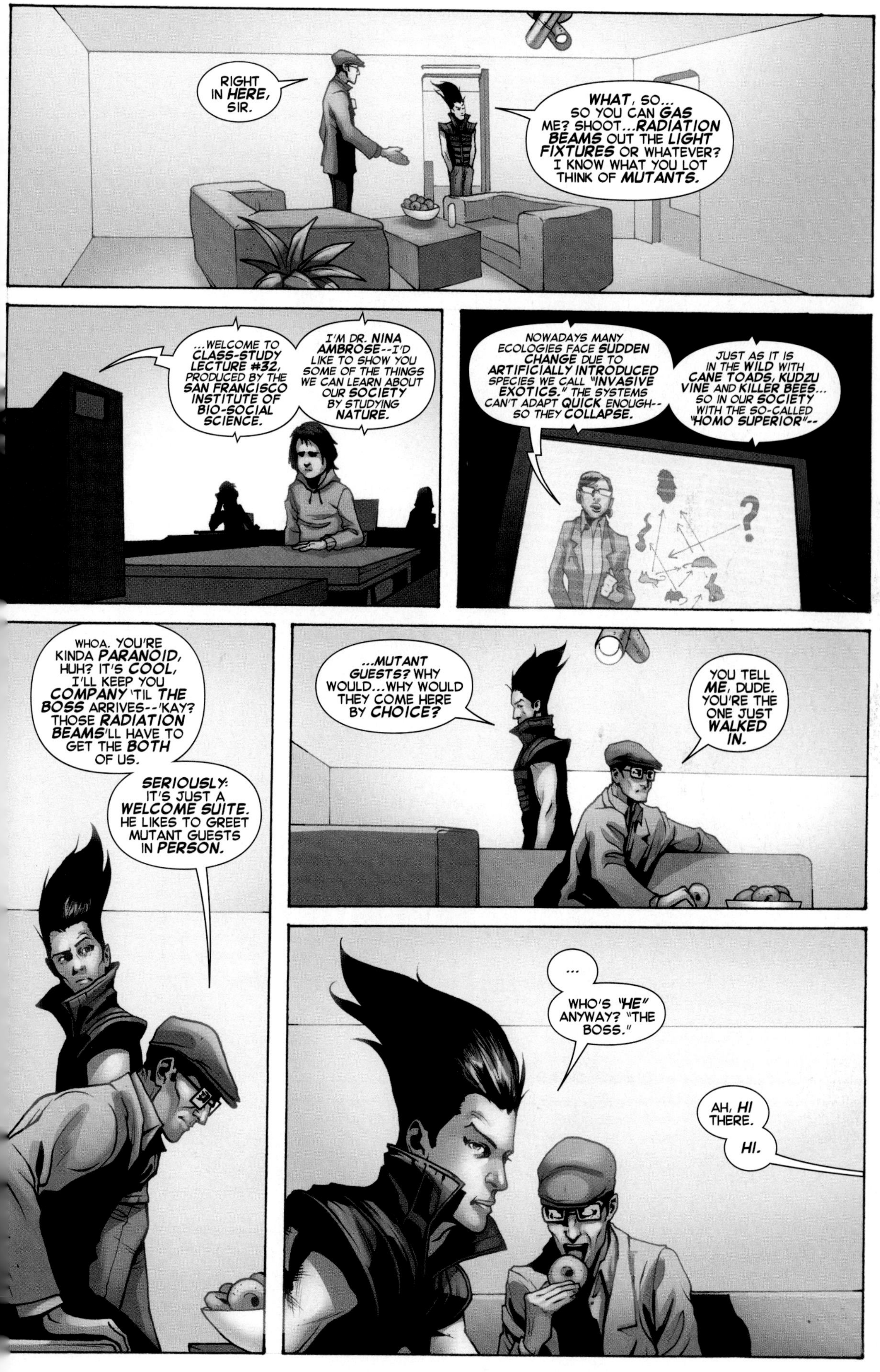
RIGHT IN HERE, SIR.
WHAT, SO... SO YOU CAN GAS ME? SHOOT...RADIATION BEAMS OUT THE LIGHT FIXTURES OR WHATEVER? I KNOW WHAT YOU LOT THINK OF MUTANTS.
...WELCOME TO CLASS-STUDY LECTURE #32, PRODUCED BY THE SAN FRANCISCO INSTITUTE OF BIO-SOCIAL SCIENCE.
I'M DR. NINA AMBROSE--I'D LIKE TO SHOW YOU SOME OF THE THINGS WE CAN LEARN ABOUT OUR SOCIETY BY STUDYING NATURE.
NOWADAYS MANY ECOLOGIES FACE SUDDEN CHANGE DUE TO ARTIFICIALLY INTRODUCED SPECIES WE CALL "INVASIVE EXOTICS." THE SYSTEMS CAN'T ADAPT QUICK ENOUGH-- SO THEY COLLAPSE.
JUST AS IT IS IN THE WILD WITH CANE TOADS, KUDZU VINE AND KILLER BEES... SO IN OUR SOCIETY WITH THE SO-CALLED "HOMO SUPERIOR"--
WHOA. YOU'RE KINDA PARANOID, HUH? IT'S COOL, I'LL KEEP YOU COMPANY 'TIL THE BOSS ARRIVES--'KAY? THOSE RADIATION BEAMS'LL HAVE TO GET THE BOTH OF US.
SERIOUSLY: IT'S JUST A WELCOME SUITE. HE LIKES TO GREET MUTANT GUESTS IN PERSON.
...MUTANT GUESTS? WHY WOULD...WHY WOULD THEY COME HERE BY CHOICE?
YOU TELL ME, DUDE. YOU'RE THE ONE JUST WALKED IN.
...
WHO'S "HE" ANYWAY? "THE BOSS."
AH, HI THERE.
HI.

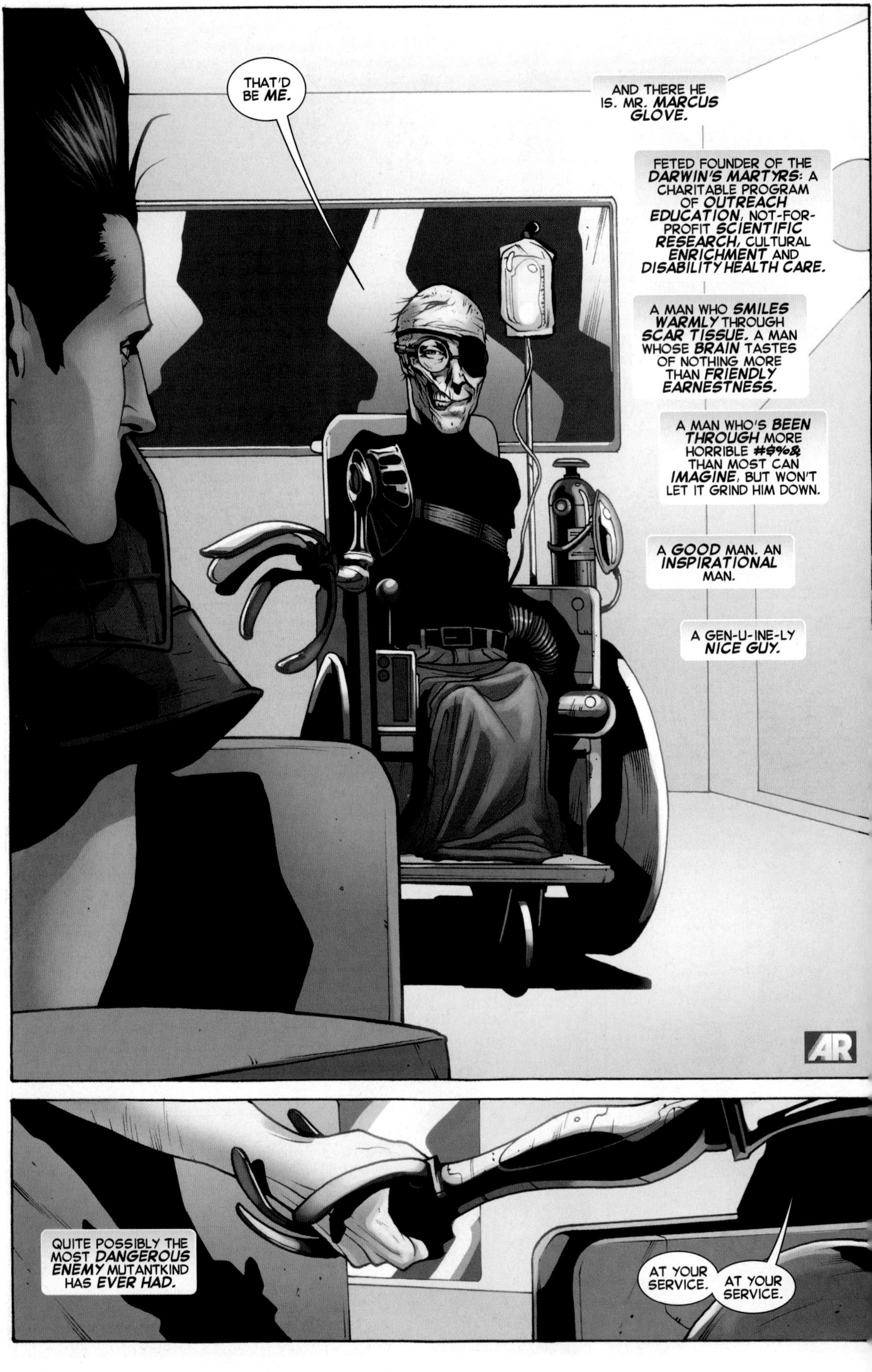
THAT'D BE ME.
AND THERE HE IS. MR. MARCUS GLOVE.
FETED FOUNDER OF THE DARWIN'S MARTYRS: A CHARITABLE PROGRAM OF OUTREACH EDUCATION, NOT-FOR-PROFIT SCIENTIFIC RESEARCH, CULTURAL ENRICHMENT AND DISABILITY HEALTH CARE.
A MAN WHO SMILES WARMLY THROUGH SCAR TISSUE. A MAN WHOSE BRAIN TASTES OF NOTHING MORE THAN FRIENDLY EARNESTNESS.
A MAN WHO'S BEEN THROUGH MORE HORRIBLE #$%& THAN MOST CAN IMAGINE, BUT WON'T LET IT GRIND HIM DOWN.
A GOOD MAN. AN INSPIRATIONAL MAN.
A GEN-U-INE-LY NICE GUY.
AR
QUITE POSSIBLY THE MOST DANGEROUS ENEMY MUTANTKIND HAS EVER HAD.
AT YOUR SERVICE.
AT YOUR SERVICE.

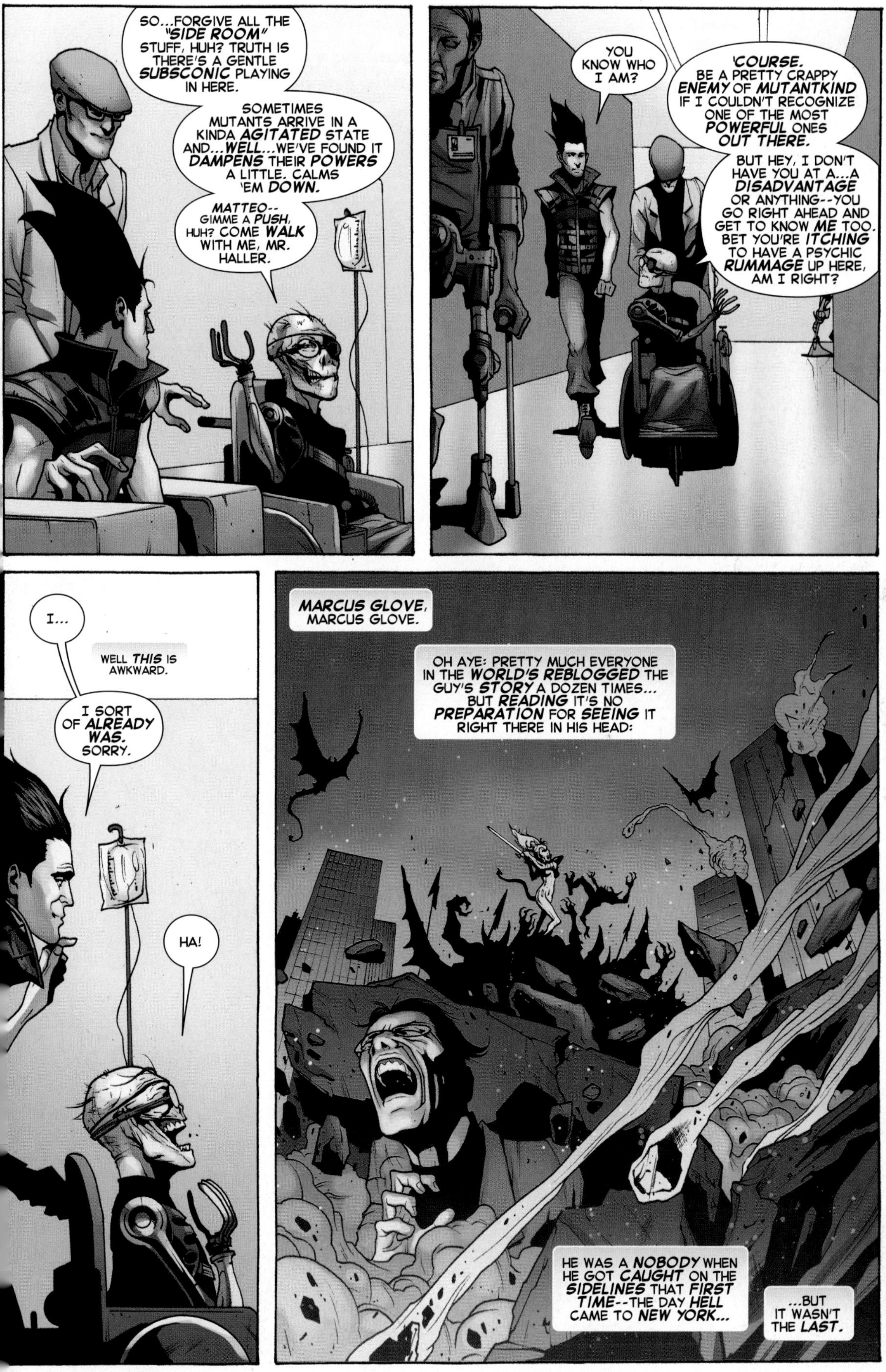

SO...FORGIVE ALL THE "SIDE ROOM" STUFF, HUH? TRUTH IS THERE'S A GENTLE SUBSCONIC PLAYING IN HERE.
SOMETIMES MUTANTS ARRIVE IN A KINDA AGITATED STATE AND...WELL...WE'VE FOUND IT DAMPENS THEIR POWERS A LITTLE. CALMS 'EM DOWN.
MATTEO-- GIMME A PUSH, HUH? COME WALK WITH ME, MR. HALLER.
YOU KNOW WHO I AM?
'COURSE. BE A PRETTY CRAPPY ENEMY OF MUTANTKIND IF I COULDN'T RECOGNIZE ONE OF THE MOST POWERFUL ONES OUT THERE.
BUT HEY, I DON'T HAVE YOU AT A...A DISADVANTAGE OR ANYTHING--YOU GO RIGHT AHEAD AND GET TO KNOW ME TOO. BET YOU'RE ITCHING TO HAVE A PSYCHIC RUMMAGE UP HERE, AM I RIGHT?
I...
WELL THIS IS AWKWARD.
I SORT OF ALREADY WAS. SORRY.
HA!
MARCUS GLOVE, MARCUS GLOVE.
OH AYE: PRETTY MUCH EVERYONE IN THE WORLD'S REBLOGGED THE GUY'S STORY A DOZEN TIMES... BUT READING IT'S NO PREPARATION FOR SEEING IT RIGHT THERE IN HIS HEAD:
HE WAS A NOBODY WHEN HE GOT CAUGHT ON THE SIDELINES THAT FIRST TIME--THE DAY HELL CAME TO NEW YORK...
...BUT IT WASN'T THE LAST.

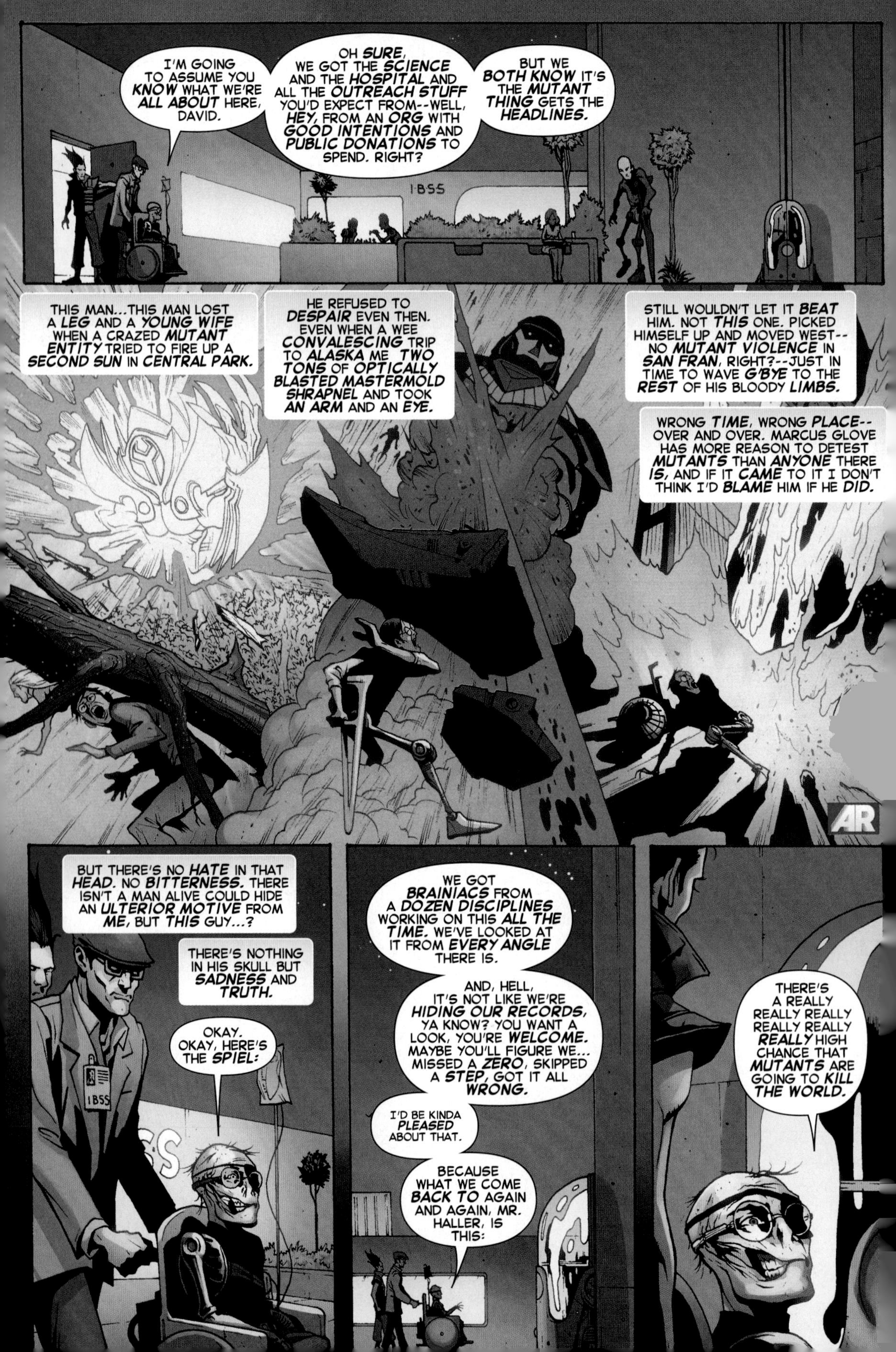
I'M GOING TO ASSUME YOU KNOW WHAT WE'RE ALL ABOUT HERE, DAVID.
OH SURE, WE GOT THE SCIENCE AND THE HOSPITAL AND ALL THE OUTREACH STUFF YOU'D EXPECT FROM--WELL, HEY, FROM AN ORG WITH GOOD INTENTIONS AND PUBLIC DONATIONS TO SPEND. RIGHT?
BUT WE BOTH KNOW IT'S THE MUTANT THING GETS THE HEADLINES.
IBSS
THIS MAN...THIS MAN LOST A LEG AND A YOUNG WIFE WHEN A CRAZED MUTANT ENTITY TRIED TO FIRE UP A SECOND SUN IN CENTRAL PARK.
HE REFUSED TO DESPAIR EVEN THEN. EVEN WHEN A WEE CONVALESCING TRIP TO ALASKA ME TWO TONS OF OPTICALLY BLASTED MASTERMOLD SHRAPNEL AND TOOK AN ARM AND AN EYE.
STILL WOULDN'T LET IT BEAT HIM. NOT THIS ONE. PICKED HIMSELF UP AND MOVED WEST--NO MUTANT VIOLENCE IN SAN FRAN, RIGHT?--JUST IN TIME TO WAVE G'BYE TO THE REST OF HIS BLOODY LIMBS.
WRONG TIME, WRONG PLACE--OVER AND OVER. MARCUS GLOVE HAS MORE REASON TO DETEST MUTANTS THAN ANYONE THERE IS, AND IF IT CAME TO IT I DON'T THINK I'D BLAME HIM IF HE DID.
AR
BUT THERE'S NO HATE IN THAT HEAD. NO BITTERNESS. THERE ISN'T A MAN ALIVE COULD HIDE AN ULTERIOR MOTIVE FROM ME, BUT THIS GUY...?
THERE'S NOTHING IN HIS SKULL BUT SADNESS AND TRUTH.
OKAY. OKAY, HERE'S THE SPIEL:
IBSS
WE GOT BRAINIACS FROM A DOZEN DISCIPLINES WORKING ON THIS ALL THE TIME. WE'VE LOOKED AT IT FROM EVERY ANGLE THERE IS.
AND, HELL, IT'S NOT LIKE WE'RE HIDING OUR RECORDS, YA KNOW? YOU WANT A LOOK, YOU'RE WELCOME. MAYBE YOU'LL FIGURE WE... MISSED A ZERO, SKIPPED A STEP, GOT IT ALL WRONG.
I'D BE KINDA PLEASED ABOUT THAT.
BECAUSE WHAT WE COME BACK TO AGAIN AND AGAIN, MR. HALLER, IS THIS:
THERE'S A REALLY REALLY REALLY REALLY REALLY REALLY HIGH CHANCE THAT MUTANTS ARE GOING TO KILL THE WORLD.

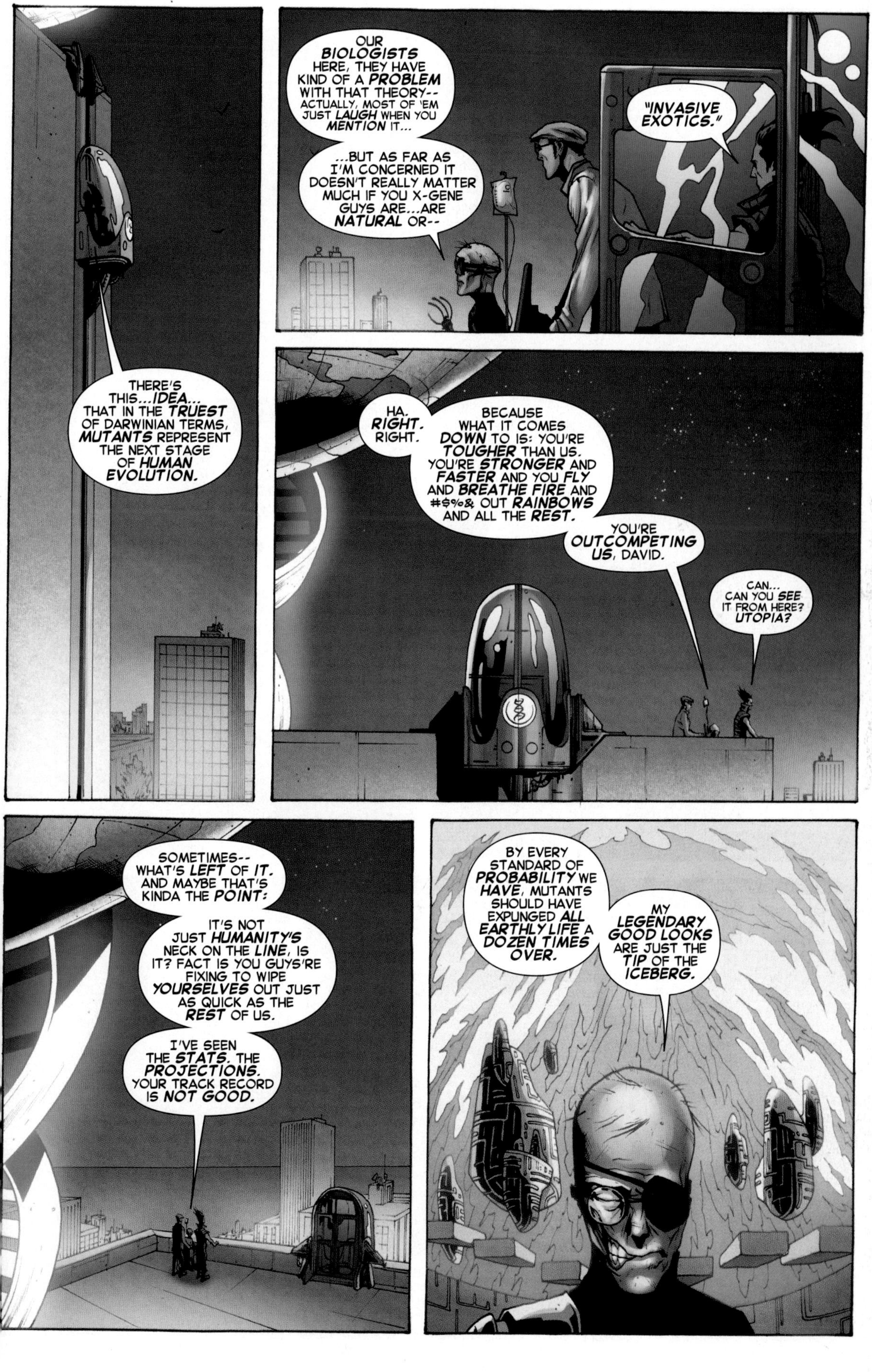
THERE'S THIS...IDEA... THAT IN THE TRUEST OF DARWINIAN TERMS, MUTANTS REPRESENT THE NEXT STAGE OF HUMAN EVOLUTION.
OUR BIOLOGISTS HERE, THEY HAVE KIND OF A PROBLEM WITH THAT THEORY-- ACTUALLY, MOST OF 'EM JUST LAUGH WHEN YOU MENTION IT...
...BUT AS FAR AS I'M CONCERNED IT DOESN'T REALLY MATTER MUCH IF YOU X-GENE GUYS ARE...ARE NATURAL OR--
"INVASIVE EXOTICS."
HA. RIGHT. RIGHT.
BECAUSE WHAT IT COMES DOWN TO IS: YOU'RE TOUGHER THAN US. YOU'RE STRONGER AND FASTER AND YOU FLY AND BREATHE FIRE AND #$%& OUT RAINBOWS AND ALL THE REST.
YOU'RE OUTCOMPETING US, DAVID.
CAN... CAN YOU SEE IT FROM HERE? UTOPIA?
SOMETIMES-- WHAT'S LEFT OF IT. AND MAYBE THAT'S KINDA THE POINT:
IT'S NOT JUST HUMANITY'S NECK ON THE LINE, IS IT? FACT IS YOU GUYS'RE FIXING TO WIPE YOURSELVES OUT JUST AS QUICK AS THE REST OF US.
I'VE SEEN THE STATS. THE PROJECTIONS. YOUR TRACK RECORD IS NOT GOOD.
BY EVERY STANDARD OF PROBABILITY WE HAVE, MUTANTS SHOULD HAVE EXPUNGED ALL EARTHLY LIFE A DOZEN TIMES OVER.
MY LEGENDARY GOOD LOOKS ARE JUST THE TIP OF THE ICEBERG.

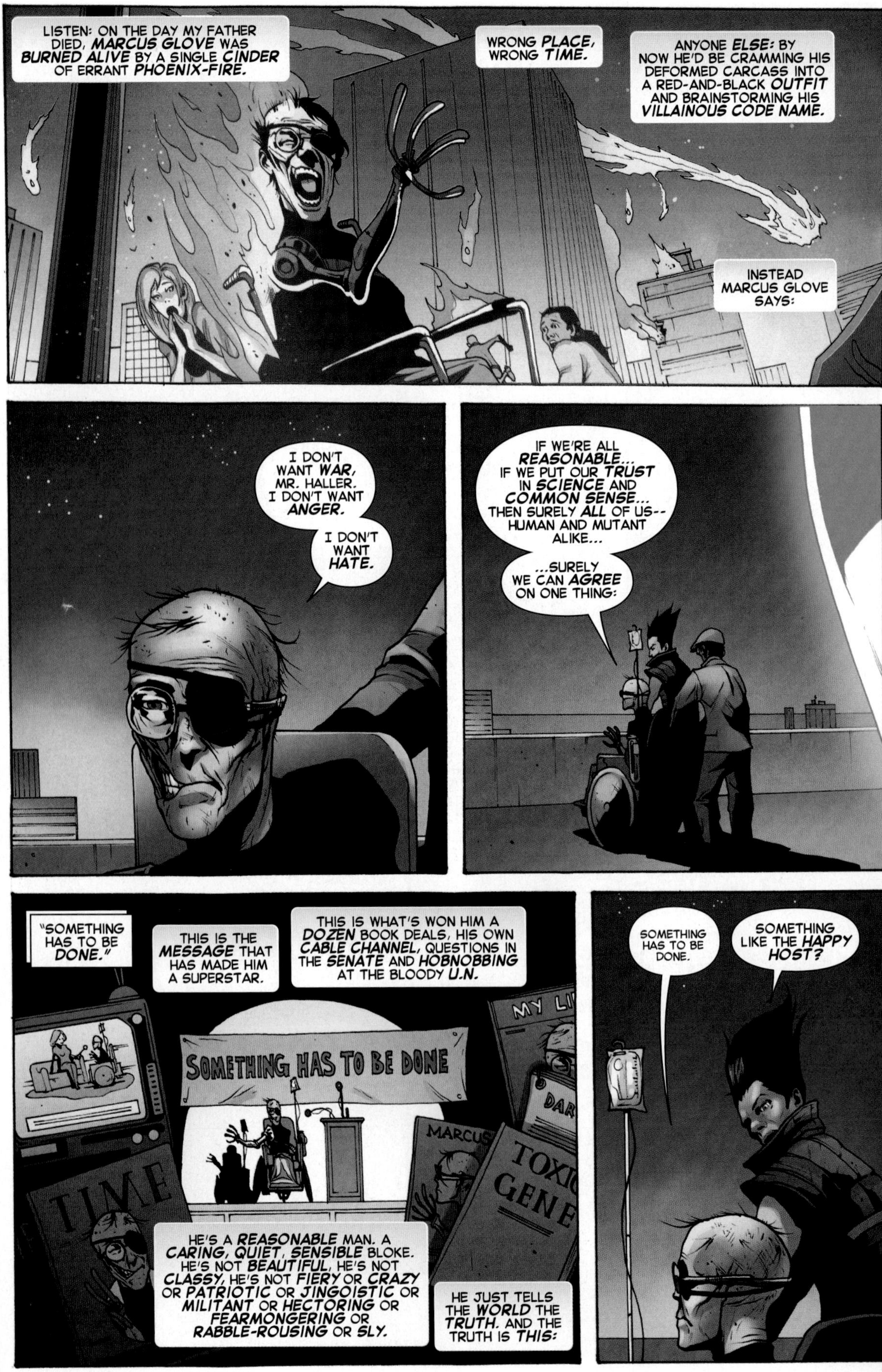
LISTEN: ON THE DAY MY FATHER DIED, MARCUS GLOVE WAS BURNED ALIVE BY A SINGLE CINDER OF ERRANT PHOENIX-FIRE.
WRONG PLACE, WRONG TIME.
ANYONE ELSE: BY NOW HE'D BE CRAMMING HIS DEFORMED CARCASS INTO A RED-AND-BLACK OUTFIT AND BRAINSTORMING HIS VILLAINOUS CODE NAME.
INSTEAD MARCUS GLOVE SAYS:
I DON'T WANT WAR, MR. HALLER. I DON'T WANT ANGER.
I DON'T WANT HATE.
IF WE'RE ALL REASONABLE... IF WE PUT OUR TRUST IN SCIENCE AND COMMON SENSE... THEN SURELY ALL OF US-- HUMAN AND MUTANT ALIKE...
...SURELY WE CAN AGREE ON ONE THING:
"SOMETHING HAS TO BE DONE."
THIS IS THE MESSAGE THAT HAS MADE HIM A SUPERSTAR.
THIS IS WHAT'S WON HIM A DOZEN BOOK DEALS, HIS OWN CABLE CHANNEL, QUESTIONS IN THE SENATE AND HOBNOBBING AT THE BLOODY U.N.
SOMETHING HAS TO BE DONE
TIME
TOXIC GENE
HE'S A REASONABLE MAN. A CARING, QUIET, SENSIBLE BLOKE. HE'S NOT BEAUTIFUL, HE'S NOT CLASSY, HE'S NOT FIERY OR CRAZY OR PATRIOTIC OR JINGOISTIC OR MILITANT OR HECTORING OR FEARMONGERING OR RABBLE-ROUSING OR SLY.
HE JUST TELLS THE WORLD THE TRUTH. AND THE TRUTH IS THIS:
SOMETHING HAS TO BE DONE.
SOMETHING LIKE THE HAPPY HOST?

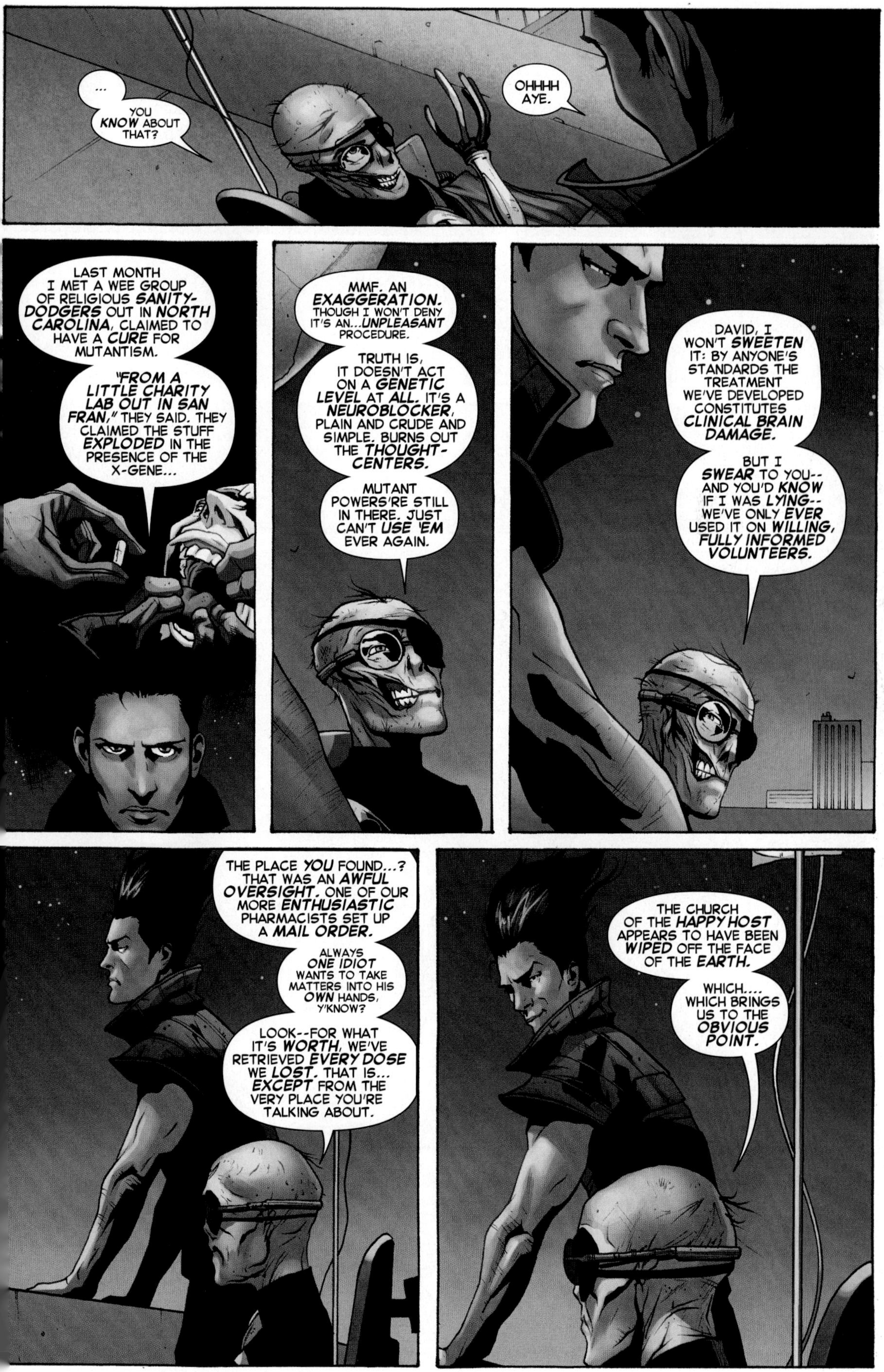
...
YOU KNOW ABOUT THAT?
OHHHH AYE.
LAST MONTH I MET A WEE GROUP OF RELIGIOUS SANITY-DODGERS OUT IN NORTH CAROLINA, CLAIMED TO HAVE A CURE FOR MUTANTISM.
"FROM A LITTLE CHARITY LAB OUT IN SAN FRAN," THEY SAID. THEY CLAIMED THE STUFF EXPLODED IN THE PRESENCE OF THE X-GENE...
MMF. AN EXAGGERATION. THOUGH I WON'T DENY IT'S AN...UNPLEASANT PROCEDURE.
TRUTH IS, IT DOESN'T ACT ON A GENETIC LEVEL AT ALL. IT'S A NEUROBLOCKER, PLAIN AND CRUDE AND SIMPLE. BURNS OUT THE THOUGHT-CENTERS.
MUTANT POWERS'RE STILL IN THERE. JUST CAN'T USE 'EM EVER AGAIN.
DAVID, I WON'T SWEETEN IT: BY ANYONE'S STANDARDS THE TREATMENT WE'VE DEVELOPED CONSTITUTES CLINICAL BRAIN DAMAGE.
BUT I SWEAR TO YOU-- AND YOU'D KNOW IF I WAS LYING-- WE'VE ONLY EVER USED IT ON WILLING, FULLY INFORMED VOLUNTEERS.
THE PLACE YOU FOUND...? THAT WAS AN AWFUL OVERSIGHT. ONE OF OUR MORE ENTHUSIASTIC PHARMACISTS SET UP A MAIL ORDER.
ALWAYS ONE IDIOT WANTS TO TAKE MATTERS INTO HIS OWN HANDS, Y'KNOW?
LOOK--FOR WHAT IT'S WORTH, WE'VE RETRIEVED EVERY DOSE WE LOST. THAT IS... EXCEPT FROM THE VERY PLACE YOU'RE TALKING ABOUT.
THE CHURCH OF THE HAPPY HOST APPEARS TO HAVE BEEN WIPED OFF THE FACE OF THE EARTH.
WHICH.... WHICH BRINGS US TO THE OBVIOUS POINT.

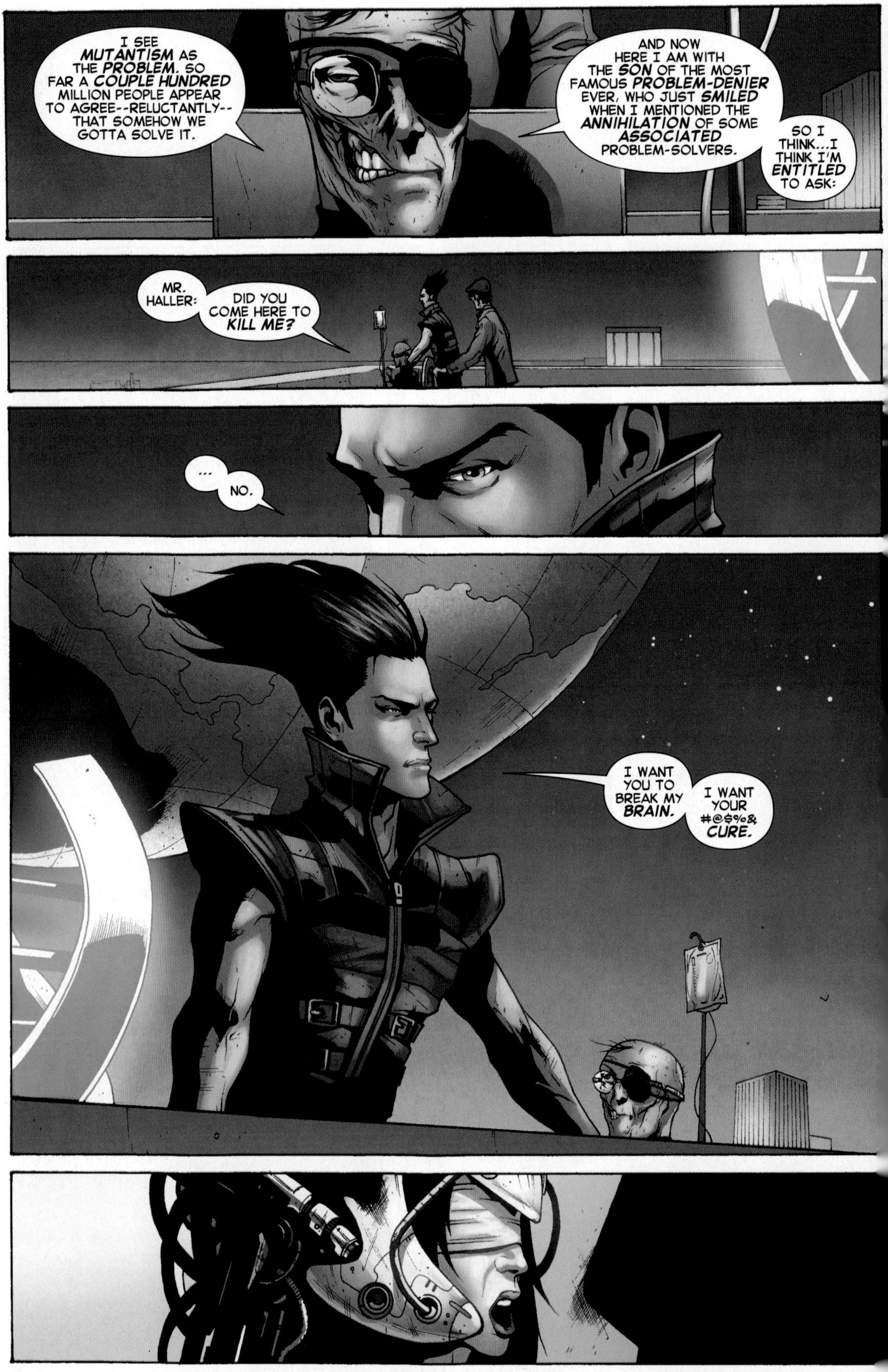
I SEE MUTANTISM AS THE PROBLEM. SO FAR A COUPLE HUNDRED MILLION PEOPLE APPEAR TO AGREE--RELUCTANTLY--THAT SOMEHOW WE GOTTA SOLVE IT.
AND NOW HERE I AM WITH THE SON OF THE MOST FAMOUS PROBLEM-DENIER EVER, WHO JUST SMILED WHEN I MENTIONED THE ANNIHILATION OF SOME ASSOCIATED PROBLEM-SOLVERS.
SO I THINK...I THINK I'M ENTITLED TO ASK:
MR. HALLER:
DID YOU COME HERE TO KILL ME?
...
NO.
I WANT YOU TO BREAK MY BRAIN.
I WANT YOUR #@$%& CURE.

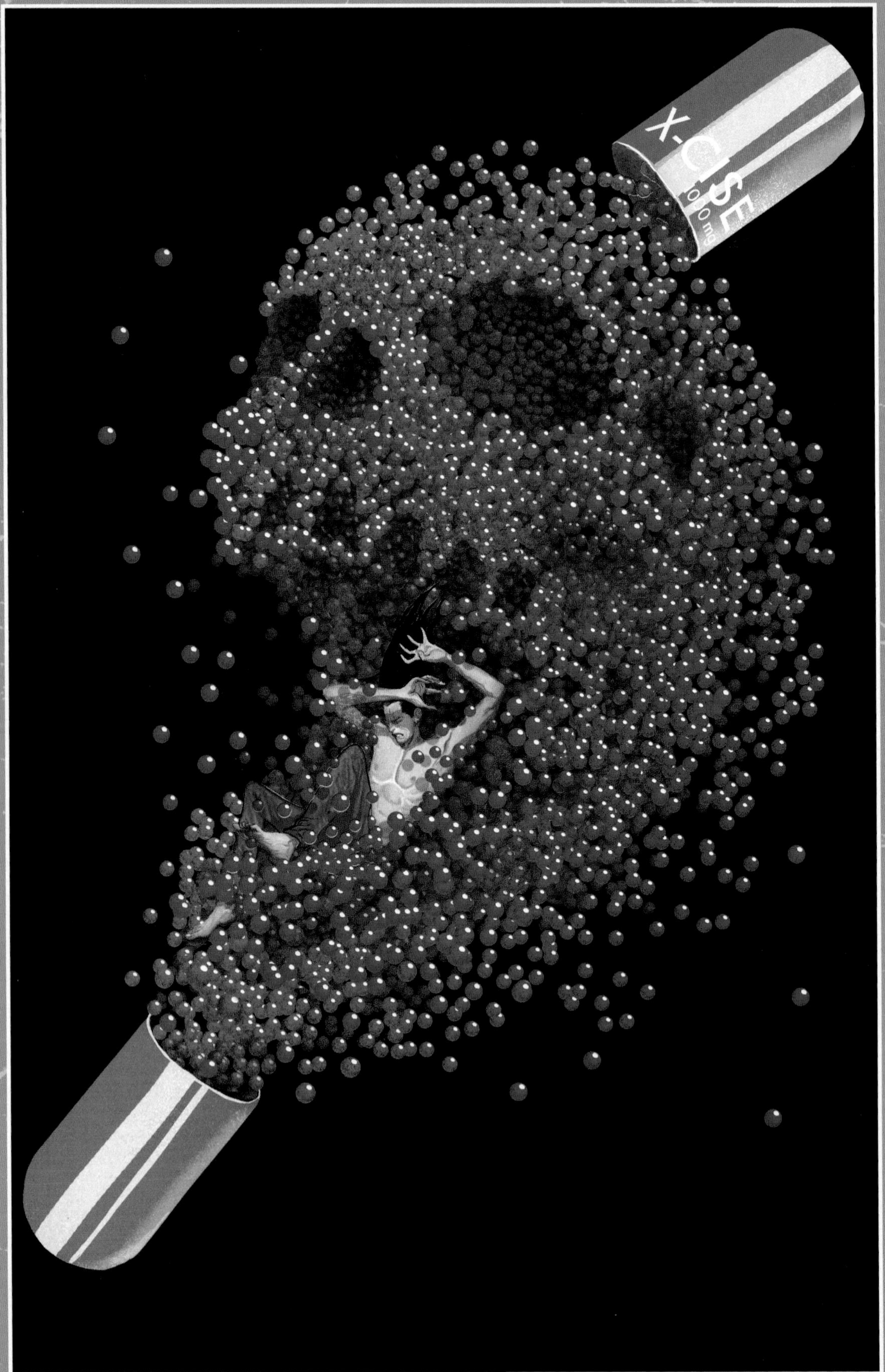
X-CISE
1000mg

ELEVEN

OCULAR *PHOTON STIMULATION.*

ICTHYOID AND *AVIAN* MORPHOLOGIES.

EVEN THE EXTRUSION OF *ORGANIZED METAL STRUCTURES,* FOR CRYING OUT LOUD.

AND YET PEOPLE *STILL* CALL IT THE *"NEXT STAGE OF EVOLUTION."*

DARWIN WOULD #&%&.

DAVID: *DR. NINA AMBROSE.*

TELLS IT LIKE IT *IS.*

"TELLS IT LIKE IT IS," GLOVE SAYS. THAT TWINKLING *EYE* OF HIS. THAT RAVAGED WEE *SMILE...*

I MEAN, *SERIOUSLY?* YOU THINK HUMAN *DNA* HAS *LATENT CODE* FOR... VEHICLE DESIGNING? JUST *WAITING* FOR THE *RIGHT* MUTATION TO *OPEN IT UP?*

DEMON SUMMONING? COMPUTER HACKING?

PLEASE.

HE *KNOWS,* DOESN'T HE? KNOWS I'M *READING HER MIND.* CHECKING FOR *HIDDEN TRUTHS.*

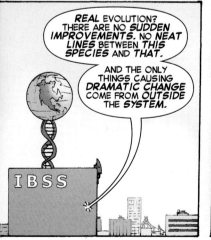

REAL EVOLUTION? THERE ARE NO *SUDDEN IMPROVEMENTS.* NO NEAT LINES BETWEEN *THIS* SPECIES AND *THAT.*

AND THE ONLY THINGS CAUSING *DRAMATIC CHANGE* COME FROM *OUTSIDE* THE *SYSTEM.*

IBSS

FRANKLY WE HAVE *NO IDEA* IF MUTANTS'RE THE PRODUCT OF *MAGIC, CELESTIAL DEITIES* OR A *DAMN GREAT FIERY BIRD*--BUT I'LL TELL YOU *THIS:*

IT'S NOT *NATURE.*

HUMANS'RE BEING *OUTCOMPETED* BY AN *ARTIFICIAL SPECIES.*

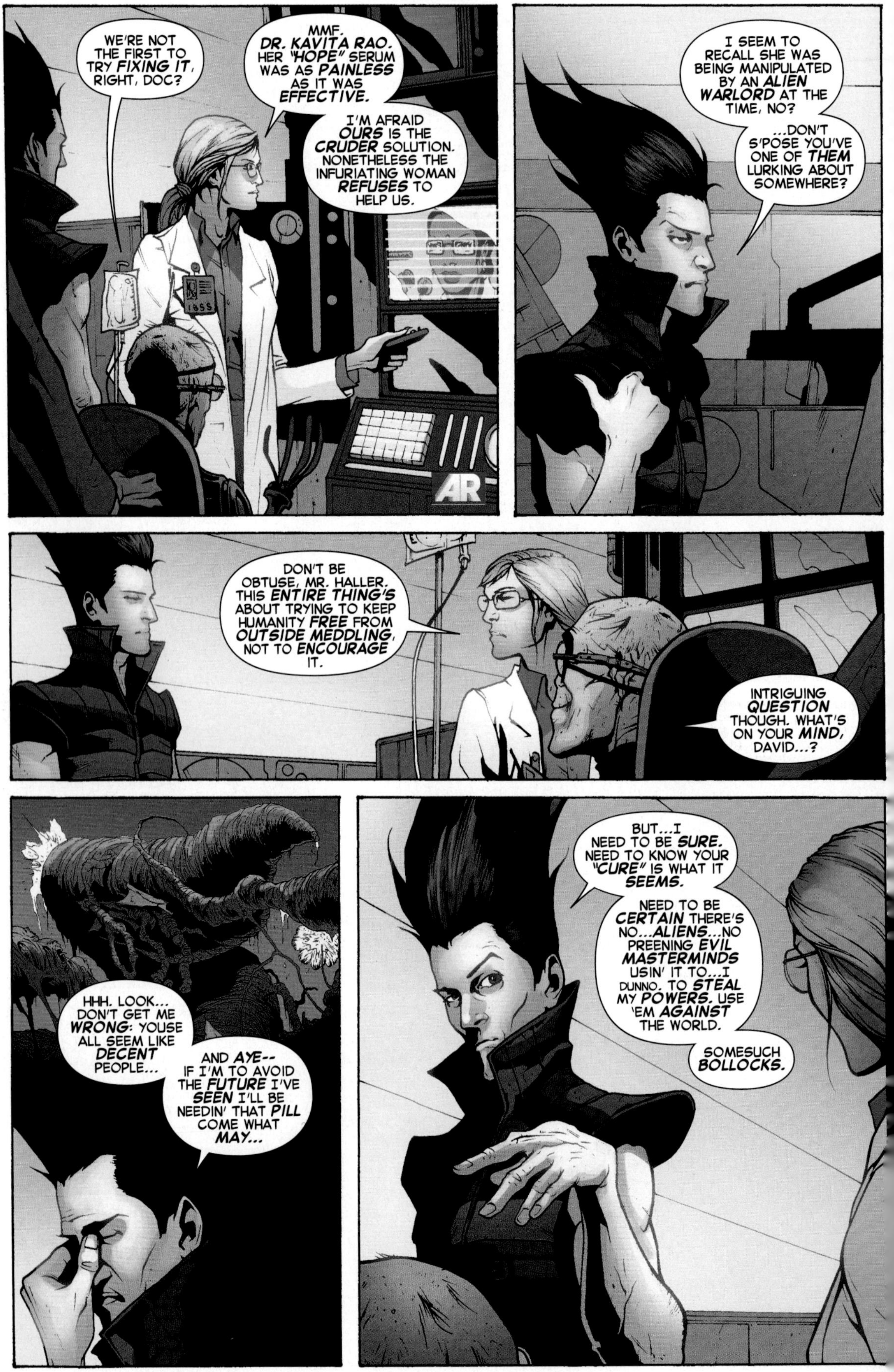
WE'RE NOT THE FIRST TO TRY FIXING IT, RIGHT, DOC?
MMF. DR. KAVITA RAO. HER "HOPE" SERUM WAS AS PAINLESS AS IT WAS EFFECTIVE.
I'M AFRAID OURS IS THE CRUDER SOLUTION. NONETHELESS THE INFURIATING WOMAN REFUSES TO HELP US.
I SEEM TO RECALL SHE WAS BEING MANIPULATED BY AN ALIEN WARLORD AT THE TIME, NO?
...DON'T S'POSE YOU'VE ONE OF THEM LURKING ABOUT SOMEWHERE?
DON'T BE OBTUSE, MR. HALLER. THIS ENTIRE THING'S ABOUT TRYING TO KEEP HUMANITY FREE FROM OUTSIDE MEDDLING, NOT TO ENCOURAGE IT.
INTRIGUING QUESTION THOUGH. WHAT'S ON YOUR MIND, DAVID...?
HHH. LOOK... DON'T GET ME WRONG: YOUSE ALL SEEM LIKE DECENT PEOPLE...
AND AYE-- IF I'M TO AVOID THE FUTURE I'VE SEEN I'LL BE NEEDIN' THAT PILL COME WHAT MAY...
BUT...I NEED TO BE SURE. NEED TO KNOW YOUR "CURE" IS WHAT IT SEEMS.
NEED TO BE CERTAIN THERE'S NO...ALIENS...NO PREENING EVIL MASTERMINDS USIN' IT TO...I DUNNO. TO STEAL MY POWERS. USE 'EM AGAINST THE WORLD.
SOMESUCH BOLLOCKS.

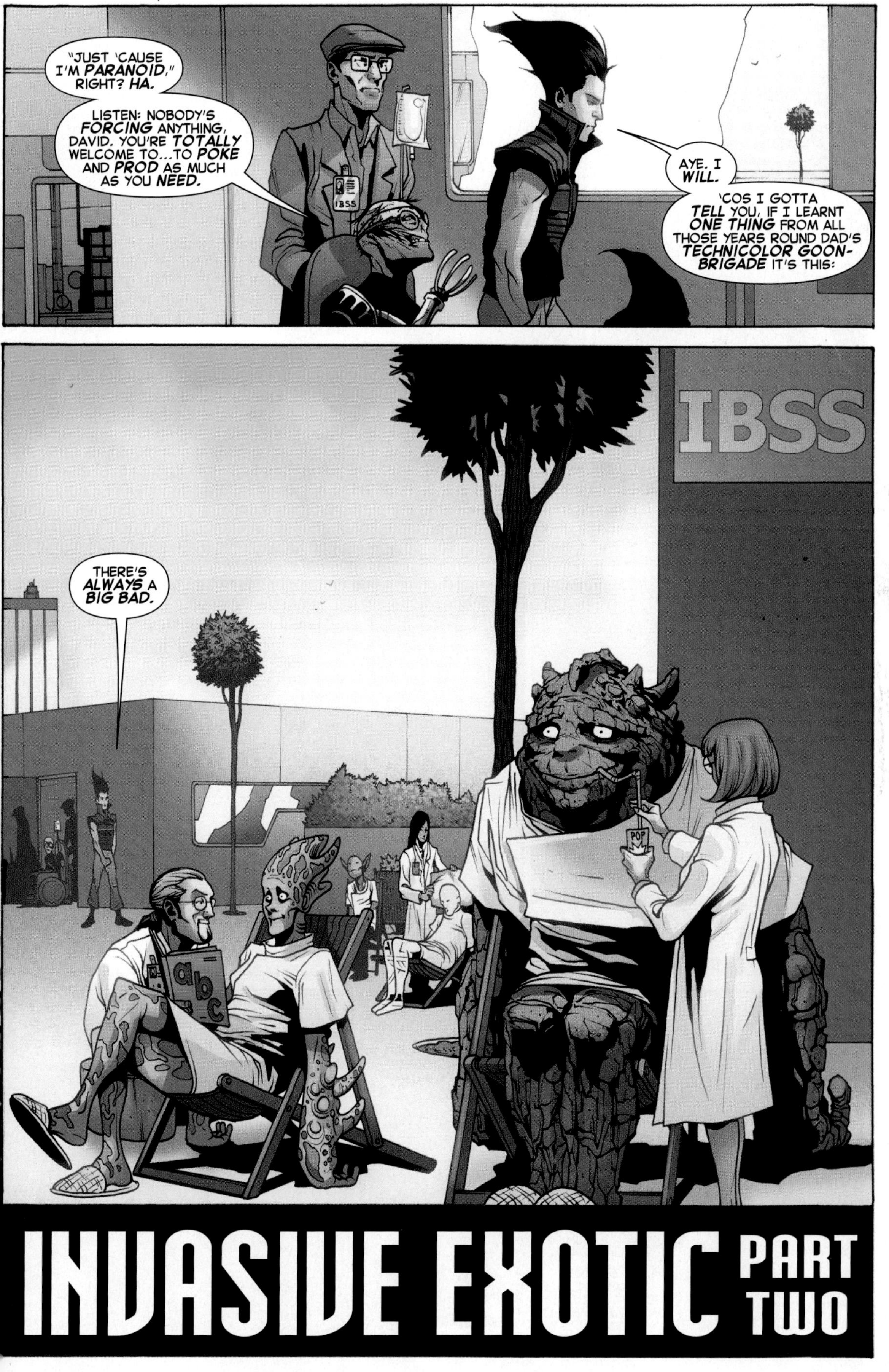
"JUST 'CAUSE I'M PARANOID," RIGHT? HA.
LISTEN: NOBODY'S FORCING ANYTHING, DAVID. YOU'RE TOTALLY WELCOME TO...TO POKE AND PROD AS MUCH AS YOU NEED.
IBSS
AYE. I WILL.
'COS I GOTTA TELL YOU, IF I LEARNT ONE THING FROM ALL THOSE YEARS ROUND DAD'S TECHNICOLOR GOON-BRIGADE IT'S THIS:
IBSS
THERE'S ALWAYS A BIG BAD.
POP
INVASIVE EXOTIC PART TWO

NEXT UP: THE *LEGION* SITUATION.

HE'S UNDENIABLY STILL ACTIVE. ABIGAIL SAYS S.W.O.R.D. HAD A RUN-IN.

NO LUCK TRACKING HIM. HOWEVER SCREWED HIS POWERS, HE'S GOT HIS TELEPATHY. CEREBRO CAN'T SEE HIM 'LESS HE WANTS IT TO.

NNF. KID'S TOO BROKEN TO STAY HIDDEN LONG. GIVE IT A MONTH, HE'LL TURN UP EITHER CRYIN' FOR HELP OR NEEDIN' HIS ASS KICKED.

EITHER WAY-- WE DRAG HIM HOME, PUT HIM UNDER.

AND EITHER WAY, HE AIN'T OUR PROBLEM 'TIL THEN.

NEXT?

OH

OHH NO, SORRY, SORRY, OHHH

HE'S... OH NO, OH PARDON...HE'S GOING TO BREAK HIMSELF...

WHAT DO I DO? NO, NO, NO. WHAT DO I DO?

ᑌ᠆᠆ᒐᎶᎤ ᏌᏁᏳᎮᎲ ᏌᎦᏁᎲᎤ

OH. I-IT'S YOU.

Ꮛ ᎤᎤᏍ ᏌᎮᏋᏁ ᏧᏌᏁᏔᏍ ᎤᏌᎤᏍᏳᏍᎤ ᎤᎤᏍᏌᎤᏁᎤᎤᏍᎤ ᏁᏌᏁᎮᎤᏓᏍᎤ

S-SORRY, SORRY...I... DON'T ACTUALLY UNDERSTAND YOU. NEVER DID. IT SOUNDS JUST LIKE SQUIGGLY SYMBOLS.

YES.

'SCUSE ME.

I GOTTA GO FIND SOME HELP.

...

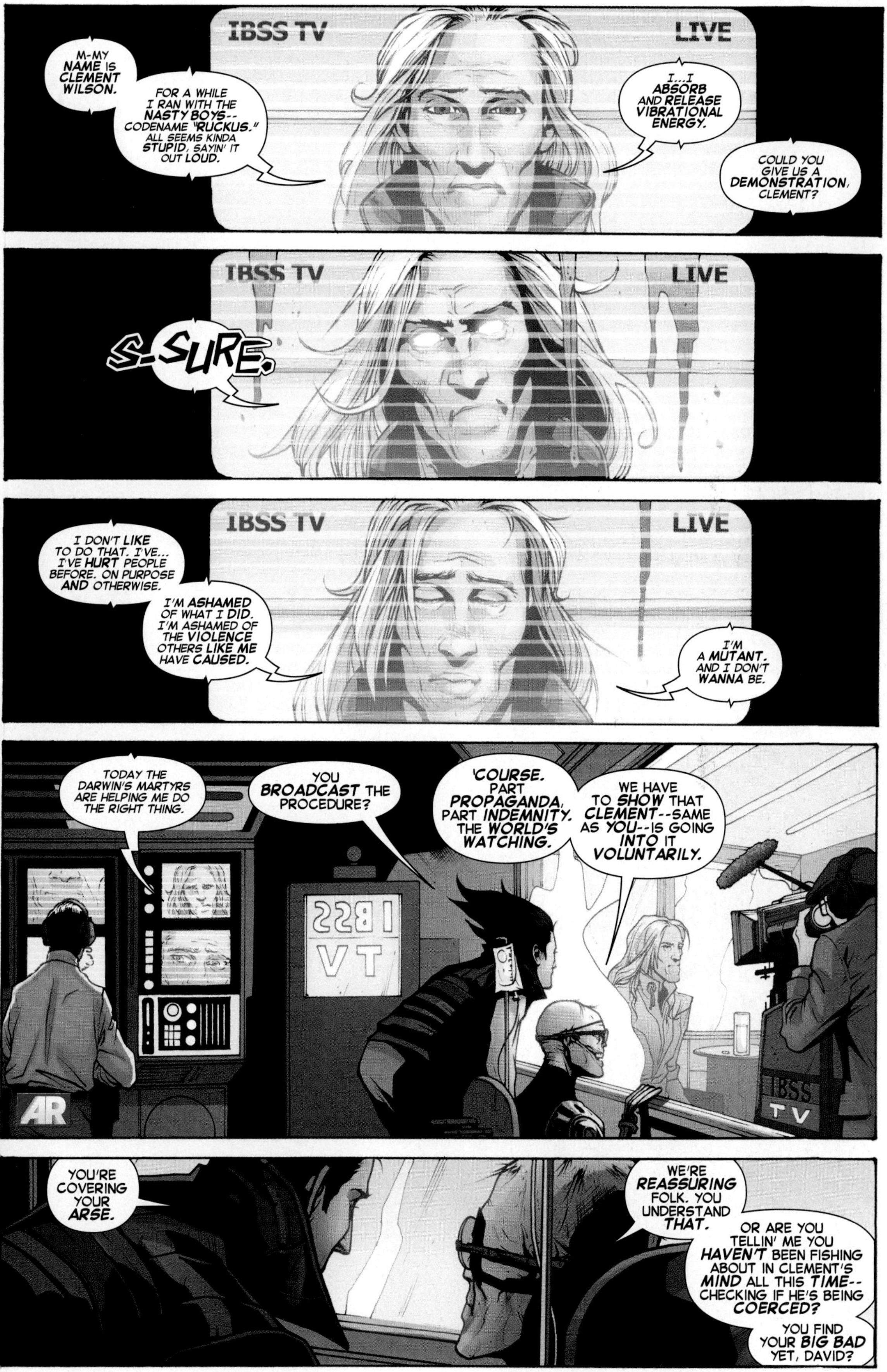
IBSS TV
LIVE
M-MY NAME IS CLEMENT WILSON.
FOR A WHILE I RAN WITH THE NASTY BOYS--CODENAME "RUCKUS." ALL SEEMS KINDA STUPID, SAYIN' IT OUT LOUD.
I...I ABSORB AND RELEASE VIBRATIONAL ENERGY.
COULD YOU GIVE US A DEMONSTRATION, CLEMENT?
IBSS TV
LIVE
S-SURE.
IBSS TV
LIVE
I DON'T LIKE TO DO THAT. I'VE... I'VE HURT PEOPLE BEFORE. ON PURPOSE AND OTHERWISE.
I'M ASHAMED OF WHAT I DID. I'M ASHAMED OF THE VIOLENCE OTHERS LIKE ME HAVE CAUSED.
I'M A MUTANT. AND I DON'T WANNA BE.
TODAY THE DARWIN'S MARTYRS ARE HELPING ME DO THE RIGHT THING.
YOU BROADCAST THE PROCEDURE?
'COURSE. PART PROPAGANDA, PART INDEMNITY. THE WORLD'S WATCHING.
WE HAVE TO SHOW THAT CLEMENT--SAME AS YOU--IS GOING INTO IT VOLUNTARILY.
IBSS TV
IBSS TV
YOU'RE COVERING YOUR ARSE.
WE'RE REASSURING FOLK. YOU UNDERSTAND THAT.
OR ARE YOU TELLIN' ME YOU HAVEN'T BEEN FISHING ABOUT IN CLEMENT'S MIND ALL THIS TIME--CHECKING IF HE'S BEING COERCED?
YOU FIND YOUR BIG BAD YET, DAVID?

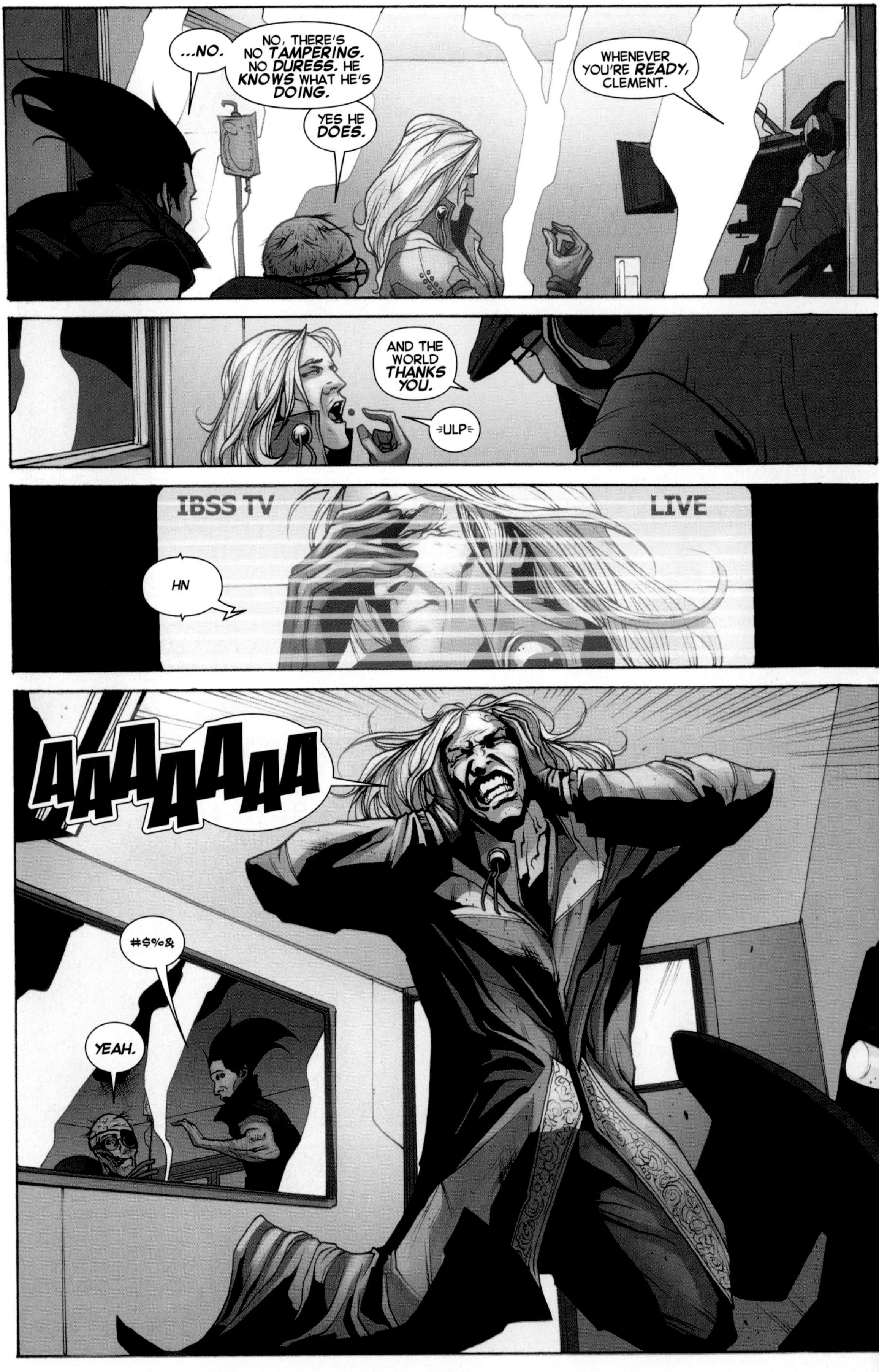
...NO.
NO, THERE'S NO TAMPERING. NO DURESS. HE KNOWS WHAT HE'S DOING.
YES HE DOES.
WHENEVER YOU'RE READY, CLEMENT.
AND THE WORLD THANKS YOU.
ULP
IBSS TV
LIVE
HN
AAAAAAAA
#$%&
YEAH.

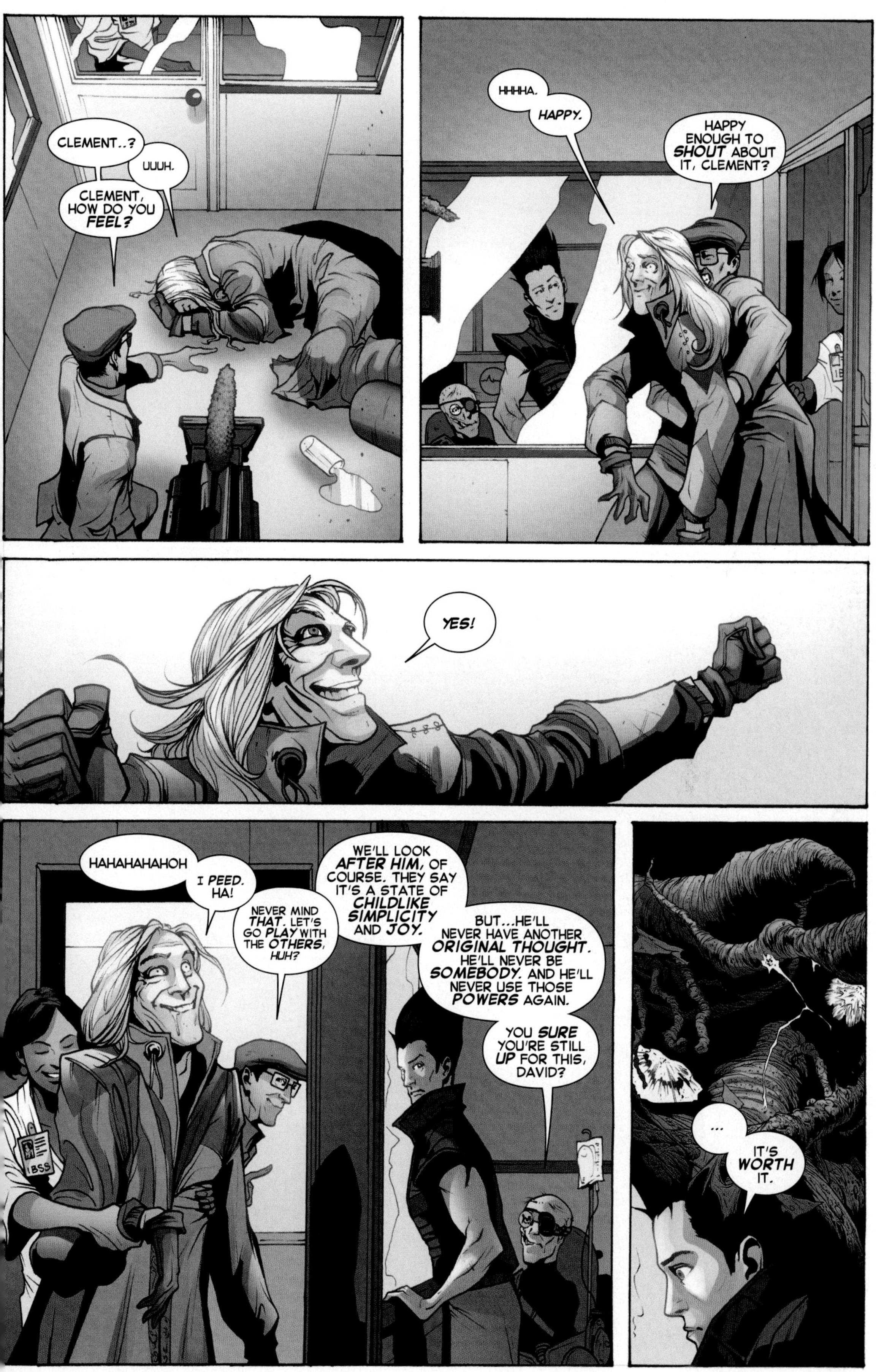
CLEMENT..?
UUUH.
CLEMENT, HOW DO YOU FEEL?
HHHHA.
HAPPY.
HAPPY ENOUGH TO SHOUT ABOUT IT, CLEMENT?
YES!
HAHAHAHAHOH
I PEED. HA!
NEVER MIND THAT. LET'S GO PLAY WITH THE OTHERS, HUH?
WE'LL LOOK AFTER HIM, OF COURSE. THEY SAY IT'S A STATE OF CHILDLIKE SIMPLICITY AND JOY.
BUT...HE'LL NEVER HAVE ANOTHER ORIGINAL THOUGHT. HE'LL NEVER BE SOMEBODY. AND HE'LL NEVER USE THOSE POWERS AGAIN.
YOU SURE YOU'RE STILL UP FOR THIS, DAVID?
...
IT'S WORTH IT.

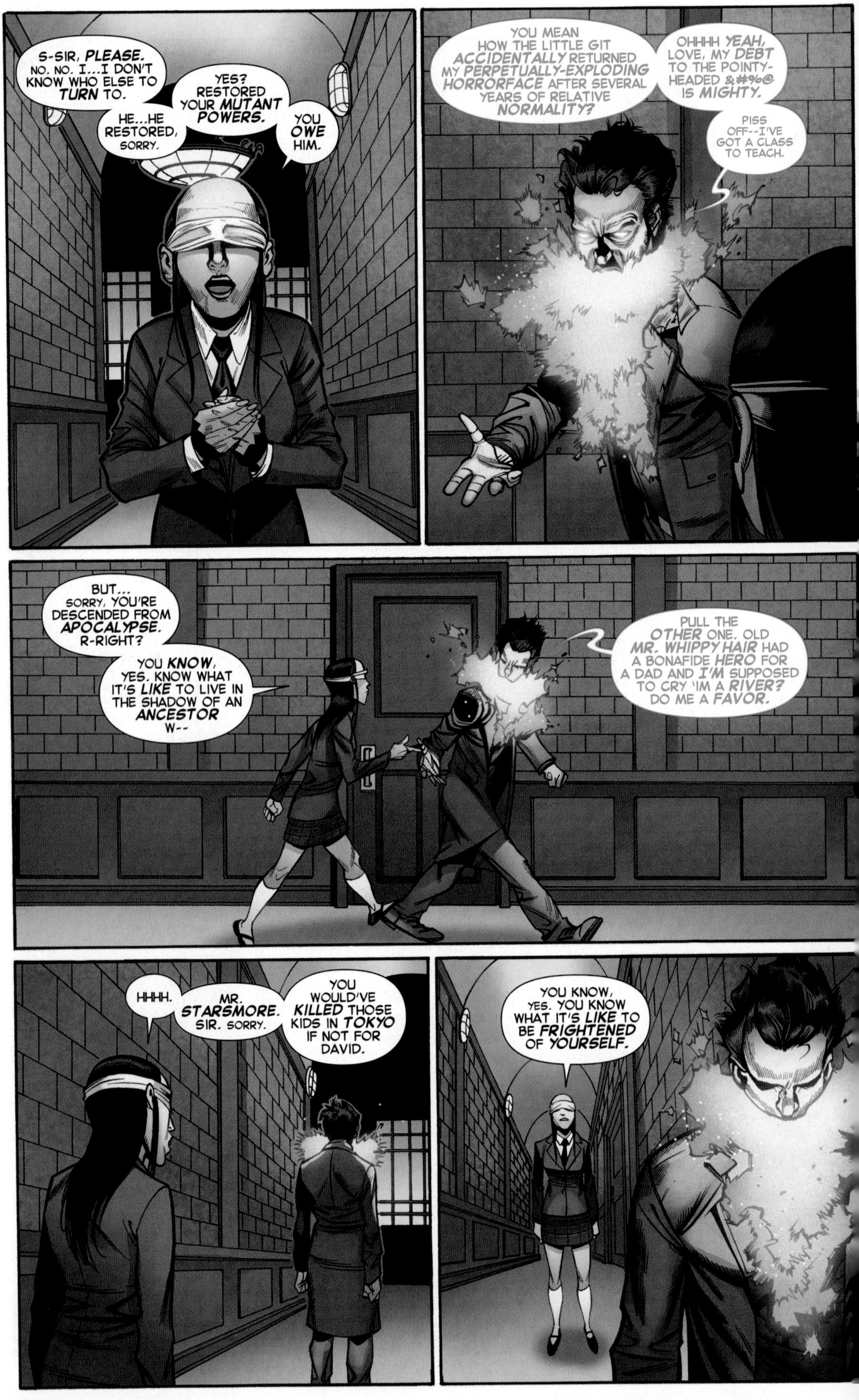
S-SIR, PLEASE. NO. NO. I...I DON'T KNOW WHO ELSE TO TURN TO.
HE...HE RESTORED, SORRY.
YES? RESTORED YOUR MUTANT POWERS.
YOU OWE HIM.
YOU MEAN HOW THE LITTLE GIT ACCIDENTALLY RETURNED MY PERPETUALLY-EXPLODING HORRORFACE AFTER SEVERAL YEARS OF RELATIVE NORMALITY?
OHHHH YEAH, LOVE, MY DEBT TO THE POINTY-HEADED &#%@ IS MIGHTY.
PISS OFF--I'VE GOT A CLASS TO TEACH.
BUT... SORRY, YOU'RE DESCENDED FROM APOCALYPSE. R-RIGHT?
YOU KNOW, YES. KNOW WHAT IT'S LIKE TO LIVE IN THE SHADOW OF AN ANCESTOR W--
PULL THE OTHER ONE. OLD MR. WHIPPY HAIR HAD A BONAFIDE HERO FOR A DAD AND I'M SUPPOSED TO CRY 'IM A RIVER? DO ME A FAVOR.
HHHH.
MR. STARSMORE. SIR. SORRY.
YOU WOULD'VE KILLED THOSE KIDS IN TOKYO IF NOT FOR DAVID.
YOU KNOW, YES. YOU KNOW WHAT IT'S LIKE TO BE FRIGHTENED OF YOURSELF.

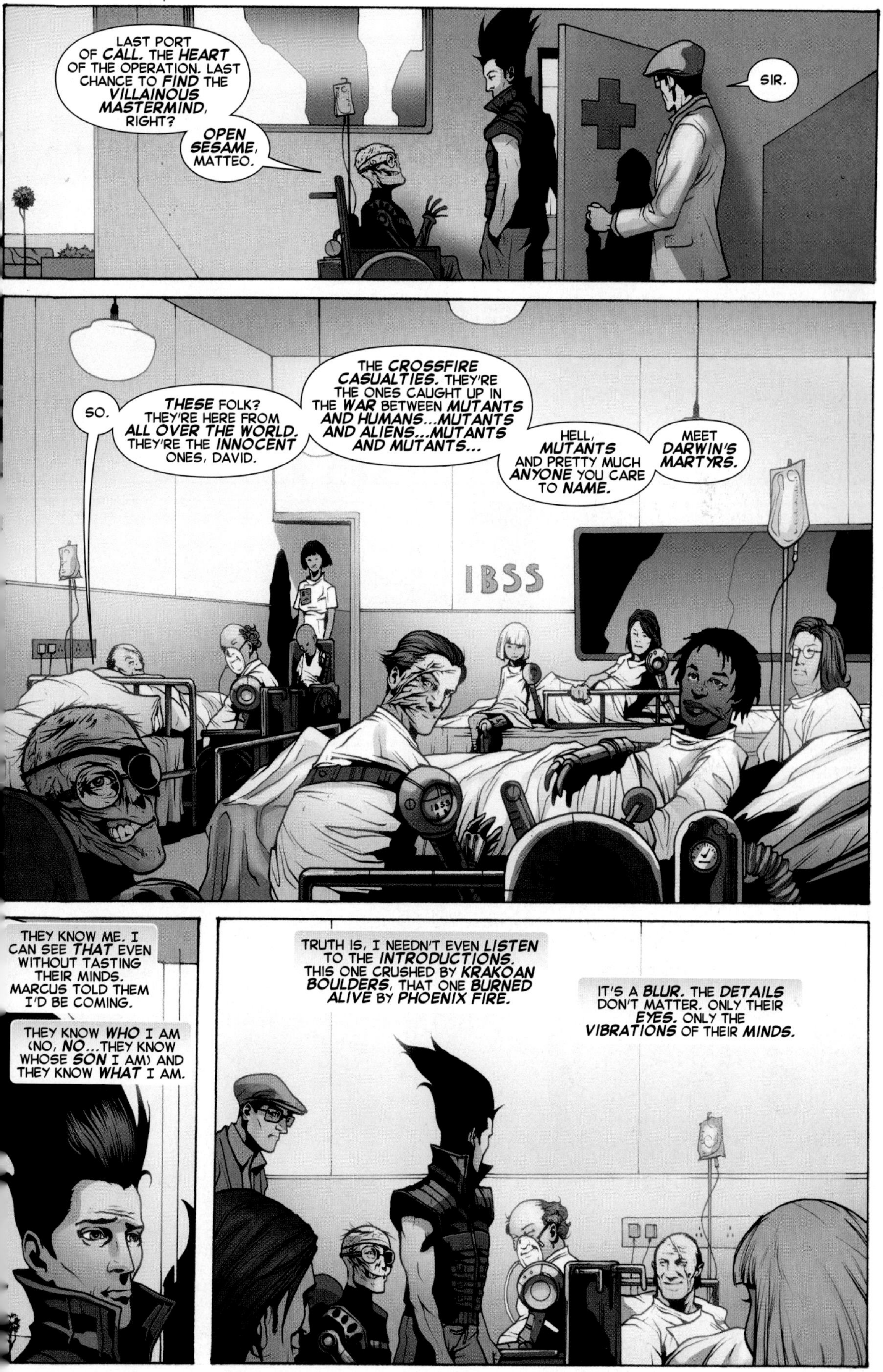
LAST PORT OF CALL. THE HEART OF THE OPERATION. LAST CHANCE TO FIND THE VILLAINOUS MASTERMIND, RIGHT?
OPEN SESAME, MATTEO.
SIR.
SO.
THESE FOLK? THEY'RE HERE FROM ALL OVER THE WORLD. THEY'RE THE INNOCENT ONES, DAVID.
THE CROSSFIRE CASUALTIES. THEY'RE THE ONES CAUGHT UP IN THE WAR BETWEEN MUTANTS AND HUMANS...MUTANTS AND ALIENS...MUTANTS AND MUTANTS...
HELL, MUTANTS AND PRETTY MUCH ANYONE YOU CARE TO NAME.
MEET DARWIN'S MARTYRS.
IBSS
THEY KNOW ME. I CAN SEE THAT EVEN WITHOUT TASTING THEIR MINDS. MARCUS TOLD THEM I'D BE COMING.
THEY KNOW WHO I AM (NO, NO...THEY KNOW WHOSE SON I AM) AND THEY KNOW WHAT I AM.
TRUTH IS, I NEEDN'T EVEN LISTEN TO THE INTRODUCTIONS. THIS ONE CRUSHED BY KRAKOAN BOULDERS, THAT ONE BURNED ALIVE BY PHOENIX FIRE.
IT'S A BLUR. THE DETAILS DON'T MATTER. ONLY THEIR EYES. ONLY THE VIBRATIONS OF THEIR MINDS.

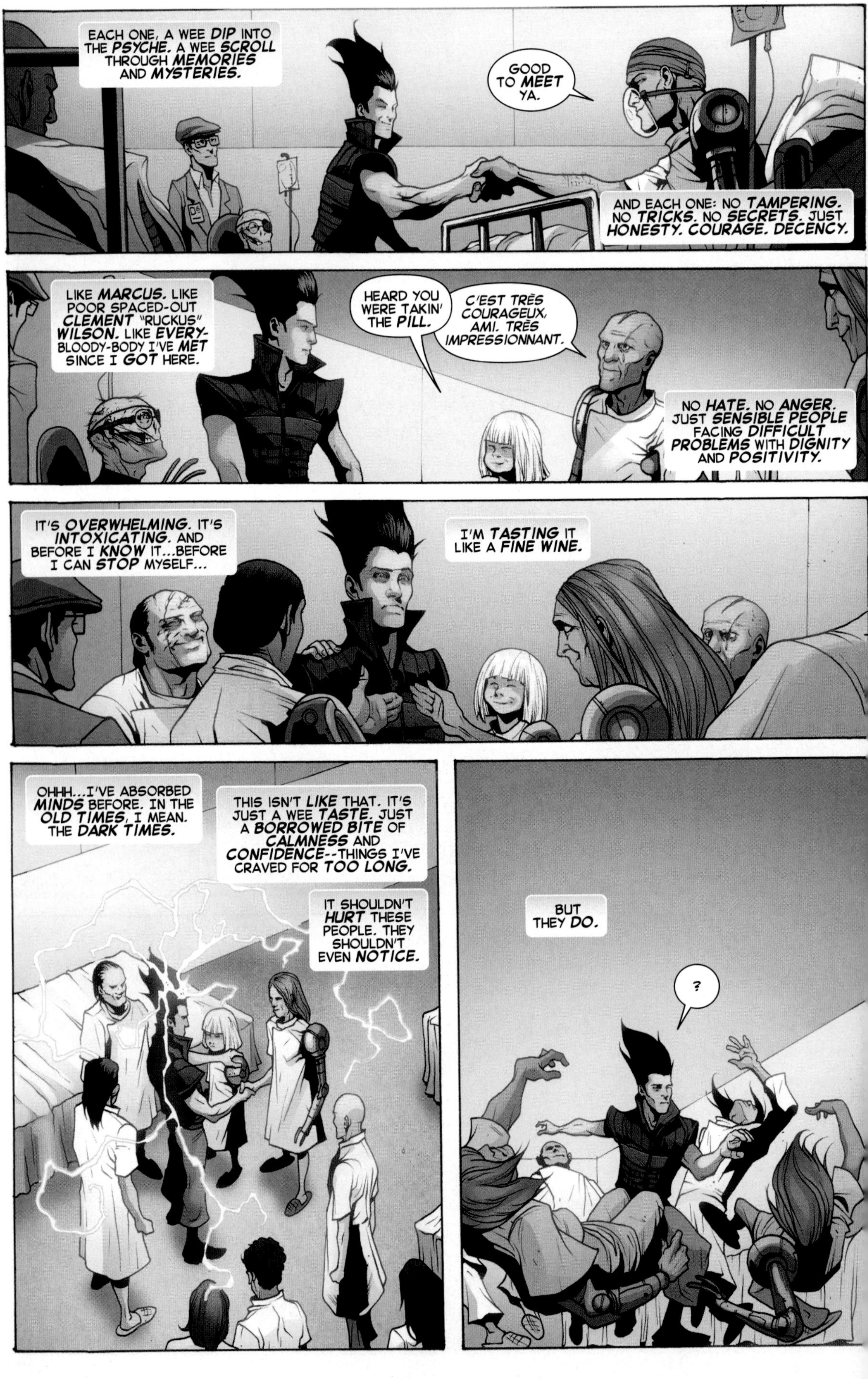
EACH ONE, A WEE DIP INTO THE PSYCHE. A WEE SCROLL THROUGH MEMORIES AND MYSTERIES.
GOOD TO MEET YA.
AND EACH ONE: NO TAMPERING. NO TRICKS. NO SECRETS. JUST HONESTY. COURAGE. DECENCY.
LIKE MARCUS. LIKE POOR SPACED-OUT CLEMENT "RUCKUS" WILSON. LIKE EVERY-BLOODY-BODY I'VE MET SINCE I GOT HERE.
HEARD YOU WERE TAKIN' THE PILL.
C'EST TRÈS COURAGEUX, AMI. TRÈS IMPRESSIONNANT.
NO HATE. NO ANGER. JUST SENSIBLE PEOPLE FACING DIFFICULT PROBLEMS WITH DIGNITY AND POSITIVITY.
IT'S OVERWHELMING. IT'S INTOXICATING. AND BEFORE I KNOW IT...BEFORE I CAN STOP MYSELF...
I'M TASTING IT LIKE A FINE WINE.
OHHH...I'VE ABSORBED MINDS BEFORE. IN THE OLD TIMES, I MEAN. THE DARK TIMES.
THIS ISN'T LIKE THAT. IT'S JUST A WEE TASTE. JUST A BORROWED BITE OF CALMNESS AND CONFIDENCE--THINGS I'VE CRAVED FOR TOO LONG.
IT SHOULDN'T HURT THESE PEOPLE. THEY SHOULDN'T EVEN NOTICE.
BUT THEY DO.
?

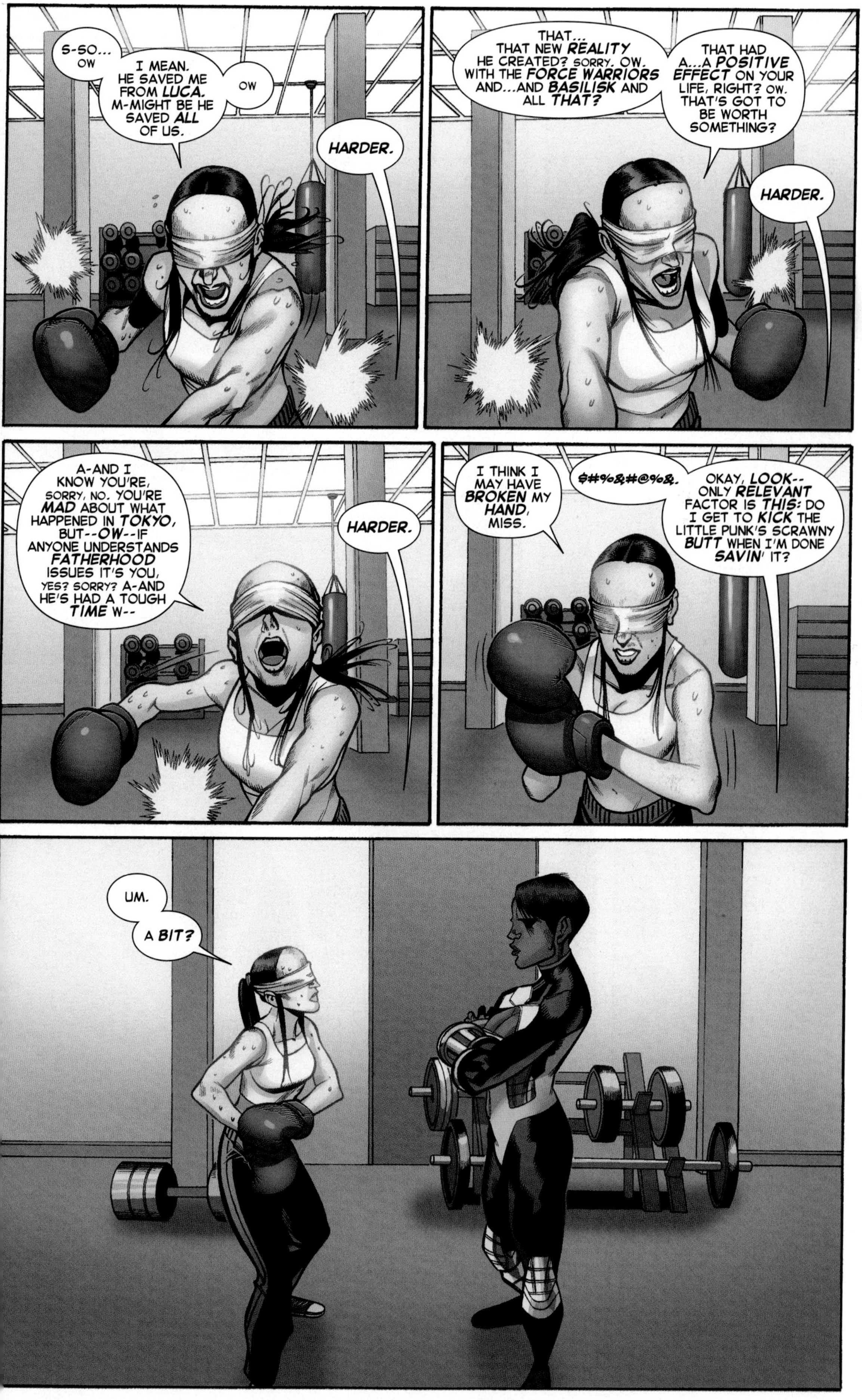
S-SO... OW
I MEAN. HE SAVED ME FROM LUCA. M-MIGHT BE HE SAVED ALL OF US.
OW
HARDER.
THAT... THAT NEW REALITY HE CREATED? SORRY. OW. WITH THE FORCE WARRIORS AND...AND BASILISK AND ALL THAT?
THAT HAD A...A POSITIVE EFFECT ON YOUR LIFE, RIGHT? OW. THAT'S GOT TO BE WORTH SOMETHING?
HARDER.
A-AND I KNOW YOU'RE, SORRY, NO. YOU'RE MAD ABOUT WHAT HAPPENED IN TOKYO, BUT--OW--IF ANYONE UNDERSTANDS FATHERHOOD ISSUES IT'S YOU, YES? SORRY? A-AND HE'S HAD A TOUGH TIME W--
HARDER.
I THINK I MAY HAVE BROKEN MY HAND, MISS.
$#%&#@%&.
OKAY, LOOK-- ONLY RELEVANT FACTOR IS THIS: DO I GET TO KICK THE LITTLE PUNK'S SCRAWNY BUTT WHEN I'M DONE SAVIN' IT?
UM.
A BIT?

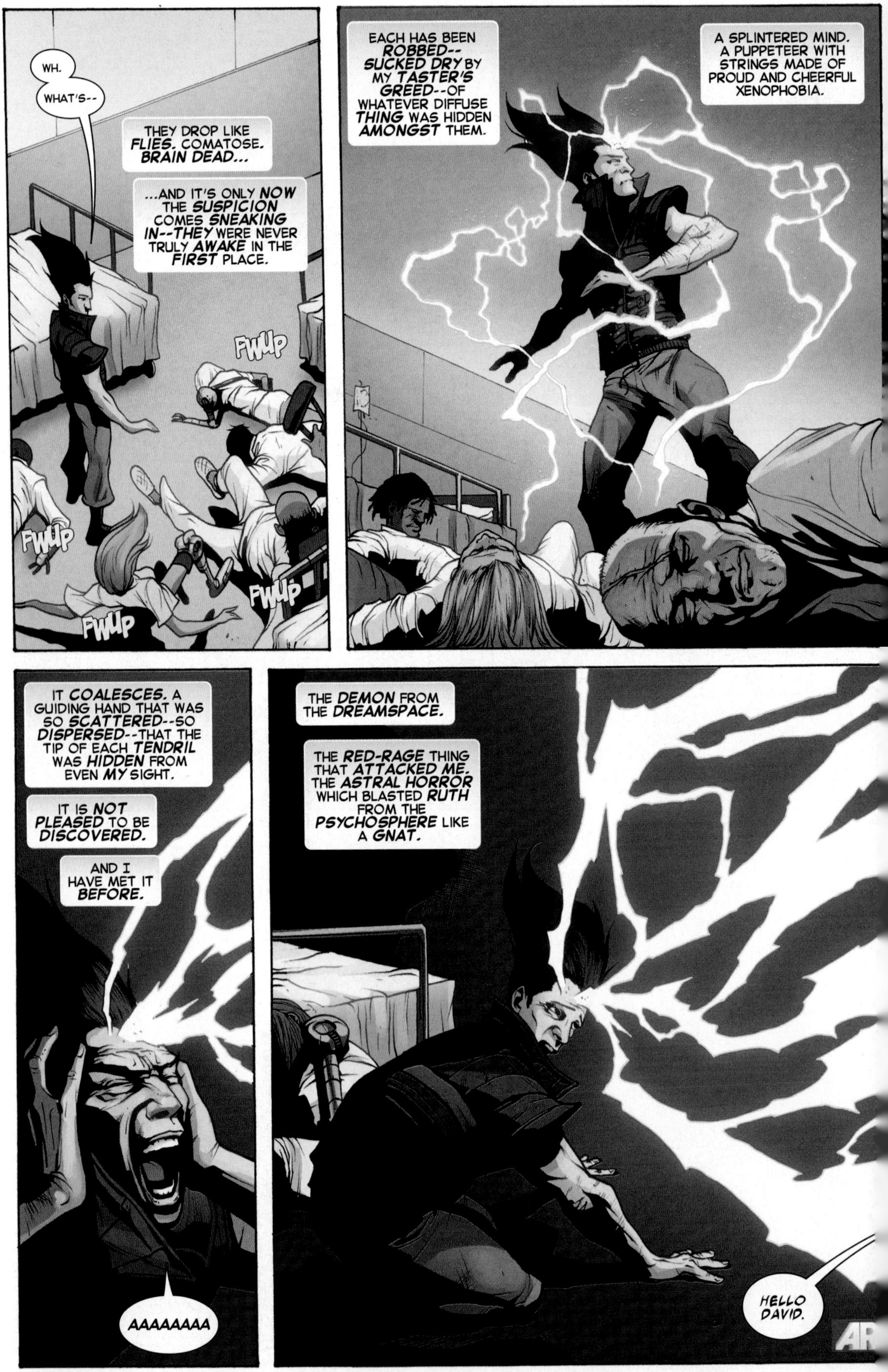

WH.
WHAT'S--
THEY DROP LIKE FLIES. COMATOSE. BRAIN DEAD...
...AND IT'S ONLY NOW THE SUSPICION COMES SNEAKING IN--THEY WERE NEVER TRULY AWAKE IN THE FIRST PLACE.
FWUP
FWUP
FWUP
FWUP
EACH HAS BEEN ROBBED--SUCKED DRY BY MY TASTER'S GREED--OF WHATEVER DIFFUSE THING WAS HIDDEN AMONGST THEM.
A SPLINTERED MIND. A PUPPETEER WITH STRINGS MADE OF PROUD AND CHEERFUL XENOPHOBIA.
IT COALESCES. A GUIDING HAND THAT WAS SO SCATTERED--SO DISPERSED--THAT THE TIP OF EACH TENDRIL WAS HIDDEN FROM EVEN MY SIGHT.
IT IS NOT PLEASED TO BE DISCOVERED.
AND I HAVE MET IT BEFORE.
AAAAAAAA
THE DEMON FROM THE DREAMSPACE.
THE RED-RAGE THING THAT ATTACKED ME. THE ASTRAL HORROR WHICH BLASTED RUTH FROM THE PSYCHOSPHERE LIKE A GNAT.
HELLO DAVID.

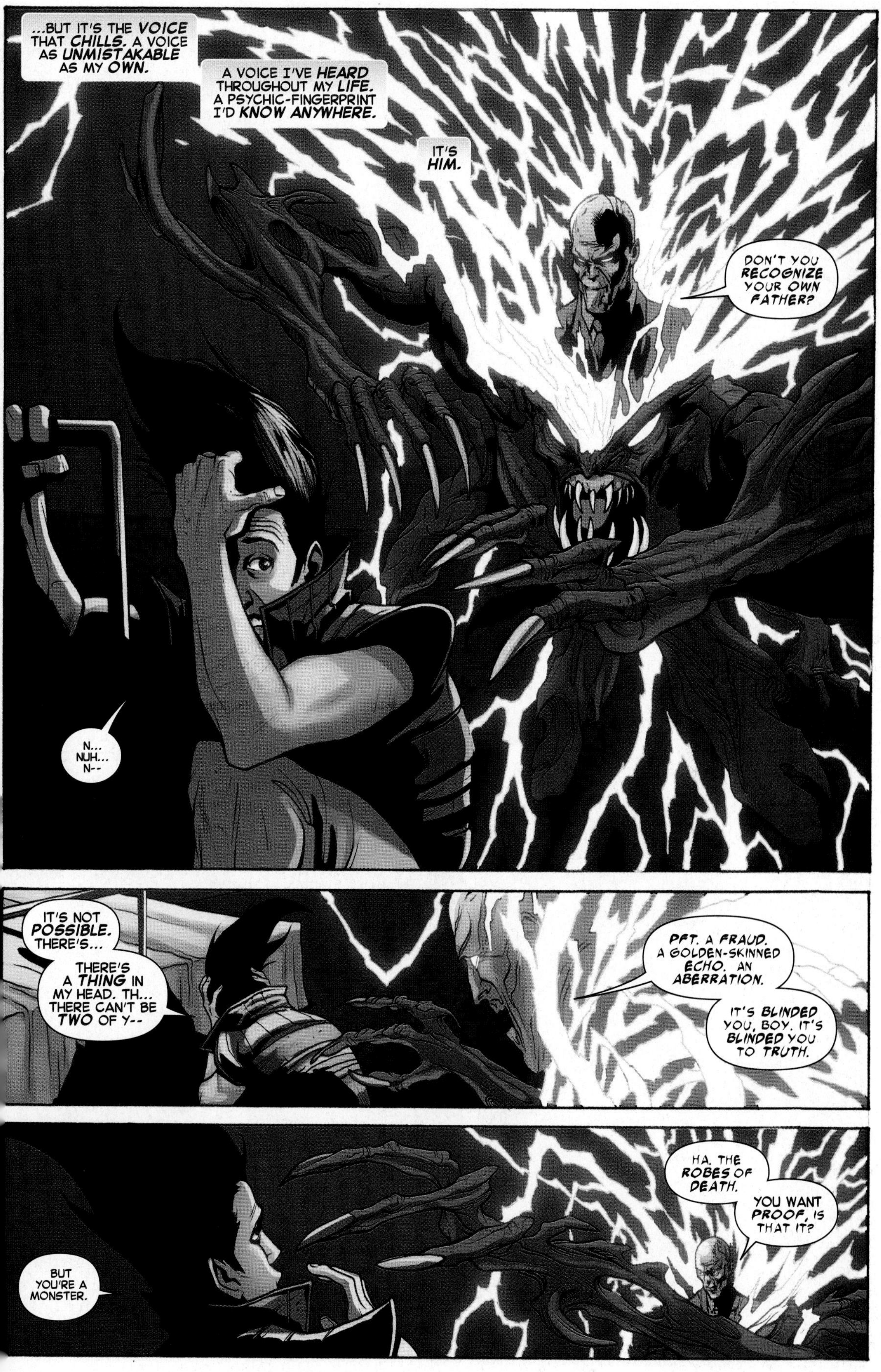
...BUT IT'S THE VOICE THAT CHILLS. A VOICE AS UNMISTAKABLE AS MY OWN.
A VOICE I'VE HEARD THROUGHOUT MY LIFE. A PSYCHIC-FINGERPRINT I'D KNOW ANYWHERE.
IT'S HIM.
DON'T YOU RECOGNIZE YOUR OWN FATHER?
N... NUH... N--
IT'S NOT POSSIBLE. THERE'S...
THERE'S A THING IN MY HEAD. TH... THERE CAN'T BE TWO OF Y--
PFT. A FRAUD. A GOLDEN-SKINNED ECHO. AN ABERRATION.
IT'S BLINDED YOU, BOY. IT'S BLINDED YOU TO TRUTH.
BUT YOU'RE A MONSTER.
HA. THE ROBES OF DEATH.
YOU WANT PROOF, IS THAT IT?

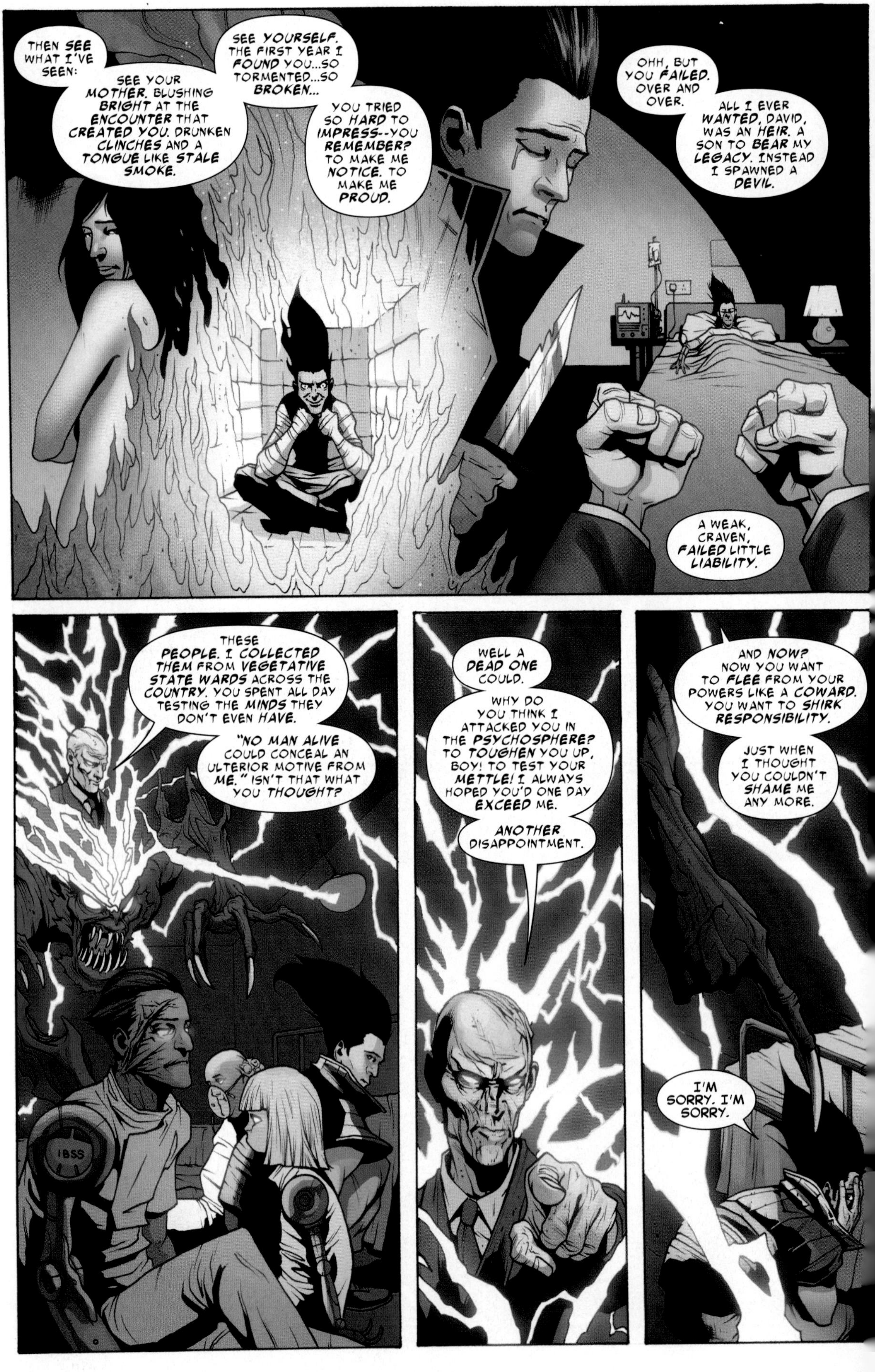
THEN SEE WHAT I'VE SEEN:
SEE YOUR MOTHER. BLUSHING BRIGHT AT THE ENCOUNTER THAT CREATED YOU. DRUNKEN CLINCHES AND A TONGUE LIKE STALE SMOKE.
SEE YOURSELF. THE FIRST YEAR I FOUND YOU...SO TORMENTED...SO BROKEN...
YOU TRIED SO HARD TO IMPRESS--YOU REMEMBER? TO MAKE ME NOTICE. TO MAKE ME PROUD.
OHH, BUT YOU FAILED. OVER AND OVER.
ALL I EVER WANTED, DAVID, WAS AN HEIR. A SON TO BEAR MY LEGACY. INSTEAD I SPAWNED A DEVIL.
A WEAK, CRAVEN, FAILED LITTLE LIABILITY.
THESE PEOPLE. I COLLECTED THEM FROM VEGETATIVE STATE WARDS ACROSS THE COUNTRY. YOU SPENT ALL DAY TESTING THE MINDS THEY DON'T EVEN HAVE.
"NO MAN ALIVE COULD CONCEAL AN ULTERIOR MOTIVE FROM ME." ISN'T THAT WHAT YOU THOUGHT?
IBSS
WELL A DEAD ONE COULD.
WHY DO YOU THINK I ATTACKED YOU IN THE PSYCHOSPHERE? TO TOUGHEN YOU UP, BOY! TO TEST YOUR METTLE! I ALWAYS HOPED YOU'D ONE DAY EXCEED ME.
ANOTHER DISAPPOINTMENT.
AND NOW? NOW YOU WANT TO FLEE FROM YOUR POWERS LIKE A COWARD. YOU WANT TO SHIRK RESPONSIBILITY.
JUST WHEN I THOUGHT YOU COULDN'T SHAME ME ANY MORE.
I'M SORRY. I'M SORRY.

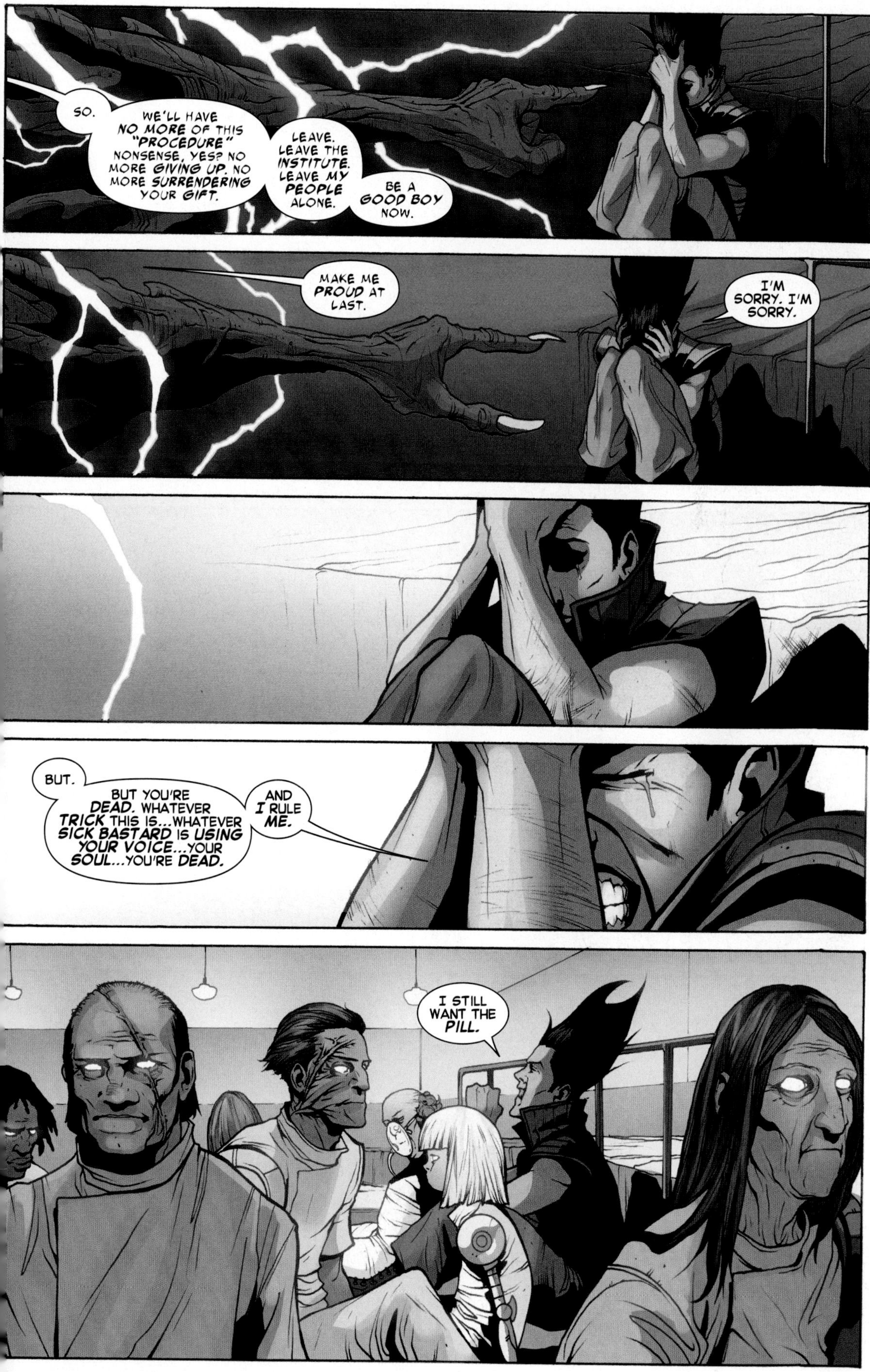
SO.
WE'LL HAVE NO MORE OF THIS "PROCEDURE" NONSENSE, YES? NO MORE GIVING UP. NO MORE SURRENDERING YOUR GIFT.
LEAVE. LEAVE THE INSTITUTE. LEAVE MY PEOPLE ALONE.
BE A GOOD BOY NOW.
MAKE ME PROUD AT LAST.
I'M SORRY. I'M SORRY.
BUT.
BUT YOU'RE DEAD. WHATEVER TRICK THIS IS...WHATEVER SICK BASTARD IS USING YOUR VOICE...YOUR SOUL...YOU'RE DEAD.
AND I RULE ME.
I STILL WANT THE PILL.

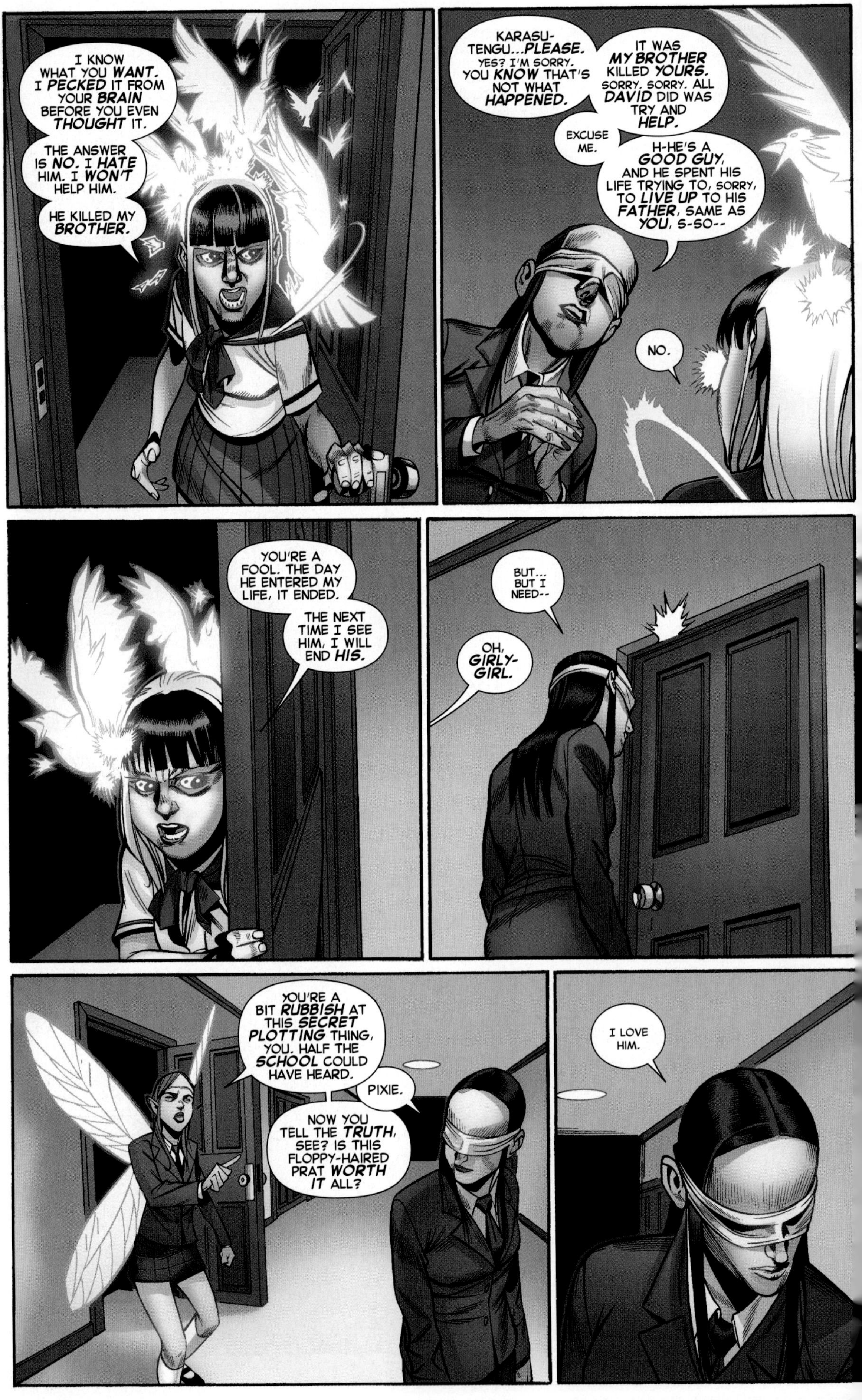
I KNOW WHAT YOU WANT. I PECKED IT FROM YOUR BRAIN BEFORE YOU EVEN THOUGHT IT.
THE ANSWER IS NO. I HATE HIM. I WON'T HELP HIM.
HE KILLED MY BROTHER.
KARASU-TENGU...PLEASE. YES? I'M SORRY. YOU KNOW THAT'S NOT WHAT HAPPENED.
IT WAS MY BROTHER KILLED YOURS. SORRY. SORRY. ALL DAVID DID WAS TRY AND HELP.
EXCUSE ME.
H-HE'S A GOOD GUY, AND HE SPENT HIS LIFE TRYING TO, SORRY, TO LIVE UP TO HIS FATHER, SAME AS YOU, S-SO--
NO.
YOU'RE A FOOL. THE DAY HE ENTERED MY LIFE, IT ENDED.
THE NEXT TIME I SEE HIM, I WILL END HIS.
BUT... BUT I NEED--
OH, GIRLY-GIRL.
YOU'RE A BIT RUBBISH AT THIS SECRET PLOTTING THING, YOU. HALF THE SCHOOL COULD HAVE HEARD.
PIXIE.
NOW YOU TELL THE TRUTH, SEE? IS THIS FLOPPY-HAIRED PRAT WORTH IT ALL?
I LOVE HIM.

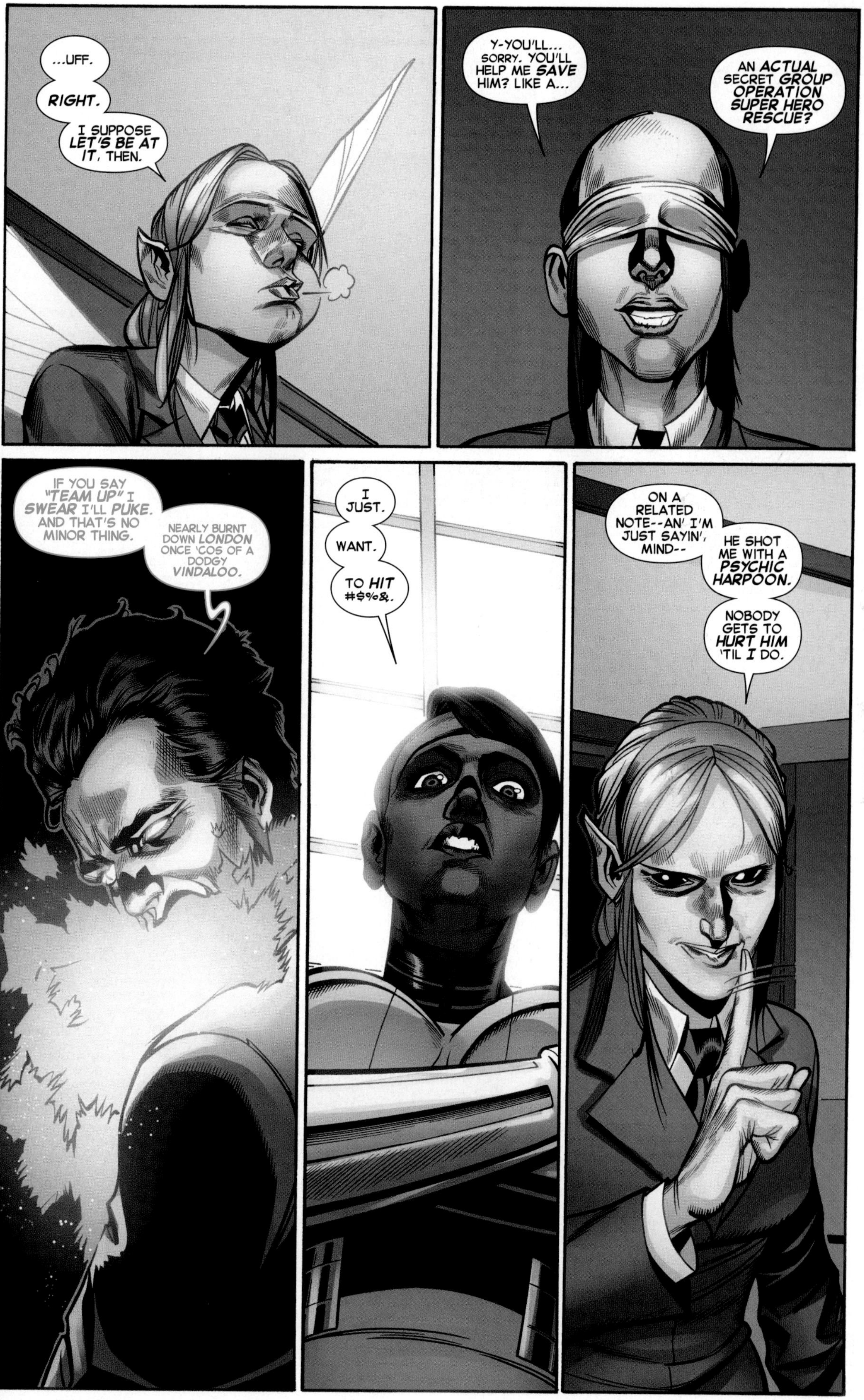
...UFF.
RIGHT.
I SUPPOSE LET'S BE AT IT, THEN.
Y-YOU'LL... SORRY. YOU'LL HELP ME SAVE HIM? LIKE A...
AN ACTUAL SECRET GROUP OPERATION SUPER HERO RESCUE?
IF YOU SAY "TEAM UP" I SWEAR I'LL PUKE. AND THAT'S NO MINOR THING.
NEARLY BURNT DOWN LONDON ONCE 'COS OF A DODGY VINDALOO.
I JUST.
WANT.
TO HIT #$%&.
ON A RELATED NOTE--AN' I'M JUST SAYIN', MIND--
HE SHOT ME WITH A PSYCHIC HARPOON.
NOBODY GETS TO HURT HIM 'TIL I DO.

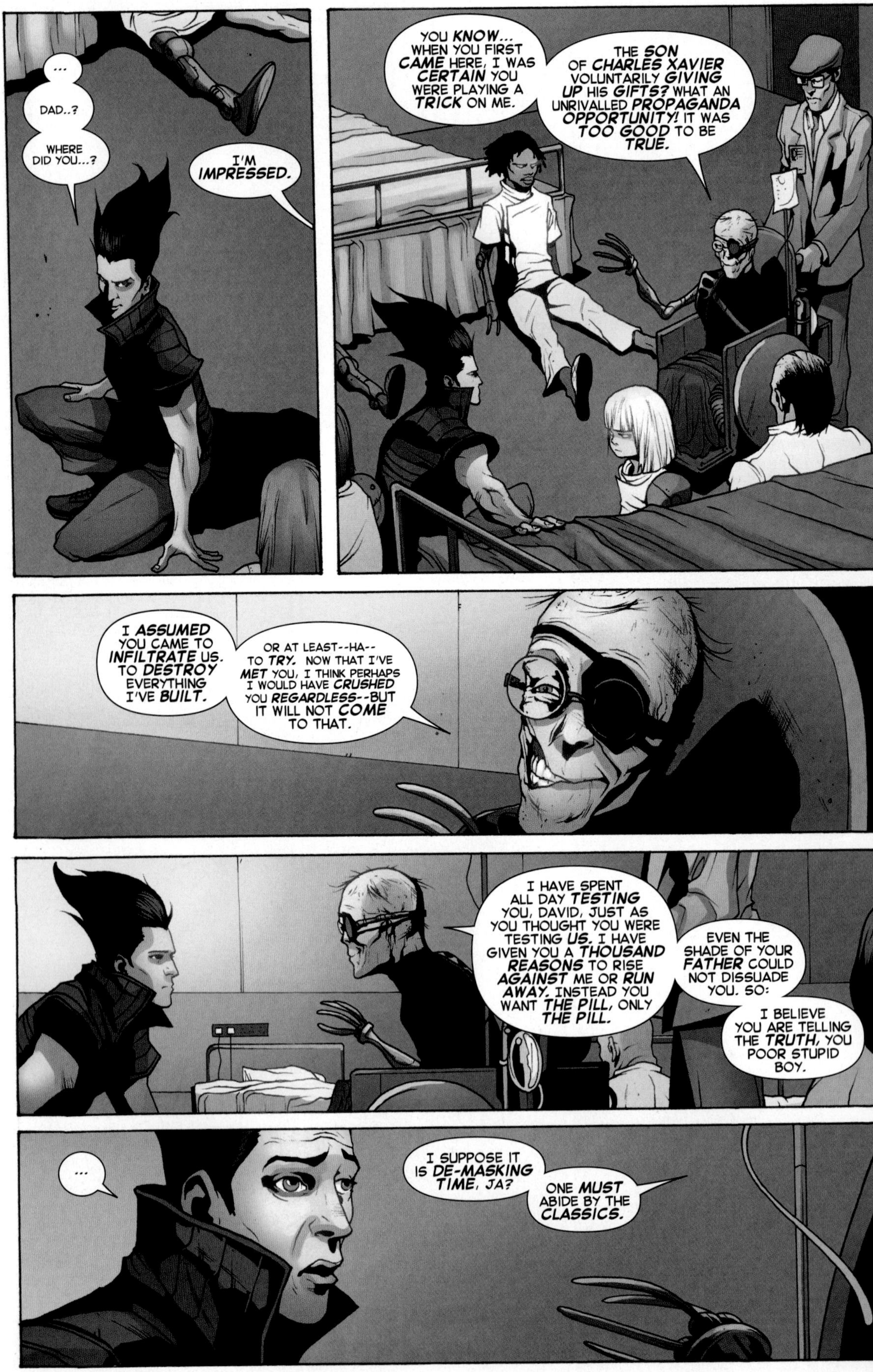
...
DAD..?
WHERE DID YOU...?
I'M IMPRESSED.
YOU KNOW... WHEN YOU FIRST CAME HERE, I WAS CERTAIN YOU WERE PLAYING A TRICK ON ME.
THE SON OF CHARLES XAVIER VOLUNTARILY GIVING UP HIS GIFTS? WHAT AN UNRIVALLED PROPAGANDA OPPORTUNITY! IT WAS TOO GOOD TO BE TRUE.
I ASSUMED YOU CAME TO INFILTRATE US. TO DESTROY EVERYTHING I'VE BUILT.
OR AT LEAST--HA--TO TRY. NOW THAT I'VE MET YOU, I THINK PERHAPS I WOULD HAVE CRUSHED YOU REGARDLESS--BUT IT WILL NOT COME TO THAT.
I HAVE SPENT ALL DAY TESTING YOU, DAVID, JUST AS YOU THOUGHT YOU WERE TESTING US. I HAVE GIVEN YOU A THOUSAND REASONS TO RISE AGAINST ME OR RUN AWAY. INSTEAD YOU WANT THE PILL, ONLY THE PILL.
EVEN THE SHADE OF YOUR FATHER COULD NOT DISSUADE YOU. SO:
I BELIEVE YOU ARE TELLING THE TRUTH, YOU POOR STUPID BOY.
...
I SUPPOSE IT IS DE-MASKING TIME, JA?
ONE MUST ABIDE BY THE CLASSICS.

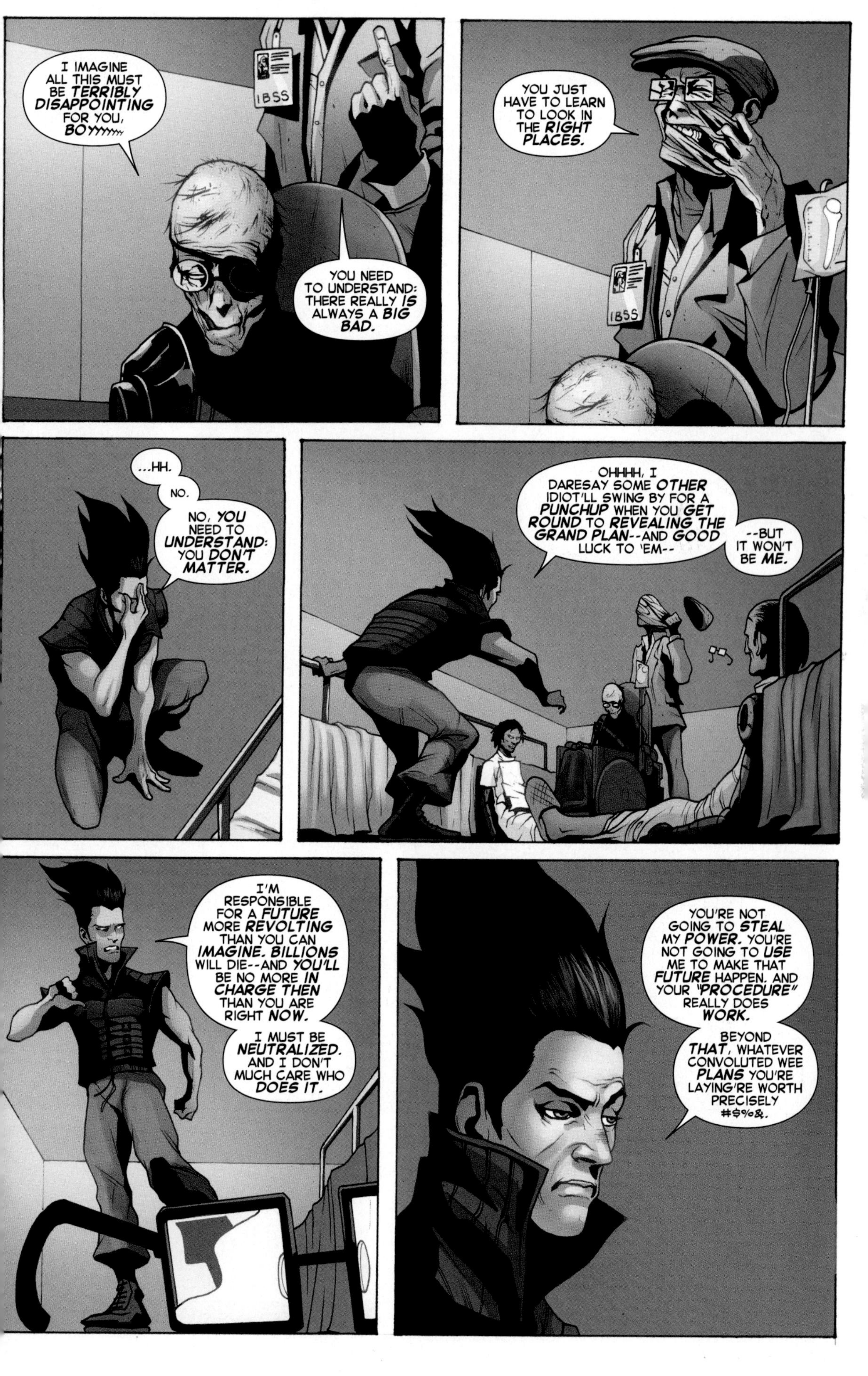

I IMAGINE ALL THIS MUST BE TERRIBLY DISAPPOINTING FOR YOU, BOYYYYYYY
YOU NEED TO UNDERSTAND: THERE REALLY IS ALWAYS A BIG BAD.
IBSS
YOU JUST HAVE TO LEARN TO LOOK IN THE RIGHT PLACES.
IBSS
...HH.
NO.
NO, YOU NEED TO UNDERSTAND: YOU DON'T MATTER.
OHHHH, I DARESAY SOME OTHER IDIOT'LL SWING BY FOR A PUNCHUP WHEN YOU GET ROUND TO REVEALING THE GRAND PLAN--AND GOOD LUCK TO 'EM--
--BUT IT WON'T BE ME.
I'M RESPONSIBLE FOR A FUTURE MORE REVOLTING THAN YOU CAN IMAGINE. BILLIONS WILL DIE--AND YOU'LL BE NO MORE IN CHARGE THEN THAN YOU ARE RIGHT NOW.
I MUST BE NEUTRALIZED. AND I DON'T MUCH CARE WHO DOES IT.
YOU'RE NOT GOING TO STEAL MY POWER. YOU'RE NOT GOING TO USE ME TO MAKE THAT FUTURE HAPPEN. AND YOUR "PROCEDURE" REALLY DOES WORK.
BEYOND THAT, WHATEVER CONVOLUTED WEE PLANS YOU'RE LAYING'RE WORTH PRECISELY #$%&.

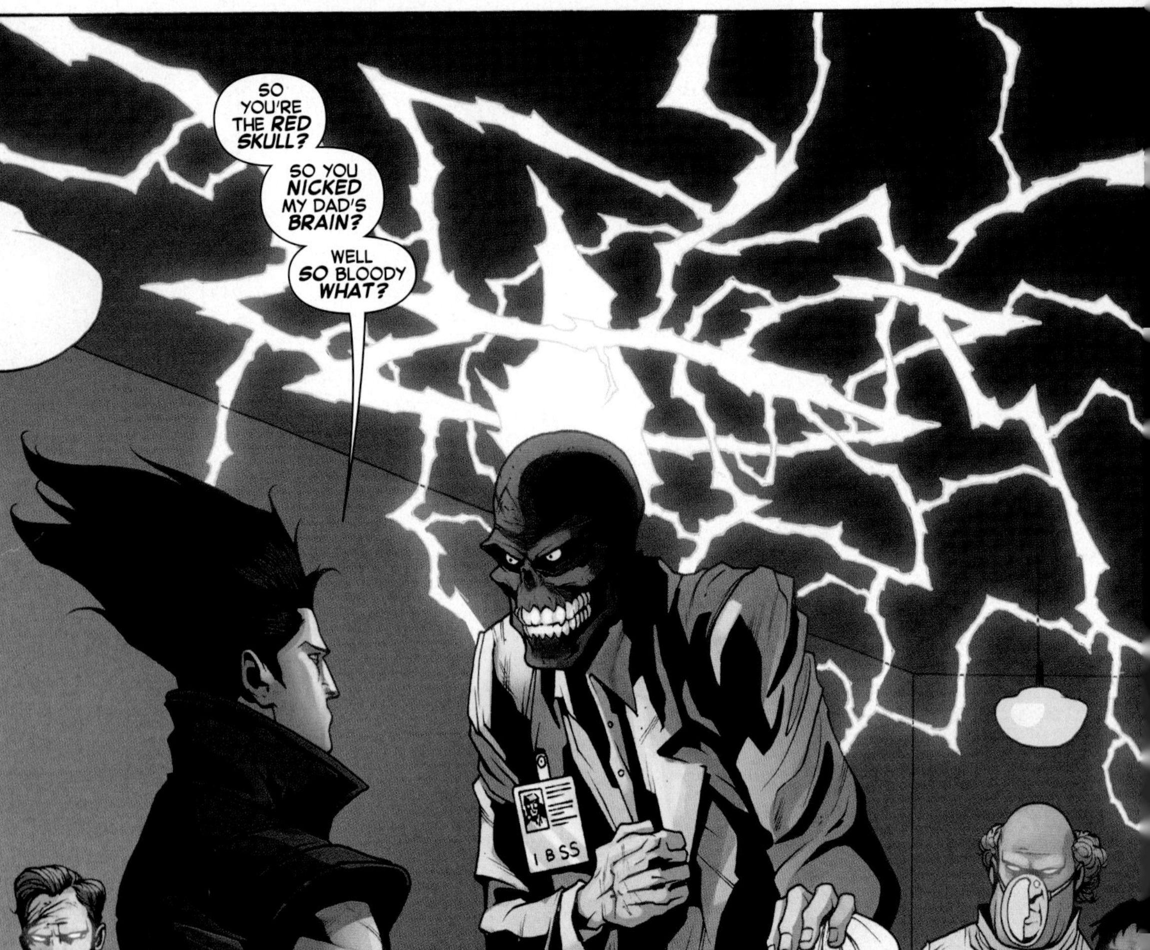
SO YOU'RE THE **RED SKULL?**
SO YOU **NICKED** MY DAD'S **BRAIN?**
WELL **SO** BLOODY **WHAT?**

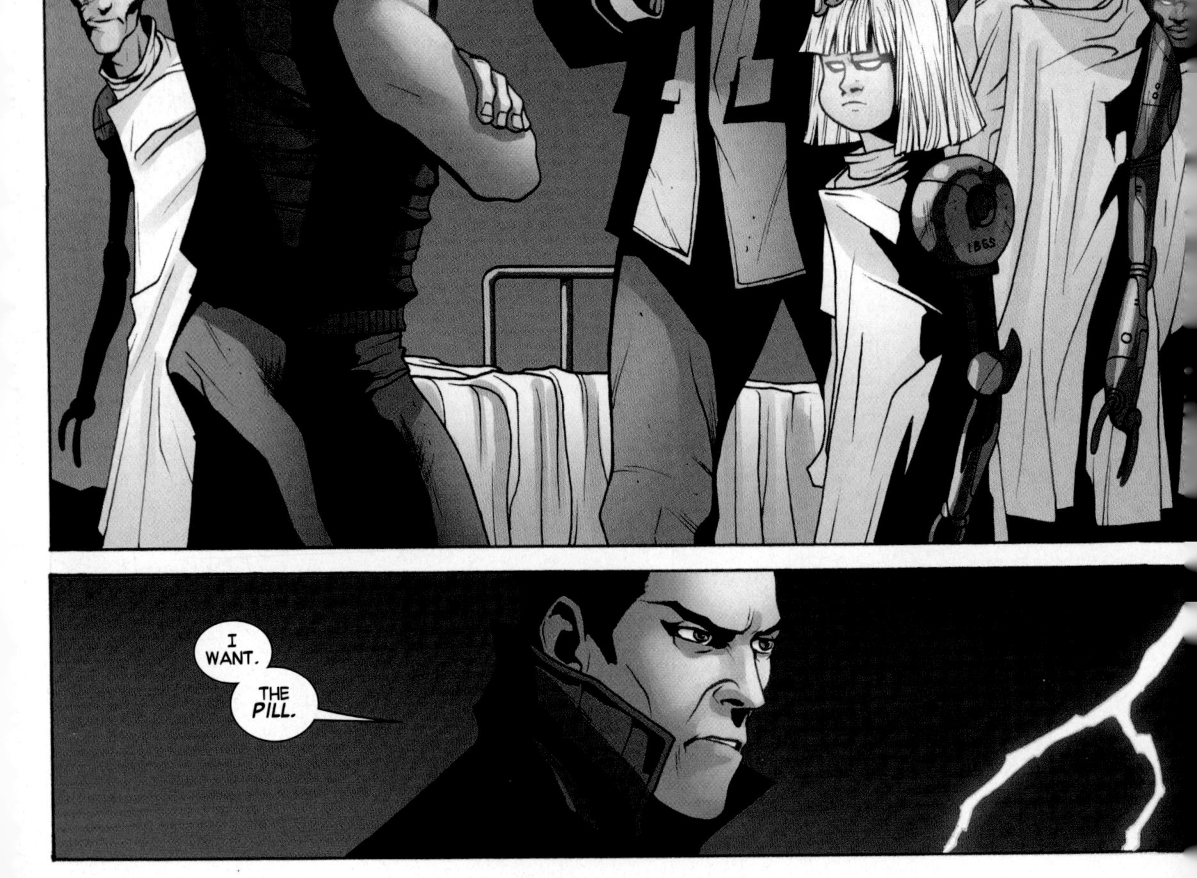
I WANT.
THE **PILL.**

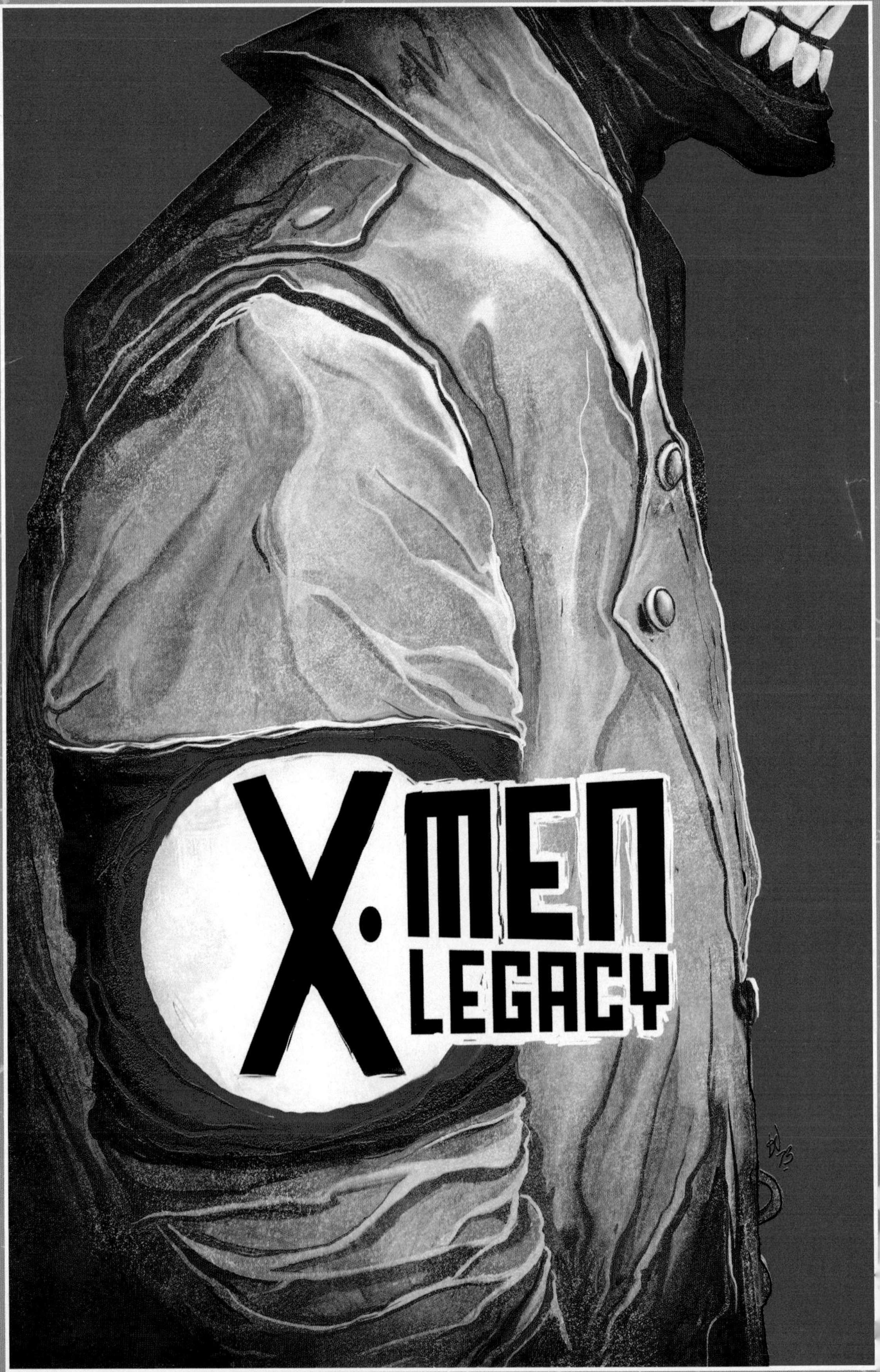
X-MEN
LEGACY

TWELVE